Gold on Blue

GRAHAM HOSKINS

DEDICATION

To Margaret

and the magnificent musicians of the Royal Marines Band Service

GOLD ON BLUE

CONTENTS

LEADERSHIP

To lead is to give vision and direction, to energise and motivate. Leaders set and enforce absolute standards of behaviour, attitude, presentation and performance. They know what they are talking about and, where necessary, they surround themselves with the expertise of others so that any gaps in their knowledge are covered. Leaders make hard decisions and follow them through to completion. If things go wrong they can explain why. Good leadership can be defined in many ways but central to it will always be the inspiration, hard work, respect, value, honesty and responsibility that the leader brings to his or her organisation to achieve results of which all can be proud.

Anonymous

GOLD ON BLUE

INTRODUCTION

Let me take you on my journey, which started in the 1930s and led to an amazing career in the Royal Marines Band Service. This is the story of a boy who left school having just turned fourteen without any academic qualifications, who joined the Band Service without ever having played a musical instrument, and yet became its Principal Director of Music.

Writing this book has enabled me to relive both the highlights and the lowlights of my life. This is not a story of one triumph after another. It is the story of someone who, occasionally, was in the right place at the right time. Someone who saw opportunities and embraced them. Someone whose life involved duty, honour, ceremony and tradition.

Let me tell you about my career that included marching through the streets of London for the coronation of Queen Elizabeth II, and many years later for the funeral of her uncle, Lord Mountbatten of Burma. A career that included playing on the pitch during the 1966 World Cup Final and sailing around the world. Let me explain what it was like to be a boy musician at the Royal Marines School of Music in the 1950s, to serve on board *HMY Britannia* and to sail the Mediterranean on the QE2. Who was Mr Utter Bilge? What sound does a Urinecorn produce? And what did the *Sheffield Five* get up to?

Share with me my pride as I had the privilege of performing at venues as diverse as Horse Guards Parade, the Royal Albert Hall and Madison Square Garden. And learn of my grief as I encountered tragedy in September 1989.

An index lists many of the people I've encountered during my career in the Band Service. In terms of their ranks, honours and qualifications, I've described them as I knew them or as they were known when they retired from active service.

I am greatly indebted to Colin Bowden of the Royal Marines Historical Society, Lawrie Bloomfield of Radio Solent, Stephen Misson of Cinque Port Music, and my son Martin for their support as I prepared this book. My memories of incidents that occurred years ago remain vivid, so I trust that you won't find me to be too unreliable a narrator.

Graham Hoskins
May 2022

CHAPTER 1

THE JOURNEY BEGINS
1935 - 1949

The boy was only seven when one evening his mother sent him on an important errand. He ran through the village to a line of terraced cottages backing onto a small river. He knocked urgently on the door of one of them until a middle-aged lady who was the local midwife appeared. "Come quickly!" the boy shouted. "My Mum is *weeing* on the floor and can't stop!" He then went on to the river to catch minnows in a jam-jar. With a wry smile the lady climbed onto her ancient bicycle, hung her *black bag* over the handlebar and pedalled her way to the address that she had been given. My mother's waters had broken and I was making my way into the world. It was the 4th of May 1935 and the address was that of my grandmother, a thatched cottage then known as *No.11, The Mount* in Drift Road, North Wallington, Fareham, Hampshire.

The cottage at No. 11, The Mount, Drift Road, Wallington, Fareham

Christened Graham Anthony Clifford Hoskins, my mother was Marjorie Olive Ruth Hoskins (nee Hill) and my father Clifford Norman Hoskins. Along with older brother Jack (the midwife caller and minnow fisher), I was to have three younger sisters. My mother's family had occupied the lonely cottage for many years. My grandfather died before I was born so I never knew him, and my grandmother died when I was still very young. I recall her only vaguely, hair in a bun and always wearing an all-encompassing apron. When she died in her 70s she was kept at home until her funeral in accordance with the custom of those days. Her open coffin and clasped arum lily is an abiding memory.

I was always told that my grandfather had been a highly respected man within the community, with political persuasions that took him to the local hustings when necessary. He was of considerable bulk and for much of his later life was not able to work owing to problems with his legs.

During her lifetime, my grandmother had been a very religious lady who belonged to a sect called *The Truth*. Members would assemble in each other's houses for services because there was no church building for them to use. In the parlour of the cottage there were two ancient harmoniums, one of which would be used during services to accompany the hymns when it was my grandmother's turn to preside. I cannot recall ever attending a service and it all seemed very secret to me.

The cottage was very basic and some of my earliest memories are of hearing mice running around in the loft above my little bedroom. Each year the loft was used to store and ripen walnuts from a tree in the garden so there was always plenty of food up there for any small animals that knew of it.

I still remember the musty smell of old hymnbooks that added to the general aged feel of the home. It had an outside toilet with no wooden seat. There was no bath, just a butler-sink attached to the wall of a downstairs room. Water initially came from a well at the back of the property, for this was an old farm cottage and, when built, was the only dwelling in the lane.

My mother had been *in service* since leaving school and had worked as a maid in London and Sidmouth, Devon, as well as in Warnford, Hampshire. In circumstances never explained to me she conceived a son, Jack Ian Stanley Hill, seven years before she met and married my father. My father fully accepted this boy who went on to attend Prices Grammar School in Fareham. After serving as an Artificer in the Fleet Air Arm of the Royal Navy, Jack became a draughtsman with the Atomic Energy Authority near Didcot in Berkshire.

Around the time of the outbreak of World War II, a row of semi-detached houses was built next to my grandmother's cottage. My mother, father, Jack and I rented and moved into the first of these, No. 13 Drift Road, where we remained throughout the course of the war. Many nights were spent in the *Anderson* air-raid shelter that was dug into the back garden The shelter, which could accommodate four people, had two bunkbeds on each side. It was damp and smelly and often very cold, probably because I do not remember the shelter having a proper door, just a ladder to climb down into it. Fortunately, our house was never bombed.

The hazard was always there because we were only nine miles from the Royal Naval Dockyard at Portsmouth and surrounded by Service Establishments – all important enemy targets. Indeed Drift Road led up to Fort Wallington, the first of several old forts built defensively along the elevated ground of Portsdown Hill, to the north of Portsmouth Harbour. The next in the line was Fort Nelson, then Fort Southwick and finally Fort Widley. It was from the third of these, Fort Southwick, that the 'D' Day landings were directed, so they were certainly prime targets for an enemy with knowledge and bombs to spare.

My father had a life-long lung condition and a curvature of the upper spine. Because of this he was declared unfit for active service but was accepted to serve as a Constable with the Royal Marine Police, formed in the 1920s to relieve the Metropolitan Police, who up to that time were responsible for the security of Naval Dockyards. Colin Bowden, who later in my life became a good friend and a celebrated Royal Marines Drum Major, told me that he was born in the married quarters of the

Royal Marine Police at Gosport and that without exception his neighbours were former Royal Marines Light Infantry or Royal Marines Artillery personnel. To join the Royal Marine Police, applicants had to have served in the Corps. Just prior to World War II, the entry criteria for the RMP was expanded and those with no former Service connections were allowed to apply.

This is the point at which my father became a policeman attached to the Admiralty. He was later promoted Sergeant and was based, until he reached retirement age, at Fleetlands, the Royal Naval Aircraft Repair Yard, between Fareham and Gosport. It was there that naval aircraft were repaired or overhauled before being returned for further war service. Aircraft would be towed from the nearby Grange Airfield to Fleetlands, crossing a railway line and the main Gosport to Fareham Road. A bridge was built over the railway line, designed to enable the aircraft to cross without their wings hitting the buttresses on either side. Nothing so adventurous was attempted for the road crossing, for here, the police merely stopped the traffic. It seems that *aircraft crossings* preceded *pedestrian crossings* – at least in Hampshire!

Before the war, my father had been a Hants & Dorset bus conductor for the country routes around Fareham. He was keen on motors and had a driving licence when only in his teens. His father had also been a member of the Admiralty Constabulary, coming initially from the Portland area of Dorset where today there are family tombstones in a local churchyard. My grandfather and his family eventually moved from Dorset to Gosport and lived in one of the police houses near to what is now the Royal Clarence Marina, the garden of which backed on to the tidal reaches of Portsmouth Harbour.

I attended Fareham Church of England Infant School from the age of five. The Second World War had recently begun, and school-lessons were often interrupted by air-raid warning sirens. The windows of the classrooms were taped over in a lattice arrangement to reduce the danger from any flying glass, and we always carried our gasmasks with us.

After school and at weekends, my pals and I would go off into nearby areas to see for ourselves the bomb damage to nearby houses and property and thought it great fun to locate pieces of shrapnel to take home as souvenirs.

As the war progressed, and the strategic relevance of the area in which I lived became more important, service personnel needed to be billeted locally wherever possible. My mother saw this as a way of supplementing the family's meagre income and she took in a succession of servicemen as lodgers. There was not much space for everyone, and our lifestyle seemed to alter somewhat. After we children had been pushed off to bed, games of cards now became very popular among the adults. There was only radio. Television was in its infancy, and we didn't have one.

As the years went on and what became known as 'D' Day approached, enemy aerial activity increased, as did the build-up of troops. 'Smokey-Joes' appeared in various places. These were mobile oil burners that belched out thick black smoke from a chimney, concealing what was around from enemy reconnaissance aircraft. The roads became rutted from tank tracks and my peaceful countryside seemed destroyed forever.

Around this time I recall a direct hit by a bomb on the Fareham gas works causing much excitement for, as children, we seemed to see only excitement in such things. I do not recall being at all frightened personally throughout these dark days.

Village life after World War II

There were huge celebrations when the end of the war was announced in 1945. Bonfires lit up the sky and street parties were held. Rationing of food was still in place and was to remain so for a further five years, but sandwiches, cakes and jellies miraculously appeared among the flags and bunting.

One man from the village was able to play a clarinet and led us children around like the Pied Piper of Hamelin. It was my first introduction to instrumental music, and it is strange that it should have included so much marching around, for my life was eventually to be professionally involved in doing so.

With freedom from the tensions of war, village life began to return to what it had been. The annual fete and gymkhana were reinstated. On the day of the fete, our trickling Wallington River was carefully dammed downstream to raise the water level in the village for the older boys, and for some fathers, to take part in water sports with tin baths, greasy poles and colourful rafts. Prizes would be awarded for the best children's wildflower collection (presented in a jam-jar with all species named), and for the child in the best fancy dress.

My mother saw this as an opportunity to show great resourcefulness and our family often won both competitions. She was very talented with a needle and had made hundreds of collars for sailors during the war years. She also made the most amazing fancy-dress outfits for my sisters and me. One year, she dressed me as Robin Hood in a suit of Lincoln green with feathered hat, and Dad provided me with a wooden quiver for my bow and feathered arrows. I even had the horn from a cow hanging at my side for use as a bugle. All I can remember about the horn is how awful it smelt.

My most embarrassing outfit was that of Humpty-Dumpty, for it required me to wear stockings and buckled shoes! The all-encompassing egg costume was in two halves made from wire frames covered with white material. The bottom half had two holes for my legs and was hung on a pair of braces. The upper half, hiding the braces, covered my head and had holes for my arms. The join of the two halves was covered with a brightly coloured waist-sash. Once inside I was not able to see very much at all, for the painted eyes on the face of the egg were about a foot apart! But, as Humpty-Dumpty, I went home clutching the winner's rosette.

Mother used to make dolls from spare material and realistically embroidered the faces before making their clothes and dressing them. They were always much admired and in great demand locally. She regularly made our Christmases totally delightful. Always, in absolute secrecy, she was able to arrange for an Aladdin's cave of gifts and presents to be available. Colour and character were her hallmarks, and these annual moments of magic on Christmas morning were beyond the imaginings of my friends. We children were kept upstairs until the fire in the *front room* – a room kept for high days and holidays – had been lit. When we did go down the stairs, in strict order of age with the youngest first, we found the room transformed from the day before into an unbelievable fairyland.

My father daily rode his bicycle to Fleetlands, where his life was very much routine. His hours as a Police Sergeant were 2pm-10pm, 10pm-6am or 6am-2pm, so his mealtimes were largely different from the rest of our family. If he was absent for his meal, Mum would keep a dinner plated-up for him and, because he liked them, she always sliced and fried his boiled potatoes. Forbidden 'fruit' for us youngsters but we were able to enjoy the aroma from the hot beef-dripping. Aahh!

One Guy Fawkes Night, father brought home a nautical maroon or signal-flare. We children went excitedly into the garden to watch from a safe distance and await the 'whoosh' from this rocket-like contrivance but, try as he may, Dad couldn't make it work. Bitterly disappointed, we went indoors to join mother who was sitting by the kitchen fire. This was contained in an old black range with oven attached, all of which she kept highly polished and blackened with daily brush-loads of *Zebo* polish. My sisters and I gathered round to benefit from the warmth of the fire and to tell mum of our disappointment when father came into the room, raised the iron lid of the range, and without speaking put the failed flare in with the coals. In no time at all there was an almighty explosion, the top of the range turned white and mother, then eight months pregnant with my youngest sister, only just avoided a premature birth. Dad usually kept rather in the background, and after this foolhardy event he tended to sit even further back!

My brother, Jack was allowed to have an air gun. I used to borrow it and shoot at tin cans balanced on the top of the garden swing. Often not being able to afford pellets to use as ammunition, I found that reasonable substitutes were hard green unripe elderberries.

Our lavatory could only be accessed from the back yard, so it was hardly a *convenience*. Mum kept a mangle in the tiny space and hanging up on one wall was a tin bath that was used on washdays. In joy, or perhaps boredom, I carved a 'Victory V' sign in the wooden roller of the mangle when the war ended. Mum was not impressed for from then on everything that was put through the mangle came out embossed! I particularly remember the mangle because it got in the way as I sat there tearing up my squares of newspaper. We didn't have toilet rolls during the war!

Climbing trees was a favourite pastime and my chum, 'Johnnie' Coker used to join me in the branches of a tree in the garden for teatime sandwiches passed aloft by mum. We used to sit in the tree wondering what would become of us as the years progressed.

Each year, I would raise a jackdaw from nestling to adult. Being a country boy, I was familiar with animals being used on the farm because tractors were not freely available and shire horses were. Keeping a bird as a pet did not seem cruel, although it meant having to clip the ends of its wing feathers to ensure that it didn't fly away. With a daily diet of warmed bread and milk the bird probably thought the inconvenience worthwhile! One year my bird went missing and I was very sad. Then a lad from across the road came to tell me that *he* now had a bird for a pet. When I saw it I recognised from a scar under its beak, the result of it falling off our garden coal-shed when very young, that it was my lost jackdaw. As it couldn't have flown to his house on the other side of the road he had obviously stolen it from my garden. End of friendship!

Graham Hoskins with his jackdaw, 1946

Schooling

Memories of my time at infant school are patchy at best. I recall the huge and impressive horse chestnut tree in the centre of the playground. Fancy, at the age of five, being able to collect conkers while at school! Bordering the school was an alleyway leading to a small shoe repair business run by a Mr. Sturgess. The workplace was his enlarged garden shed and the smell of new leather and polish emanating from the premises has remained with me over all the years.

When seven or eight years old, I was befriended by one of the school dinner-ladies, a Mrs. Raggett. She was very busy after the serving of the food as the 'washer-up' of all plates, cutlery and dishes. She inveigled me into helping her with this chore and paid me in dinky toys and coloured glass marbles brought from her home, no doubt after her own children had grown beyond the need for such things. I preferred the dinky toys because I quickly lost marbles in playground competitions with my peers, and often went home with nothing to show for my hard work at lunchtime in the school kitchen. My job there was usually cleaning the long cylindrical *roly-poly* tins, hinged along their length, in which steamed puddings had been cooked. They were always very greasy and hardly hygienic but, hey! who cared in those days. At the age of ten, I was one of those hopelessly infatuated boys whose preferences at playtime was to 'accidentally' fall at the feet of the girls just to check on the colour of their knickers!

At the age of eleven, I had to move from Infant to Secondary School. I had failed my 11-plus examination and was therefore ineligible to follow my brother Jack at the local Grammar School, so I attended Fareham Secondary Modern School. It was a segregated school with a playground adjoining that of the corresponding girls' section. As the hormones raced, we boys could only look on with hangdog expressions. No chance now of falling at girls' feet.

After school activities

I was probably perceived as becoming 'a bit of a loner,' so it was suggested that I join the local Boy Scouts group in which Jack had been a leading light. The night I joined, the scoutmaster fell out with the scout mistress and the unit was disbanded! I was beginning to feel that there was something not quite right about me!

Fears were dispelled, however, when I then joined a Sea Cadet unit that was based in Fareham creek on an ex-wartime motor torpedo boat. I was given a diminutive naval uniform and proudly began a loose association with the Royal Navy. The boat had been de-engined and either rested on the mud or floated just above it, depending upon the state of the tide. To us youngsters, its 'crew', the boat was all an embryo sailor could have hoped for. We learned all about knots and splices, *nautical rules of the road* when afloat – *Green to green, red to red, perfect safety go ahead* or *If upon your port is seen a steamer's starboard light of green* ... etc. We pulled on the oars of boats as we learned basic seamanship and safety while afloat and were encouraged to go dinghy sailing.

One evening, on the conclusion of a 'cadet night' on board, I was invited to smoke a cigarette and later to puff from a pipe of shag tobacco. I was green within seconds and deeply affected as I struggled onto the upper deck, gasping for air. The experience put me off smoking for life, and although I didn't know then that it would be so, I have been grateful to this day for that life-enhancing experience.

Youngsters in those days were able to take seasonal work on local farms, of which there were several in the area. I recall the potato-picking in particular. We would go to a designated farm early on frosty autumn mornings and be allocated to a particular field. We would spread out along one side and 'pitches' would be marked out along the line of the furrows so that each 'picker' had an equal amount of ground to cover. We would strip off all the parched greenery (haulms) from the ground and a horse-drawn spinner would come down the line spinning out the potatoes and earth in front of us. We had baskets in which to put the potatoes as we picked them up. They were then tipped into sacks to be taken away later. As the day progressed, and we went further and further across the field, the stick-markers for each pitch would be taken forward as well. This is when the bigger boys would ensure that their 'pitch' got smaller and smaller whilst the ones alongside got bigger and bigger! During breaks for lunch, etc., we would have to collect the haulms into piles and burn them. We made baked potatoes in the hot ashes and feasted on them once the blackened skins had been removed.

Encountering predators

Each year a funfair or a circus would come to town. The circus would set up its big top in the water meadows at Wallington. It all seemed very colourful and adventurous with acts like motorbike riding on the upright inner cylinder of the 'Wall of Death'.

One year, I recall watching a couple setting up their equipment in readiness for an act that involved spinning together on roller-skates at great speed on a round reinforced tabletop.

That afternoon, with the female well out of the way, the man invited me into his tent to see his white leather skating boots. Green as grass, I went with him and became immediately aware that I was in some form of danger, though I knew not what. I managed to extricate myself from this situation - but not before I had been made aware that he wore a leather hernia-truss near to his groin.

I was too embarrassed to tell anyone about this incident which was one of two in my childhood. The other involved a soldier camped on the lower slopes of Portsdown Hill by the side of a tracked vehicle whilst awaiting embarkation for D-Day. I was a good-looking youngster with fair curly hair and the two of us were all alone in that country lane. He didn't physically hurt me, but I learned far more that day than a lad of my years should have done, and the memories have remained with me to this day.

Leaving school

On leaving Grammar School, brother Jack joined the Royal Navy as an Artificer in the Fleet Air Arm. When my 14th birthday approached I became concerned about what I would be able to do with my life, for the school leaving age in 1949 was fourteen. I had no qualifications to my name, and it was a worrying time.

It was decided that I should apply to be taught a trade at the Portsmouth Building School. I was accepted but, before I could take up my place, an uncle serving in the Royal Navy and knowing that I had been in the church choir, suggested I might be an ideal candidate to join the Royal Naval School of Music if I could get up early in the mornings! This seemed to be the only requirement and, as I had been doing a paper round for some months, I felt that I might qualify, even though I had no musical experience.

As a sea cadet, I had obtained a commendation from the Commanding Officer when my sea cadet uniform was returned to the Unit. My mother received a very warm appraisal saying that the condition in which it was returned "augured well" for my future. Perhaps this was a lesson in life, for cleanliness and smartness became necessary bywords in the career that was to come.

Musicians in the navy

Having musicians in Royal Navy ships started as a private venture, probably by captains who appreciated the value of a little music in the life of a man-of-war. The time of the Napoleonic Wars saw the appearance of bands in most flagships, and after a time the Admiralty began to encourage this new development. In 1847 the naval rank of Bandsman was introduced, and they remained naval ratings until 1903. From 1856, bands served in many large ships.

With no central authority or organisation, the quality of personnel varied considerably and many bandsmen with proven musical expertise came from abroad. In 1863, the first tentative steps were taken by the Admiralty towards training their own musicians, recruiting youngsters with musical potential to perform on ships. Four years later, a grant was provided to help with the purchase of their musical instruments. In 1868, the rank of Bandmaster, equivalent to the rank of Petty Officer, was established. In 1874, a uniform specifically for musicians was introduced, and the Adjutant General Royal Marines became responsible for inspecting naval bands.

Just after the turn of the century, the Royal Naval School of Music (RNSM) was established as an integral part of the Corps of Royal Marines. Its members were enlisted into the Corps in the same way as those who would train to become General Duty Royal Marines and were given the title of Musician. As they became available, musicians serving in ships' bands were disembarked to Eastney Barracks in Portsmouth to be absorbed into the RNSM. The first musicians to arrive were 34 ratings from *HMS Impregnable* and the ship's band of *HMS Leviathan*. They were under the leadership of Chief Bandmaster Harry Lidiard, who would later become a Major within the new organisation. It was he who conducted the *HMS Impregnable* band at the RNSM's opening ceremony at Eastney Barracks on 22nd July 1903.

Twenty years later, it was decided that the School of Music would move to Deal in Kent where, apart from relocating to Malvern, Scarborough, the Isle of Man and Burford to avoid possible enemy action during World War II, it remained until it returned to Portsmouth in 1996.

GOLD ON BLUE

CHAPTER 2

TRAINING AT BURFORD AND DEAL
1949 - 1953

My application to join the Services was processed through the Royal Navy & Royal Marines Recruiting Office at Portsmouth. An audition to access my suitability to be trained as a musician was arranged. I went along at the appointed time to find that I was the only candidate present. I was taken into a room, empty except for an upright piano placed against one wall and with a small man in Royal Marines uniform pacing up and down. He told me that he was going to test my 'aural perception'. This was a bad start because I didn't know what that was! He raised the lid of piano keyboard and, having asked me to stand by his right arm, played a couple of notes. My 'audition,' which I passed, seems to have consisted of being able to indicate which was the higher of those two notes!

I later learned that my Report on Entry noted that I had 'very slight knowledge of the piano keyboard,' a 'very good ear' and that I was 'quite a musical boy and bright.'

I didn't know it at the time but, with the war over, those who had survived it were leaving the Services in droves to return to civilian employment, and there was an urgent need to replace them.

The wartime death toll of Royal Marines musicians serving in ships had been enormous. Over 25% of those serving at sea were lost. The action station for musicians was down below the waterline of the ship. Their duty was to man the Transmitting Station, the gunnery control centre of capital ships, where information was collated on the distance of the target, state of the sea, wind speed, speed of the ship, etc. When accurately plotted, the data was passed to the upper deck guns. It wasn't until the musicians had calculated and sent this vital information that firing from the six, eight, or twelve-inch main armament turrets could commence.

Sadly, the Transmitting Station was in the bottom of the ship, often between the fuel and ammunition stores. Below the water line, hatches to compartments were sealed from above during action stations. Torpedo damage from the enemy caused enormous loss of life in these compartments. Many ships that were sunk, including *HMS Hood, HMS Barham, HMS Gloucester and HMS Neptune,* took their entire complement of musicians to the bottom of the sea with them.

Buglers and drummers, of which each ship usually had a complement of two, lost many of their number. Their action stations were on the ship's bridge and the after steering position. The youngest Royal Marine to be killed in action during the First World War was Boy Bugler Charles Timmins, aged fourteen, on board *HMS Cardiff,* as the ship intercepted

German minesweeping forces that were clearing British minefields in the North Sea. One of the youngest British servicemen to be killed in action during World War II was fourteen-year-old Boy Bugler Peter Avant on board *HMS Fiji*, off Crete. His fellow bugler, a sixteen-year-old lad named Kenneth French, also died.

Burford

I was thirteen years old when I applied, and only fourteen and one week when I joined the Band Service. I travelled by train to Burford in Oxfordshire on 11th May 1949 where, at the Royal Naval School of Music, I was formally inducted by swearing due allegiance to the Sovereign. I was told that in return for *The Queen's Shilling*, I had signed to serve for twelve years from the age of eighteen and would receive musical training until I reached that age. The powers-that-be had four years to turn me into a proficient musician before I would join an adult band.

I was to be taught to play the clarinet and the viola. It had long been a requirement for musicians in the naval service to play in both military band and orchestra, so students were taught to play combinations of instruments similar in pitch that allowed for this. The combinations included clarinet/violin, saxophone/viola, euphonium/cello and tuba/string bass. Some instruments could be played in both military band and orchestra, i.e. French horn, trombone, oboe, flute, bassoon, trumpet and percussion, and these players were only trained on their single instrument. Buglers and Drummers were an autonomous group trained in all aspects of Band Ceremonial, wherein they have become world-leaders.

Within weeks of joining, my instrumental category was changed to clarinet/violin, possibly on the intervention of a Bandmaster relative of mine whom I had never met. He was E.G.R. (Ted) White a violinist, who recognised that playing melodies on the violin would be more interesting than playing supporting parts on the viola. It was sage advice, and I am grateful to him for it.

As a new intake of boys numbering about forty, we were billeted in two Nissen Huts. My hut was called the Churchill Room, while the other half of my intake was housed across a colonnade, in the Battenburg Room. Each barrack-room contained toilets and a washroom as well as beds and lockers along the sides for each boy.

In Churchill Room, Corporal Dunckley, a drill instructor, together with a senior boy from an earlier intake, was in charge and responsible for the daily parades and the general non-musical training of us recruits. He was an example to all in cleanliness, fairness and honesty. I lost touch with him for several decades and only became acquainted again after he had become an old man. I was able then to thank him for showing me the way all those years ago, and to explain that had it not been for him, I would never have become a successful commissioned officer within the Royal Marines.

Another man whose guidance I valued during those first weeks and months was a drill instructor called Fred Yardley. Some fifty years later, I would often see him walking through the streets of Deal. I never ceased to admire his ability as an instructor in life skills and to appreciate the kindness with which he taught us youngsters. Kindness is not a word usually associated with drill instructors of any Service, but Fred was, as a committed Christian, an exception to the rule.

Fred may well have had something to do with the fact that we were each given a poem by Margaret Swanton to keep in our pay books:

FOR HONOUR AND FOR HER

Somewhere a woman, thrusting fear away
Faces the future bravely for your sake.
Toils on from dawn till dark, from day to day.
Fights back her tears, nor heeds the bitter ache.

She loves you, trusts you, breathes in prayer your name.
Soil not her faith in you by sin or shame.
Somewhere a woman — mother, sweetheart, wife —
Waits betwixt hopes and fears for your return.

Her kiss, her words, will cheer you in the strife
When death itself confronts you, grim and stern.
But let her image all your reverence claim,
When base temptations scorch you with their flame.

Somewhere a woman watches — filled with pride;
Shrined in her heart you share a place with none.
She toils, she waits, she prays, till side by side
You stand together when the battle's done.

Oh! Keep for her dear sake a stainless name.
Bring back to her a manhood free from shame.

The establishment at Burford was not very secure, just a three-foot high Cotswold dry-stone wall separated it from the adjoining fields. Trysts over the wall with local girls were fairly common although, at the tender age of fourteen, I was never involved. We all heard stories about one girl who had earned the name *Black Rita*. Poor girl, I wonder what became of her?

Being only a hutted camp, most facilities there were basic. The sports field, for instance, had no pavilion or changing area. It did, however, have the fuselage of a crashed wartime glider near to the side of the football pitch, the top of which we used as a vantage point to view the sports action.

As the winter of 1949 approached, I became very poorly after queuing in the snow to collect my weekly laundry and was admitted to the Sick Bay, where there was considerable concern because my temperature had risen alarmingly to well beyond the point of safety. In some concern, my uncle, Bandmaster White, paid me a visit. Up to that point in my recruit training, he had avoided any form of contact with me so that my colleagues should not see me as having any form of preferential treatment. This was despite the fact that, at the time, he was an instructor of violin and cornet for a senior class of students at the School. Eventually, he invited me to spend an occasional Saturday or Sunday afternoon with him and his wife at their cottage in a nearby Cotswold village. It was always such a welcome change from the reality of my days in training within the camp.

My first clarinet was a 'simple-system' model with very few keys. I was later issued with a modern 'Boehm system' clarinet with thirteen keys, a far superior instrument. When I joined, I had no musical knowledge at all. My father had been a conductor, but of a bus, and that didn't count! Some of my fellow recruits had been playing instruments throughout their earlier years. One chap, Jan Kessell, told me that he played a cornet. I thought a cornet was something that ice-cream came in!

Each day, after early morning parade, we would focus on our music practice. We stood beside our beds, erected our music-stands and made a cacophony of sounds as we tried to coax notes out of the instruments we were holding. An instructor was always present to coach each boy in turn, before bringing everyone together for scale and arpeggio practice.

If the morning was taken up with practice on an orchestral instrument, then the afternoon would be given over to one's military band instrument, and the pattern would be reversed the following day. It was all very new to me. I was very unsure of myself and doubtful of my ability to progress as a musician.

My first violin instructor was Band Corporal George Clarke. He looked at me rather oddly for some days, and then asked me the name of my hometown and whether I had a job there. I told him that I came from Fareham and that my only regular job had been as a paper-boy. "I knew it!" he said. "You used to deliver along Hartland's Road, didn't you?" I confirmed that I did. He recognised me because he had been living there at the time and his front door was at the end of a long garden path. A hedge divided his path from an identical path to the neighbour's front door. He grabbed me by the ear and made me apologise for bursting through his hedge each day to deliver his neighbour's paper. I learned the lesson that there could be no escape from one's past!

One day, a rumour spread that some of us may be made redundant. I had very mixed feelings at this point. An initial surge of enthusiasm that I would be one of those selected welled up in my chest as I thought of home, but I then began to hope that my name would not be among those chosen. Although very homesick, I could not face the embarrassment of returning home to my village as the failure I knew I would be seen to be. After all, being accepted into the Royal Marines had been the high point in my young life. As it turned out, the rumour was a false one, and things went on as normal. My sister, who had taken over my room in the family home, would not have been at all impressed had I returned at that point!

We wore blue serge siren-suits with boots and berets during the working day. Around our waist, we wore webbing belts with clasps at the front, and buckles at the back, made from dull gun-metal. Like everything else, these metal parts had to be cleaned. They never ever shone, for it was like polishing pewter. When my father saw the belt during my first spell of home leave, he did no more than unpick the stitching at the back of the belt to free the buckles and took them, together with the front clasps and runners, to be professionally chromium-plated by a friend at work! When I appeared on parade after leave wearing my newly modified belt - mother had sewn the buckles back on - I was the object of much interest. There was some jealousy, and I couldn't believe it when one NCO wanted me to be punished for *defacing government property*. Common sense prevailed, however, and throughout my training I never had to use polish on those metal parts again.

The violin class 1950. B/Cpl George Clark i/c

Boy Musician Hoskins 'At ease' in the back garden, 1951

In 1950, the Staff Bands of the Royal Marines were located at Chatham, Portsmouth and Plymouth. Until 1947, these bands had been known as Divisional Bands and recruited locally. In the 18th century, Divisional Bands were financially supported to a large degree by the Divisional Officers, although in later years these Officers were only obliged to help with the upkeep of their band in the form of one day's pay per year!

Deal

General Duty Royal Marines had always joined at Deal, and it was decided that the Royal Naval School of Music would move early in 1950 to Deal from Burford. It was also decided that the 'Royal Naval School of Music' would be renamed the 'Royal Marines School of Music,' and that the Commanding Officer of the Royal Marines Depot in Deal would become the Commandant of the new School of Music.

Major Vivian Dunn, the Director of Music of the Portsmouth Divisional Band, which provided musicians for Royal Yachts, was brought to Deal and, on promotion to Lieutenant Colonel, was appointed the first Principal Director of Music Royal Marines. He held the appointment for the next 17 years!

This was a momentous decision, for it heralded the beginning of the present-day Band Service. Professional music tutors (Professors) were recruited from non-military music circles for instrumental and theoretical tuition. Initially, they were paid by the hour with no remuneration during leave periods and no pension rights. Prior to this, music instructors had been restricted to uniformed members of the Band Service, whose instrumental teaching ability was questionable - after all, they had fought through a world war when musical performance had taken a low priority.

A special train was laid on to take some 400 RNSM personnel from Burford to Deal and we were each issued with bag rations that had been prepared many hours before the journey. The train was put into a siding at about the time we ate our lunch. The sandwiches were very stale and the meat-pies were considered by most to be inedible. Windows of the train were opened, and all the pies were thrown out. When the train eventually pulled away, it looked as if the area had been subjected to a plague of leg-less tortoises, as the debris of a very poor lunch lay scattered in the grass.

On our arrival at Deal railway station, we were met by a marching band, civic dignitaries and uniformed personnel. We then realised that we would have to march to wherever the barracks was. Being January, we were wearing greatcoats and had marching-order haversacks on our backs. We fell in behind the Depot Band and, amid crowds of onlookers, marched through the streets of Deal and up The Strand to East Barracks where, twenty minutes later we wheeled right, under the clock-tower and heard the gates, prison-like, clang shut behind us.

As we entered, I had my first glimpse of a Regimental Sergeant Major. His name, I was eventually to learn, was Tom Franks. He was tall and reed thin. Every part of his uniform glistened in the late afternoon sunshine. With his sardonic smile, he seemed to us boys to be the devil incarnate. We just knew we were to be *on his menu* and so it transpired.

Many years later, I was to appreciate his true value when we really needed him. I was a member of the Plymouth Band and we were at the Bath & West Agricultural Show, together with the King's Squad of the Royal Marines who were under the command of RSM Tom Franks. A group of youths were causing difficulty in the early evening gloom as we waited to go into the arena for our ceremonial display. They began to bait the squad of Royal Marines, who ignored them. Then came a moment I shall never forget: RSM Franks called his men to the position of attention and, with an ice-cold stare towards the tormentors, gave the command: *Fix Bayonets!* I hardly need say that the troublemakers turned on their heels and ran!

Although of no military significance today, Deal had, for centuries, played an important role in securing the nation's defences. Situated on the Kent coast, just 25 miles from France, it was about a mile north from where Julius Caesar had first landed his armies in 55 and 54BC. In the 1530s, King Henry VIII had built three castles along Deal's coastline to deter European forces from invading the country, and it was here where the Admiralty had later established a sizeable presence. Deal was a town very familiar to soldiers as illustrious as the Duke of Wellington, and sailors as illustrious as Lord Nelson.

Just to the north of Deal Castle was a Naval Yard, which is now mainly occupied by Victorian homes. Established in 1672, the Yard was responsible for the logistical support of warships anchored offshore in The Downs, an area of sea between the beach and the Goodwin Sands. Its importance grew during the Napoleonic Wars (1794 – 1815) when Deal harboured the Fleet and was the base for several raids on the French coast.

The yard closed in 1863, just two years after a Royal Marines Depot had opened in the town to train recruits destined for the Royal Marines Light Infantry.

The Royal Marines initially occupied a large building near Deal Castle. With its distinctive white clocktower, it was built in 1809 as a hospital to replace an earlier Royal Naval Hospital that the Admiralty had purchased in 1796 but had been struck by lightning. Originally known as Hospital Barracks, the site became, on 7th May 1861, the home of the Depot Royal Marines. Hospital Barracks was later renamed East Barracks.

By 1860, servicemen were also using three other large barrack blocks in Deal. The cavalry and infantry occupied North and South Barracks, alongside which was a separate hospital for army personnel (known as Infirmary Barracks).

In 1950, when I first arrived in Deal, the barrack areas were used in the following ways:

South Barracks, accessed from Dover Road and Canada Road, contained administrative offices for the Commanding Officer, Second in Command, Principal Director of Music and others, accommodation for Women's Royal Naval Service personnel, also the Gymnasium, Officers' and Sergeants' messes, a church and the sports fields. Halfway along the barrack wall facing Dover Road was Jubilee Gate, which had been installed to commemorate Queen Victoria's Golden Jubilee in 1887. It gave the public a stunning view of the long drive that led to the Officers' Mess. To the left of Jubilee Gate was the finest hockey pitch in Kent, and possibly the country. Originally often waterlogged, the surface had at some stage been dug up, then wattle and brushwood had been laid on the earth before the grass turf was replaced. This cushioning effect was very popular with the sportsmen on the pitch. To the right of Jubilee Gate was an open-air bandstand that was used for public concerts. The massive sports field behind the Officers' Mess, beyond which was an obstacle course, was known as the Drill Field. Because of its size, it was extremely useful after 1950 for Massed Band rehearsals prior to the Royal Tournament, Edinburgh Military Tattoos and Horse Guards Parade performances. The final dress rehearsals for these events were open to the public and always attracted large audiences.

North Barracks was a large complex opposite South Barracks, on the other side of Canada Road. It contained the adult Royal Marines accommodation blocks, the main parade ground, a NAAFI shop, the main galley, the Globe Theatre, stables and Officers' houses. A modern drill shed was erected, but it had hopeless acoustic qualities rendering it virtually useless for parade work.

Infirmary Barracks contained the Sick Bay, school rooms and wood and metal workshops that had previously been used as zymotic (infectious disease) wards. Instruction for these latter subjects was part of our general educational curriculum.

Lastly, there was *East Barracks*, the home of the Royal Marines School of Music, where we boy musicians lived and studied.

We were allocated barrack-room accommodation according to our instrumental categories and without regard to our ages. The barrack-rooms were situated on three levels on either side of stone staircases.. Each set of barrack rooms was designated a capital letter: M, N, O, P and Q. 'M' Block housed the buglers and drummers; 'N' Block, the string bass/bombardon and euphonium/cello instrumentalists; 'O' Block the oboists, bassoonists and French horn players on the upper two floors, whilst a communal bathroom was situated at ground level. 'P' Block housed the cornet players, saxophonists, clarinettists, violinists and viola players. 'Q' Block contained smaller rooms with a piano available in each for the pianists to practice on.

No one actually lived in 'Q' block, which was just as well for it also sported a well-documented ghost that switched lights on and off in locked rooms during the night, much to everyone's consternation!

In common with other academic institutions at the time, a *house system* was incorporated for boys under training. The four houses were given the names of Royal Navy ships that had been sunk during World War II, taking with them the musicians that were trapped in their duty stations. Each *house* had its designated colour for sportswear, etc. 'M' block was *Barham* (blue), 'N' block *Gloucester* (green), 'O' block *Eagle* (yellow) and 'P' Block *Neptune* (red). This house system brought with it considerable sports-field rivalry and a certain amount of individual pride when success was achieved.

The barrack rooms became instrumental classrooms during the day, with access to individual tutorial rooms leading from the stairwells. Music stands were erected between the beds and a uniformed instructor supervised the students during working hours. The cacophony was such that at times, when windows were open, complaints were received from nearby houses. The answer to them was always, "Sorry, but the Royal Marines were here first!"

East Barracks was also where the clothing store, central music library, tailor's shop, boot repair shop, barber's shop and musical instrument store were located. Nearby was a little room known to all musicians as *The Crotchet Factory,* where Band Sergeant Paul Schmitt sat every day writing out music from composers' full scores to make individual instrumental copies.

The lower room of 'N' block was a dining hall and across the parade ground was a small galley, with suitably barred windows, where our food was prepared and cooked by Royal Marines chefs each day. At mealtimes the food had to be carried across the parade ground in all weathers in uncovered metal trays by boys whose duty it was when nominated.

A new dining facility was eventually built in North Barracks to serve the entire barracks population. Once it was available, we had to march there from East Barracks for our food three times a day. An early 'tea and supper combined' meal was served at weekends so that the duty chef would not be inconvenienced by having to work in the evening! Those of us that could went ashore later in the evening for egg and chips in a local café.

An unheated corrugated-iron shed-like building stood near the galley on the other side of the parade ground from the accommodation. This was the toilet block. It contained eight cubicles on one side and an open urinal on the other. The doors to the cubicles were hinged so that they hung well above floor level and any occupants clearly visible. Even in winter it was 'air-conditioned,' for there was an eight-inch gap between the top of the walls and the roof. The toilet paper was hard and shiny, with every sheet marked *Government Property*. There was no heating of any sort, so winter brought with it huge discomfort. Our mothers never knew of our predicament for we bravely withheld such information from them. During working hours, this was the only facility for all boy musicians and buglers under training. Other small toilets were built into the sides of the barrack blocks, but these were kept locked during daylight hours and only available from 9pm until 6am.

Baths were allowed once a week, whether needed or not, in a room at the bottom of 'O' block which contained eight tubs. Bath nights were supervised by an adult musician who checked barrack-room lists for absentees and ensured that only a minimum amount of hot water was put into each bath.

Harsh, short back and side, haircuts were administered each fortnight by an adult musician whose name was 'Twin' Hember - selected, no doubt, because he was better at cutting hair than playing his instruments. His barbershop was on the southern side of East Barracks main entrance gate.

'Twin' Hember, so named because his twin brother also served in the Band Service, eventually set up a thriving hairdressing business in Hampshire. His expertise came from the fact that musicians serving in ships of the fleet were not permitted to play their instruments in the afternoons, when the night-time watch-keepers were asleep. This meant that on board ships, spare time on a regular basis was available and enterprising musicians used this time to their advantage. The ship's photographer, tailor, barber and shoe repairer was often a member of the band, and these artisans took their trades with them into civilian life when the time came for them to leave the service. Basil Kidd, who had served in the Arctic Convoys during the war, was one of the many who did just that, becoming a highly respected staff photographer for the East Kent Mercury group of newspapers.

Bundles of soiled clothing were collected and returned each week by Lambert's laundry. It was not a cheap service, so some of us relied on an old lady who used to appear daily at the side gate of the barracks with an ancient pram. She would accept bundles of clothes for washing and bring them back the next day, often still damp, for she had no means of properly drying it. We used to put the items under the bottom sheet in our beds and let our body heat 'air' it through the night! When I eventually told my mother that this is what we used to do she was horrified and didn't believe me, but it was true. In an emergency, it was another way to press our trousers, but never entirely successful. It should have worked better than it did with the trousers sandwiched between the hard mattress and our body weight. We had to try not to wriggle about too much through the night!

Our lives were governed by the clock and days began when a duty bugler sounded *Reveille* at 6am. This was the signal for the duty NCO to enter all the barrack rooms in turn, shouting and banging on locker doors. Anyone still in bed when he revisited in about five minutes was required to run around the parade ground scantily clad.

There was one communal washroom for all! It had originally been the operating theatre when the premises had been a Napoleonic hospital. Semi-circular in shape, the room had taps hanging every three feet around the perimeter wall. A black slate base held individual metal washbowls, while the water splashed away through a central waste. Limited supplies of hot water were available from a nearby gas boiler that fed into a large, covered tank. Getting to and from the washroom meant leaving my barrack-room, negotiating the stone staircase down into the open air and on through a colonnaded area, often sparsely dressed!

Each barrack-room housed about sixteen trainees plus an adult Band Corporal or trained soldier (addressed as *Troop*). He had a corner bed and would use the kit lockers to gain some privacy for himself, whereas we boys just had a small steel locker between each bed. Bedspaces were allocated along both sides of the long room. A shelf and hooks were fixed on the wall behind each bed, where items of kit were displayed.

Each day, we would polish the wooden floor before we had our breakfast. Throughout the day, blankets and sheets were folded and placed neatly at the head of the bed with a spare blanket covering the mattress. Under the foot of each bed, immaculately cleaned boots, shoes and whitened plimsoles were displayed.

Once a term, kit-muster inspections were ordered. This entailed placing a blanket on the floor and laying upon it every item of kit with which we had been issued, clearly marked with our name and service number. There was a strict display order for this procedure so that each item could be easily located when called from the inspection list.

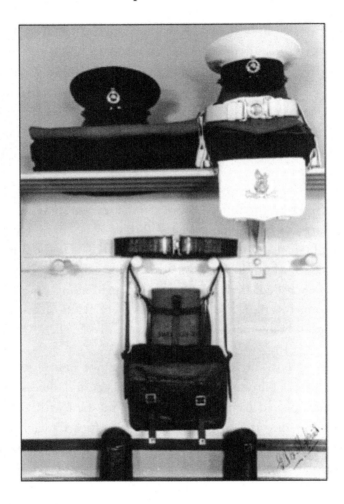

Marching order kit layout

Shirts had to be rolled up individually and placed at the top of the blanket. We were required to roll them around a copy of the Royal Marines magazine, *Globe & Laurel*, to ensure that they were always rolled to the correct size We thought it was a crafty way of ensuring that we bought the magazine, although it seemed never to contain anything about the Band Service.

Presented properly, the kit muster was a work of art and a source of great pride. I can recall the Sergeant calling out things such as: "Shirts khaki, three" and my bright reply: "One down, one on, and one at the laundry!" We had each been issued with a fold-up piece of cloth containing small compartments. It was called a 'housewife' and had to hold - from left to right - knife, fork, spoon, comb, type, and button-stick. Handles had to face upwards, and the ribbon tie tapes, properly ironed, to the right! Failure to comply probably meant jail, but I never found out!

East Barracks had no central heating. Each barrack-room had a fireplace halfway along one wall, with a coal-bunce to each side of it. These large iron bunces were embossed with insignia from a previous century, for they were, in fact, cannon-ball boxes. Coal was brought by a working party of boys carried in round metal containers each with two handles. Filled from the nearby coal-yard, the boys would haul the containers up the wide stone stairs to deliver coal to each room. This was done on Saturday mornings and formed part of general fatigue duties undertaken by all boys. Once fuel for the week had been delivered, the inside of the bunces had to be whitened down to the level of the coal!

Boys Wing family open days were held prior to Christmas leave each year. Boys festively decorated their barrack rooms and tea parties were arranged in them for families visiting their sons. Junior orchestral and band performances were held, as was a Boys Wing pantomime in the Globe Theatre.

Returning from Christmas leave in early January to cold, bleak and empty barrack rooms was, for me as a fourteen-year-old, a never to be forgotten experience. The departure of steam trains from London's Waterloo Station meant that people returned in dribs and drabs not altogether, so if you were one of the first to get back, the loneliness, chill and isolation of East Barracks was palpable.

Other things happened on Saturday mornings. With lots of exercise, boys grew fast and some, like me, who had joined when we were barely in our teens, were under training for up to four years. We naturally grew out of the service clothing we had been issued with. So, on Saturday mornings, items now too small or worn out could be replaced after 'survey' at the Clothing Store. The Officer would often look at the item and tell the boy holding it for inspection that there was at least another week's wear in it!

I once took my white ceremonial pith helmet for exchange. Lengthy exposure to rain during parades had made the peak all floppy. When the Officer asked me what was wrong with it I held it by the peak and wiggled it to indicate the problem. He erupted with indignation, accused me of doing the damage there and then in front of his eyes and made me contribute financially to its replacement! You could never appeal such decisions, and the money was taken directly from our pay.

Having left school at fourteen with no qualifications, I was fortunate to find that, at the School of Music, general educational subjects were taught alongside music. The weekly curriculum covered such subjects as Maths, English, Geography, Musical Appreciation and Religious Education.

Instruction in handicrafts was also given and we were encouraged to make useful items from wood and metal. The metal-work instructor was called, for reasons obvious to those who had met him, 'Gandhi' Rule. He allowed one boy in my class to make an eight-inch-long naval cannon. When finished, the boy brought it back to the barrack-room and loaded the breach with what we were told were the scrapings of match-heads – *lots* of them! Finally he inserted a beautifully made cannon ball into the barrel and lit the fuse. The cannon ball went straight through the barrack-room door and on into the next room, whilst the cannon hurtled backwards in our room at the same speed!

A very sensible compulsory saving scheme was introduced for boys under training where a small amount of money was put aside from their fortnightly pay and placed in a Post Office savings account. The money that accrued, by then often a substantial amount, was available to individuals on completion of training when they were presented with their Post Office bank book. Advice on insurance and investments was also given to trainees. The Prudential got the lion's share of any business for their agent, a Mr Gordon Booth, was alone permitted access to the band-boys in East Barracks and appeared on target at least once a week.

Shore leave was granted on various days and for a designated number of hours. The younger boys were only allowed out at weekends and had to be back by 7pm, whilst others could stay 'ashore' until midnight. Best blue uniform had to be worn at all times, and each boy was inspected at the guardroom before being allowed through the gate, often to join a girlfriend waiting patiently there. We had to wear our white gloves and would not be allowed to proceed without showing a clean white handkerchief. The older boys were also allowed out on Wednesdays and could wear their civilian clothes. Shore leave was extended to midnight for those approaching their eighteenth birthday.

Band Boy Hoskins ashore in Deal, 1953

An afternoon each week was reserved for sports activities. Following the 2pm parade, we would be marched to the gymnasium in South Barracks. We would be dressed in shorts and coloured cotton sports shirts according to the *house* we were from. Teams would be picked for the various sports and those left over had to go cross-country running. I became quite good at the latter - but only because I was so keen to avoid boxing and rugby! Running on the shingle of the beach was not something I looked forward to, however.

Some boys would manage to avoid sports activities altogether by hiding away in the loft under the clock-tower of East Barracks. We always knew who had been up there because when they reappeared they were filthy and covered in cobwebs. Some proudly showed clay-pipes and other artefacts they had found in the darkness of the loft that had been placed there during the previous century - probably by artisans fixing the clock that was powered by huge weights that hung down within the cavity wall. The weights needed to be hoisted regularly with a large cranking handle. Oddly, the clock was more reliable then than after it was converted to electric power.

I remember clearly playing my clarinet for the first time as a member of a parade band. We just stood still and played a march called *On the Square*. It was an altogether uplifting experience to stand amid the sparkling sounds of the different instruments, all individual yet part of a scintillating whole. I warmed to the rhythm, the tune, sensible phrasing and musical punctuation and, in particular, the way the trombones declared "Tum, tum tum, tara-tum-tum" at the end of our woodwind tune! I wasn't yet fifteen and I loved being part of it all. Suddenly, there was a reason for me to spend so many hours practising individually every day. Playing in a band was a team game that I really wanted to be part of, and my spirits soared. A light was switched on that has never dimmed.

Swimming lessons

One period a week was allotted for swimming in the covered Royal Marines Swimming Pool, built in 1900 and located opposite the Commanding Officer's house on The Strand. At the pool we were each given slips, tied at one side, to wear in the water. Before getting out of the pool at the conclusion of each session, we were required to take off the slip and squeeze the water out of it. This was my first experience of 'skinny-dipping' and I looked forward to it as perhaps the most enjoyable moment of my week!

As Royal Marines musicians would be expected to serve on ships at some point in their career, we each had to pass various tests. We had to swim a designated number of lengths wearing long cotton trousers and tunics tied at the middle with a sash, and dive into the water to recover house bricks from the bottom of the pool. Standing on the side of the pool would be a PT instructor clutching a stopwatch in one hand and a long wooden pole in the other. I thought the pole was for us to grab hold of if we got into difficulties, but quickly found that it was a device to prod us with to keep us from getting to the side and giving up.

Another requirement was for us to run and jump, one by one, into the water from the high diving board. Leaving the end of the board, we had to try to touch a roof support some way forward in the ceiling before plummeting down. This was actually to ensure that we would be upright when hitting the water, reducing the risk of bellyflops. Some boys were at home in the water and entered it from a height with barely a ripple. Others, less blade-like in build, left the end of the diving board brittle with anxiety at the thought of the impending impact below.

A favourite 'dare' at weekends was to swim out and around a wrecked ship lying just off the beach at Walmer. The fear was that a conger eel would grab the unfortunate swimmer, for it was well known that these monsters frequented such sunken ships, and Walmer beach was world-renowned for the excellence of its fishing!

Section leader

When I reached my sixteenth birthday I became eligible for promotion to Section Leader, the badge for which was an elongated red diamond worn above the left elbow on all uniforms. I was immediately selected and, with my new badge to spur my ambitions, was informed that I would now have to move from P10 room, wherein I had spent the previous two years, to the room below, P6, where I would be in sole charge. My heart sank, for P6 contained boys much older than me. Some were nearly eighteen years old and were coming to the end of their training.

The Company Sergeant Major, Staff Bandmaster Bill Wells, saw my concern and taking me to one side, gave me the best advice of my life: once I had moved into a corner bed in P6 room, I was to look around for something that needed to be done and then tell the biggest and most frightening person in the room to do it. With considerable trepidation, I followed his advice. Looking around I saw that the rubbish bin was full and in need of emptying. In the silence and crackling tension of the moment I told 'Lofty' Beatty, a rugby player and a *BIG* chap, to empty the bin by taking it to the dump across the parade ground. Nobody moved and I could feel the damp hand of failing courage on the back of my neck. Beatty then got up and without a word did as he had been ordered to do. I never had the slightest problem from that day forward!

The Coronation procession

I recall the sadness surrounding the death of King George VI in February 1952, but how quickly our spirits were raised when we were told that some of us boys would be selected to march in an adult Royal Marines band during the Coronation procession of the new Queen Elizabeth II on 2nd June 1953. I was one of the boy musicians that went to London, to be billeted in the Earls Court Exhibition Centre prior to marching in the procession. Here were upwards of 5000 soldiers, sailors and airmen living in the building for the duration of the rehearsals and the actual event. We slept in three-tier bunk beds. Mattresses were palliasse covers filled with straw that had to be collected from the main arena on the day we arrived. Old hands made sure that they stuffed huge amounts of straw into the covers, because they knew that in use, the straw would break down into not much more than dust. Lads like me just took what we thought was necessary - and paid the price of our ignorance!

On the day of the Coronation, I was one of the lucky 30,000 servicemen that marched in the teeming rain for some fifteen miles through cheering crowds. Sadly, because of where our band was in the overall procession, we didn't see much at all. All I saw of the colour and majesty of the occasion was the backside of the police horse that walked the route in front of the band. I didn't qualify for the Coronation medal. I was told that these were reserved for the Royal Navy, Royal Marines, Army and RAF servicemen who stood to attention outside Westminster Abbey, and the members of the Portsmouth Group Band who paraded with them.

Privacy and predators

There was no such thing as 'privacy' for boys under training living cheek by jowl in barrack-rooms. Within this community, we were instinctively forged into something where the key to success in 'beating the odds' was only achieved by our unity. For me this was a learning curve that necessarily lasted for the four years I was under training. It is uncomfortable all these years later to accept how institutionalised we were. I don't recall any boy having a personal radio, for instance, nor a record-player. There was a centrally controlled *Rediffusion box* on the wall of our rooms giving access to the BBC Home Service and the Light Programme, and that was it.

Any form of sexual activity was forbidden and contained in loneliness and silence beneath the blankets during long dark nights. Even moderate porn was treated like gold dust. Just as rare and twice as valuable! To us youngsters truly cooped up like prisoners, it was a class 'A' drug and almost as addictive as heroin.

At this point, I must record an event which caused great embarrassment to us boys and considerable anxiety for our distant families. A very Senior Non-Commissioned Officer and the Padre shared a room in East Barracks as a repository for their uniforms and personal items. One evening the Padre entered the room unexpectedly to find the NCO sexually abusing a boy musician. The Padre immediately reported the matter to the Commanding Officer. At his eventual Court-martial, the NCO was found guilty, given a custodial sentence and dismissed from the Service. The worst, for us trainees, was yet to come, for the local East Kent Mercury newspaper reported lurid details of the case - some true, many false - under a banner front-page headline: *Every Barrack-room has its Tart!* It took a very long time for the furore to die down and for us to be able to walk the local streets without embarrassment.

In my final year of training, as School (and Neptune House) Captain and the senior Section Leader, I must have been the logical choice to be appointed to be the first 'Boy Sergeant Major' when badges of rank were substituted for Section Leader diamonds. With this new position, I was given a small room of my own and my administrative duties increased. I was entrusted with the whole routine of Sunday Church Parades, for instance, when up to this point adult Senior NCOs had always been involved. It was good preparation for what was to come in later years.

The Cassel Prizes

In the late 1940s Sir Felix Cassel Bt., then Master of the Worshipful Company of Musicians - a London Livery Company - decided to endow annual awards of silver and bronze medals for musical ability in each of the three Services. These *Cassel Prizes*, open through competition to all students under training, are still awarded. The Royal Marines decided that a silver and bronze medal should be awarded to the best and runner-up musician under training, and that a silver medal should be awarded to the top student on the adult Bandmaster course.

In 1952, at the age of 17, I was entered for the competition and won the bronze medal. A concert was held in the Gymnasium in South Barracks at which, in front of my proud parents, my colleague Patrick Flynn, who had won the silver medal, and I performed. Patrick was a brilliant pianist who, on leaving the Corps, became an extremely distinguished composer and conductor. Accompanied at the piano by Professor Kenneth Mettyear, of whom you will learn more later, I performed part of Mozart's *Clarinet Concerto*.

I was told that I would have the honour of receiving my medal at a Worshipful Company of Musicians' Dinner in London. Finalists from all three Services attended, and on arrival at the appointed venue in our best uniforms we were given sandwiches before being ushered into the room where the dinner was in progress. At an appropriate time the medals were duly presented. These days, I am happy to report, medal winners are invited to dine with the assembled Company as guests.

In the 1930s, King George V had decreed that the best all-round Royal Marine in the senior recruit squad, to be known as *The King's Squad*, should be awarded a *King's Badge*. It would consist of his personal royal cypher surrounded by laurel leaves in gold wire and sewn onto the left shoulder of all uniforms. It was to be worn throughout the recipient's career, even if they were eventually commissioned as an officer. The Band Service equivalent was the Commandant General's Certificate of Merit, and I was awarded this distinction in 1953.

My training came to an end on my eighteenth birthday. On 4th May 1953 I was marched into the Commanding Officer's office. *Left, right, left right, HALT … Salute!* barked the Sergeant Major. I had arrived in front of the Commandant who was sitting behind a large desk. "Ah! – Hoskins," he said, "I see you have done very well over the past four years and that you now play violin, clarinet, and saxophone." (The latter, I had taught myself. I was not officially designated a saxophone player, but from the moment I had heard the American saxophonist Dick Johnson play, I was hooked, and I desperately wanted to emulate his sound on a saxophone. I had received no formal training on the instrument and had not yet been given an opportunity to play it in a dance band – something I had longed to do!) The Commandant went on to say: "I am pleased to tell you that, for your first commission, you are going to serve on the American & West Indies Station on board the cruiser *HMS Sheffield* and that the ship will be based in Bermuda. More importantly however," he said, looking me straight in the eyes: "As today is your eighteenth birthday, I am able to tell you that you have become a man!"

I was so excited that after I had left his office I went back to the barrack-room to have a look – but that was another of life's bitter disappointments!

CHAPTER 3

HMS SHEFFIELD: THE AMERICAN & WEST INDIES STATION
1953 -1954

In 1953, Service personnel were transported to their units overseas in troopships. No air travel was available. Ships of the fleet were based around the globe on designated stations ready to respond to incidents and to *show the flag* for Britain. When it was time for a ship to end its allotted period of duty, a replacement would be sent and, after a dignified hand over of command, the original vessel would return to its home port in UK for de-commissioning and a possible refit. Every capital ship had a Royal Marines Band of around eighteen musicians, led by a Bandmaster. Capital ships are the Royal Navy's most important warships, and include vessels such as cruisers, battleships and aircraft carriers.

Individual bands for ships were formed at Deal prior to embarkation. They would be issued with the necessary stores they would need together with a *Sea Service* library of music.

The library was largely the same for all ships, so going to a new ship did not entail learning an entirely new repertoire.

The *Sheffield Five*

I moved from the School of Music in East Barracks to an adult accommodation block in North Barracks, where I remained until the time came for me to make my way to *HMS Sheffield*. Those of us who had been nominated for *HMS Sheffield's* band met up for the first time under the expert guidance of its Bandmaster, 'Jeff' Jefferson. He was an experienced and accomplished musician and many years later became Director of Music of the South African Police Force in the rank of Colonel. The Captain of the *Sheffield* came to Deal to pass his band for duty after listening to them performing in various musical combinations. A date was then confirmed for the band to board the ship at Portsmouth prior to its sea trials with its new crew of officers and men.

We were to board on a Monday, so weekend leave was granted for members of the band. Five of us had relatives in the Portsmouth area, so we didn't take advantage of this offer as we would be seeing our relatives after the weekend anyway. We five stayed in Deal and looked after the instruments, music stands and other band paraphernalia that we would take with us.

Because of long-standing animosity between the regular marines and the members of the Band Service, bands going off to sea tried to find ways of leaving their mark at Deal in a way that would demonstrate their spirit and refusal to be suborned. The Regimental Sergeant Major may arrive at his office after a band had left to find his office windows whitewashed over, or some large item would have been mysteriously taken by the draft band only for them to return it to Deal in a kitbag, 'cash on delivery'!

As my career throughout training had, up to that date, been distinguished, I was glad that so many of my new band's members had gone on leave for my final weekend at Deal, because this meant that I was unlikely to have to be part of anything likely to bring discredit. Imagine then, my concern when, after dark on the Saturday evening, I answered frantic tapping on the barrack-room window. Sliding it up, I was faced with my four colleagues who between them hoisted up a three-foot long brass and highly polished shell-case and pushed it through the window for me to secrete beneath my bed before joining me in the barrack room. What had they done? They had taken the *ceremonial gong* from its hook at the edge of the main parade at North Barracks, where it had had visual pride of place. Each morning, it was struck by the Duty Bugler with a mallet at 8am, when all those on parade would stand to attention.

I was numb with shock, for I was now immersed in what could have become a career-ending jape, totally at odds with what I had been building towards over the preceding four years.

I had to decide whether to be part of this rite of passage by siding with my new comrades, or face ridicule and ostracization before the commission on *HMS Sheffield* had even begun. In fear and trepidation, I chose the former and joined in the discussion as to what could now be done with the shell-case. After all it couldn't stay under my bed! Fuelled by the beer they had consumed, my colleagues suggested that somehow we get it out of barracks. Military patrols abounded – for this was a military training establishment - and getting it past the guardroom personnel at the main gate was just not feasible.

A new accommodation block was being built nearby. Dressed in dark clothing, we dragged the shell-case to the builder's perimeter fence, passed it through a large hole in the fence where it met the barrack wall, and humped it over the wall. It was now past midnight, and we were out of barracks with our booty. "What now!" was the cry. At this moment, around the corner came a car, so we stood the shell-case on its end, draped a coat over it so that it resembled a hunched-up figure, and pretended to be a bunch of youths messing about. The car slowed but then moved on, leaving us to resume whatever we were about to do.

We carried the shell-case along Gladstone Road and headed for the beach. Being night-time, we got there without further concern and, with the tide out, we spent the next hour digging with our hands in the shingle at low water mark. Anyone who had tried to dig a hole in a shingle beach will know that twice as many stones seem to slide back than are taken out. Eventually, however, we were able to bury the shell-case in a deep hole and to sing *Auld Lang Syne* around it in farewell.

We then had to smuggle ourselves back into the barracks, over the eight-foot barrack wall and onto the parade ground, from where we slunk off to our beds. It was 2am and I didn't get a wink of sleep thereafter. I was the only one of the guilty to go to breakfast the following day. Without warning the Duty Officer, accompanied by irate staff, appeared in the dining hall and we heard a shrill blast on a whistle. In the silence that followed we were told that *The Gong* had been taken during the night and that all shore leave was cancelled until it had been returned!

The immediate suspects were, of course, the *HMS Sheffield* Draft Band, of which I was the only visible member. I was able to convince those around me that we could not have had anything to do with it because almost all the band members were on weekend leave. Leave for the barracks remained cancelled until the afternoon, when it was decided that nothing was to be gained by keeping the restriction in place.

The next day, we left the barracks at Deal with all our kit and equipment for the journey to join our ship at Portsmouth. It had been almost worth the anguish of the previous hours to see the looks on the faces of the Guard Commander and his staff as we waved a cheery goodbye from the back of our lorry. We thought the Adjutant would in future have to give the order *Strike the Hook!* rather than *Strike the Gong!* at the start of each day.

Thus the story remained untold until now, for the mystery of the disappearing shell-case has, to my knowledge, never-before been revealed. *HMS Sheffield* band had succeeded in embarrassing the system. I had personally survived the fire of initiation into manhood, and from then on avoided any possible chance of anything remotely like it ever happening to me in my life again.

The gong was eventually replaced with a superb chromium-plated *ship's bell*, welded securely to its housing. Interestingly, two of those involved on the night the original gong disappeared went on to become Directors of Music although, naturally, their names entirely escape me! The camaraderie of the *Sheffield Five* lives on.

The ship's bell that replaced the missing ceremonial gong, 1953

Aboard *HMS Sheffield*

From Portsmouth, *HMS Sheffield* steamed up and into the Denmark Strait between Iceland and Greenland to undertake sea-trials. A severe storm engulfed the area whilst we were there and caused extensive damage to the ship. All the ship's boats secured on their davits on the upper deck were smashed into matchwood; heavy ice several inches thick formed on all wires and supports. This was of great concern to me, experiencing life at sea for the first time. We sailed south to Greenock, where we berthed for extensive repairs. It had been my first taste of life at sea and, particularly as I was a poor sailor, not at all an experience I wanted to repeat.

Part of our sea trials involved firing the upper deck six-inch guns. The band mess in which we lived was on the starboard side in the fore part of the ship below and to the right of 'B' turret. We were warned that the ship was about to fire a broadside of its six-inch guns. When it happened, the guns were obviously trained to the port, or left-hand, side. The enormous recoil from the guns seemed to move the whole ship in the opposite direction from the target and the noise was unbelievable. Among other things to happen in that split second was that the doors of our aluminium mess-cupboards containing tea, sugar, jam, sauce and milk rations flew open. These cupboards were attached to the outboard side of the ship at the end of long mess tables. When the ship and the cupboards lurched to the right, what had been inside them didn't and, being unlocked, the contents spilled out on the table as a mass of sticky debris.

There were no chairs in the mess, only long wooden stools along the length of the mess tables. When off duty, we just sat around the mess table writing letters, reading books or, as happened a lot of the time, playing cards. This was not my scene, for I quickly realised that although the stakes were only matchsticks whilst the game was on, these sticks were redeemed for cash on pay-day. We were paid only once a fortnight and some of my colleagues gave away almost all their pay in card playing debts. We slept in hammocks, often up on deck in the open air if the weather would allow it. Some slept stretched out on the mess stools alongside the tables. How they ever managed to stay on such a narrow surface all night, I never understood.

The ship's galley was only there to *cook* food. Vegetables, etc., were prepared on the messdecks by the mess members. The trays of food were then taken to the galley, where the chefs would cook it. At mealtimes, a selected individual from each mess would go to the galley to retrieve the trays they had left earlier and return with them where the hot food would be eaten by the mess members. Getting up and down ladders from deck to deck with trays of hot food was no easy matter, especially during bad weather. This was sometimes complicated by the daily issue of rum at lunchtime. Every man in the ship above the age of twenty was entitled to a daily tot of rum at noon unless he had elected to be *teetotal*, when he received a few pence per day in lieu of the rum. Chief Petty Officers and Petty Officers were permitted to drink their rum neat, while the lower ranks had their tot mixed with water before it was issued. The reason for this was that rum with water added wouldn't 'keep' and had to be quickly consumed. Navy rules dictated that neat rum also had to be quickly consumed, but such rules were often ignored. Rum was an illegal currency on board and used to repay debts or favours. It would be informally dispensed as *Sippers* for something trivial, *Gulpers* for something major and *Grounders* (drink it all) if the recipient had saved your life!

During the commission, our Captain, Keith Campbell-Walter was promoted and flew his broad pennant as Commodore of the American & West Indies Station on our arrival in Bermuda. His daughter, Fiona Campbell-Walter, a professional model of great beauty, eventually married the aristocrat Hans Thyssen-Bornemisza and became one of the richest women in the world. The Captain of Marines on board, *Old Joe* in naval parlance, also had a double-barrelled name. His was Bullock-

Webster. We used to call him *Bollocks-Webgear!* He was so unsure of himself that, prior to an Armistice Parade in Hamilton, Bermuda, he allegedly arranged for the orders he would have to give the Royal Marines Guard of Honour to be chalked along the inner edge of the pavement that he would be standing in front of!

Throughout the commission, we gave spectacular shore-side ceremonies of Beat Retreat which featured a drill display by the ship's detachment of Royal Marines. On these occasions, the drill squad was always commanded by *Young Joe*, an able Royal Marines Lieutenant, whilst *B-W* mingled with the guests on board.

Our travels in and around the West Indies took us down the East Coast of South America and north to Newfoundland and Canada. Alongside in Montreal, we had an official visit from senior members of the nearby Kahnawake Indian reservation. With the Royal Marines Guard & Band paraded to greet him, Red Indian Chief Poking Fire arrived dressed ceremonially complete with trailing feathered headdress. Commodore Campbell-Walter then had to submit to being draped in a colourful Indian blanket and to wearing a similar feathered headdress to the Chief. He was given a tomahawk and made to smoke a pipe of peace before he and the ship were given indecipherable Indian names, now almost certainly lost in the mists of time. It was all very colourful for the ship's company to witness, and this was a cultural part of Canada that we had not thought to see.

During our time on the America & West Indies Station, many cities along the shoreline of North America were visited.

Returning southward via New York, *HMS Sheffield* docked at Pier 90 to be overwhelmed with offers of tickets for Broadway productions, concerts and radio and TV shows. I went along to Radio City Music Hall for a show that was mind-blowing. I had seen nothing like it before. Wonderfully colourful presentation of exotic dancing and music on stage was further enhanced by musicians all the way along the sides of the auditorium.

During our time in New York, the Duchess of Kent and Princess Alexandra visited the ship and inspected Ship's Company Divisions. A souvenir photograph of the visit was taken with the yachtsmen, gathered on the fo'cstle and the senior yachtsmen and officers above on the upper decks and bridge area. From his position right up in the bow, the photographer was able to get a memorable shot. This was my second experience of being in the presence of Royalty, albeit again at a distance!

The band was often disembarked to perform at specific venues. In Cuba, we appeared in a live TV studio broadcast when our dance band was featured. In New Orleans, we paraded through the crowded streets during the annual *Mardi-Gras* festival. Entertaining the ship's company with all manner of musical events throughout the commission was an ongoing interest. Ray Woodfield (violin/saxophone), Peter Hughes (violin/cornet), John Maddy (basses) and Chas Champion (trombone) formed a *Barber-shop Quartet* that was very popular on and off the ship.

After arriving at the port of Acapulco, the whole band was required to travel overnight by train up into the mountains to entertain at the British Embassy in Mexico City.

In Boston, Massachusetts, I first experienced the full force of a hurricane. I was ashore when Hurricane Edna hit the city and had to take refuge in a hotel while the ship left harbour to ride out the storm. Remaining alongside to be battered against the jetty was, apparently, not a good option! The pictures of hurricane devastation can only show part of the reality that hurricane winds bring. In the storm's path, it is impossible to remain standing, and what I experienced at that time in Boston was frightening in the extreme. I had no way of knowing if the situation was going to get even worse before it got better! Things did get better, however, and the ship returned to harbour. We were soon heading south to enjoy the balmy breezes of the tropics.

Some way into the commission, *HMS Sheffield* was required to act as guard-ship to the *SS Gothic*, which was being used as a Royal Yacht to take the Queen and Prince Philip on a world tour. We met up with *Gothic* in the Caribbean and headed for the Panama Canal. Sailing constantly in formation behind the *Gothic*, I never had the chance to glimpse the Royal couple as we trailed their ship across the ocean.

After passing through the Panama Canal, we sailed into the Pacific Ocean and over the equator, on which occasion a ceremony was held for those whose first time it was to *Cross the Line*. It involved King Neptune's Court and a lot of water and shaving foam.

Having *observed the proper rites of ceremony,* I was *baptised at the hand of His Most Gracious* **Majesty King Neptune**, *who according to the Law of the High Sea, pronounced him a* **Son of Neptune** *thereby permitting him to cross the line at any future date unmolested by any creature of the Deep.* I still have my certificate to prove it!

Crossing the Line, December 1953

After the excitement of this ceremony, we had an uneventful passage as far as the Marquesas Islands, where our duties as guard-ship to the *Gothic* were transferred to the Royal New Zealand Navy, who had come from the opposite direction to meet us. *Shore leave* in the islands was given to our ship's company. One evening, we were entertained in the local village by hula-hula dancing girls. I have to say that this was something of a disappointment, for all the pictures I had ever seen of such beauties showed them wearing not much more than golden raffia skirts. In reality, the skirts that these girls wore had been made during the day from green fronds, beneath which the girls wore long blue shorts - much the same as our sailors were wearing!

There was no air-conditioning in the ship, but when at sea, outboard messes could open *scuttles* (port holes) to allow fresh air into the ship, whenever the weather allowed. Wind scoops were allotted to each mess that were pushed into the portholes to direct the air inboard. We had to be a bit wary because our mess was not very far above the waterline. We constantly hoped that we wouldn't catch a rogue wave with a scoop. One evening, sitting around the mess table, we heard a thump and a large silver flying fish made its startled entrance. It slithered along the table and ended up flapping among the members of the card school, whose concentration was badly affected. One stood up, went to the porthole, stuck his head out into the salty air and demanded to know from King Neptune why the hell he hadn't delivered chips as well!

Several times during the commission the ship's company was required to *air bedding*. This entailed taking all blankets up onto the upper deck and lashing them loosely to the perimeter guard-rails. Leaving blankets for several hours in the sun and wind was considered good for our health and not at all beneficial to bedbugs. At these times I felt we must have looked, from afar, like a refugee ship and was always rather pleased that we never met up with any other ships during these evolutions. I suspect that the Captain ensured that this was so. I spent a lot of time up on deck, especially in the afternoons when the playing of instruments was not allowed for the reasons given earlier. I decided that this time could best be used to study the musical subjects I would require if I was to further my career. I was able to put my hand on various books and treatise so with paper and pencil in hand I would spend afternoons sitting quietly on an upper deck ammunition locker tackling the intricacies of harmony, orchestration, instrumentation, musical history and form. Spending so much of my time in the fresh air was an unforeseen bonus.

One lesson quickly learned in one of Her Majesty's ships is not to be late back from *shore leave*. There are several reasons for this, one being the fact that the ship may have had to sail unexpectedly for operational reasons. When you arrive late at the jetty to find your ship gone, the rule is that you pay your own way to its next port of call!

Four young sailors were late returning on board on the evening of our arrival at our first West Indian Island. To make an example of them they were charged with being late, and next day brought before the Executive Commander for disciplinary action to be taken. The Master of Arms, the senior policeman in a ship, marched the first sailor into position before the Commander. *Halt ... Off Caps!* he ordered, for in the Royal Navy, defaulting sailors are required to remove their head-dress when about to be interrogated. When asked why he was late back from shore leave, the sailor explained that there were no taxis on the island and that horse drawn vehicles were used instead. He went on to spin a long yarn about the journey. It came to a head when, on arrival at the top of a particularly steep hill, the horse drawing his cart dropped down and died in the shafts. The sailor explained that having paid the driver, he made his way back to the ship on foot but was unavoidably late by about fifteen minutes. There were no witnesses who could be called so, although the Commander was a bit sceptical, he decided to let him off with a caution. "Admonished," he said. "Case dismissed." *On Caps!* ordered the Master at Arms: *About turn, quick march!* Off went the sailor who was seen to give a wink to his three comrades still waiting to be dealt with.

Numbers two and three came up with the same story. They explained that their horses too had died at the top of that same hill and each in turn had his case dismissed. When the fourth sailor got in front of the Commander, who by then had realised that he had been conned by these chaps, he was verbally set upon. "I'll tell *you* what happened," he told the sailor standing there with a new tattoo burning into his forearm. He then went through the story up to the point where each horse died. As soon as he stopped for breath the sailor sprang to his own defence saying that this was not entirely true in his case. "What do you mean?" asked the Commander. "I've heard the same story three times." "Ah!" said the sailor, "But I was last one up the hill and when we got there we couldn't get past all them dead horses!"

Musician Hoskins on board HMS Sheffield, 1954

CHAPTER 4

PLYMOUTH GROUP BAND
1954 - 1961

Having been relieved by *HMS Superb* at the end of our commission, *HMS Sheffield* sailed for Portsmouth, anchoring briefly at Spithead on 26th October 1954 before entering harbour and subsequently No14 dock for a three-month refit. My family home was only nine miles away, in Fareham. On leaving the ship to go home, every step I took was on concrete. This was very strange after being in the West Indies where earth, compacted by the bare feet of the local population, had been the norm for anywhere except the roads. The next surprise was how my home seemed so small after the enormity of *HMS Sheffield* and how very alone I now felt without the constant company of men all around at every turn. I had to learn how to be an individual again and quickly realised why sailors throughout the world have distinct personalities and are often at their happiest only when surrounded by *their own kind*.

Margaret Humphrey

During my two-weeks leave I met up again with a childhood pal, John Coker, who told me that there was to be a party at his house on the up-coming Boxing Day, to which I was invited. He and his sister were having a combined party, so when I arrived there were several girls present whom she, rather than he, had invited. One that particularly took my eye, sufficiently for me to spill my wine all down the front of her dress, was named Margaret. She accepted my apologies but insisted on applying my handkerchief in a clean-up procedure without my personal help! I realised that I had some 'brownie points' to make up so I took my saxophone from its case and proceeded to serenade her – possibly to the consternation of the other guests! I think she took pity on me at that moment for she gave me a look that said: "I give in, I give in." Putting the instrument back into its case, I sat near her for the remainder of the party and, remembering that I had brought some photographs back from my time in the West Indies, I suggested she may like to come to my house the next day to look at them. She did – and the rest is history, as they say. We fell in love immediately. She was my first real girlfriend and became my life's treasured companion. We were married in September 1956 and are still enjoying a happy life together.

Plymouth

At the end of *HMS Sheffield's* commission, its band was split up and its members were drafted to serve elsewhere. I was sent to Deal to await appointment to another band. I learned that I had been selected to serve in the Plymouth Royal Marines Staff Band and was sent forthwith to its Durnford Street Barracks in Plymouth. The Plymouth Band was renowned as one of the finest military bands in the country. It broadcast regularly on the BBC and was comprised of excellent civilian-trained musicians. It was such a good band that one of its Sergeants, Les Brown, had earlier relinquished his rank as a Bandmaster in the Royal Naval School of Music to join it. Throughout World War II, it had boasted a superior Director of Music in the shape of Major Ricketts, alias Kenneth J. Alford, famous as a British march writer in the mould of the great John Phillip Sousa. The band's music library contained unique material from Major Ricketts' pen, and I quickly became involved in grand concerts staged all over the country.

Moving, in 1955, to join this band with its highly motivated and professional musicians was the very best thing that could have happened to me, and I was to stay with the band for the next six years. As part of our barrack duties we were required to support all Officers' Mess functions and played regularly for Regimental Dinners, etc. The atmosphere on these evenings was almost Victorian, for little had changed since that Queen's reign. *Extras* were always played to entertain guests immediately after the loyal toasts had been drunk. One item often asked for required all violinists to put their violin bows down and take up long feathered quills instead. The hard end of the quill was then bounced rhythmically on the strings to produce a delicate melody. Amid the candlelit diners, all we needed now were powdered wigs!

I really enjoyed being a member of a broadcasting band, but looking back now, I cannot believe how basic the arrangements for our broadcasts actually were. The band assembled on the small *Globe Theatre* stage in the barracks. BBC technicians would arrive to set up microphones and a signal-light panel. The sound picked up by the microphones, was then relayed into speakers set up in a nearby bathroom where the signal, enhanced with the ambience of the tiled walls, was sent by landline to the BBC in London for immediate transmission. When the orange light went off and the red one below it came on we were 'live-on-air'. There was no other way of knowing, for the announcer was in Bristol and we just had to wait for the red light that was our signal to begin! We did a lot of *Music while you work* programmes. These entailed performing without a break for exactly twenty-nine and a half minutes starting at 10am. It must have been quite an undertaking to select a programme of that length using tunes from many different shows and films. Rhythm, key sense and variation of tempo were all important. We started with a sheaf of music scores on our music-stands but at the end, the floor around us was littered with them. As soon as a tune from one score had been played that music sheet was cast onto the floor in order that the next item could be accessed without interruption.

The programme's well-known signature tune, *Calling All Workers*, started everything off and led without break into the selected music programme. After twenty-nine and a half minutes, it was back to the lilting tones of the main theme of the melodic signature tune. Whilst this was being played everyone had their eyes on the red light because if it did not go out before we reached the end of the tune we would have to begin the tune again - but this time starting with its intro. Unfortunately, this was in the form of a short fanfare with a series of top *A* notes for the cornet section. After playing without let-up for half an hour it was very possible that one of them would *crack* this high note and thus spoil what may have been a tip-top performance. If the red light went out in time there was joy amongst us all and another live broadcast had been successfully undertaken.

I very quickly realised that even to reach the rank of Band Corporal, I would have to obtain some formal educational qualifications, for although as a boy at school and under training at Deal I had been given instruction, I didn't have any. So, together with Eric Sharp, a viola and clarinet player from the band, we went to civilian adult night school classes in Plymouth. I remember the delightful female English teacher for two reasons. First, I had used a non-existent word, 'ingrimed', in an essay, not realising that the correct word was 'ingrained'. My pride was really hurt that evening! The second reason for remembering her is that she would perch on the front of her desk at the front of the class, wearing a pencil slim fitted skirt that burst into pleats about eight inches from the hem. She looked gorgeous! Anyway here I was struggling to reach the first rung of the promotion ladder.

Tommy Lang and Vivian Dunn

Captain 'Jake' Stoner had taken over as Director of Music of the Plymouth Group Band from Major Ricketts after the war, and Captain Tommy Lang followed him in that position. His son, Michael, had been under training with me as a boy musician. Both he and his father were always *squeaky-clean*. In fact, Michael's father was known as 'Dizzy' Lang as much for his smartness as the sudden movements that often emanate from a small man. He was not always well-liked, for he was often angry and deeply introverted.

This was largely because Lt. Colonel Vivian Dunn, on assuming the mantle of Principal Director of Music Royal Marines, had put a damper on the promotion prospects of those officers then serving. His plan for the future of the Band Service was that the better tuition he was now instigating must be allowed to quickly work for younger possible Director of Music candidates, such as the up-and-coming Paul Neville. A hold was placed on those currently serving and Lang, caught in this trap, knew that his career had nowhere further to go. He had a particular talent for Band Ceremonial at a time when even massing bands together was unusual. Lang was responsible for the appearance of the first Royal Marines Massed Band at the 1948 Royal Tournament, held in London's Olympia Exhibition Building. It was a spectacular success and Lt. Colonel Dunn wisely adopted Lang's ideas for significant future events, leading up to the acclaimed Beat Retreat Ceremonies that are now held on Horse Guard's Parade. The initial ideas for complicated drill patterns to allow these displays to go ahead came from 'Tommy' Lang, though he was never given the credit he deserved.

Lt. Colonel Dunn often wrote new marches for these ceremonies. In 1960, his new composition was called *Soldiers of the Sea*. Two weeks of long and tedious daily rehearsal on the Drill Field at Deal had worn everyone down, when Captain Lang was ordered to take control of an unscheduled rehearsal of the massed bands. It was Friday afternoon, and everyone expected that after one run-through, the order would be given to reassemble on the following Monday morning. This would have given the massed band members the opportunity to go home for the weekend. However, Lt. Colonel Dunn ordered an unscheduled rehearsal for Saturday morning, thereby ensuring that many could not get home and back by Monday morning!

On the Saturday morning, the massed bands duly fell in on the drill field. Lt. Colonel Dunn was absent and had ordered Captain Lang to take charge. The Corps Drum Major, Charles Bowden, had a broken arm, so Drum Major Geoff Knox from the Portsmouth band was leading from the front. A plan for a pianissimo performance had been hatched over the NAAFI bar during the weekend and, following the introductory drum rolls, the massed bands marched up and down with only the weakest of sounds coming from just a few instruments. Captain Lang then dashed across the field and ordered Geoff Knox to halt the bands, which he did. He then announced that as it was obvious that as everyone's lips were obviously tired, they would continue the rehearsal with instruments in the playing position, but not being played. Only the Corps of Drums would carry on normally. The bands performed this charade for about ten minutes, before Captain Lang stopped the proceedings again to announce that as the lips would by now have recovered, there would be a full run through with everyone playing their instrument. After the subsequent full performance Captain Lang, dismissed the bands telling them to return on Monday morning.

The Edinburgh Military Tattoos

In those days, when it was difficult to obtain early release from the Services, many people were angry and antagonistic. They were embittered by the rigid regulation of their lives and some never lost a chance to be difficult and to kick against those in authority over them, especially after situations such as the one

GOLD ON BLUE

outlined above. Continuous service for twelve years from the age of eighteen was the norm, and to wait until one was thirty to get out of uniform was considered by many to be a waste of their young lives. They had probably only joined to get away from home and what seemed a good idea in their teenage years became a noose around their necks as real maturity kicked in. Sometimes annoyance with authority was the only seed necessary to bring on thoughts of retribution.

My band colleagues and I never looked forward to playing at the world-famous Edinburgh Festival Tattoo. Transport was our first gripe – for after completing the dress rehearsal at Deal, we musicians were conveyed to Edinburgh, 500 miles away, in double decker busses provided by the local East Kent Bus company! Mid way along the route we spent the night in an RAF camp, since not even hardened musicians could be expected to travel in such discomfort without a break.

Being billeted in nearby Redford Barracks meant living in less-than-ideal circumstances for the duration of the Tattoo that took place daily on the esplanade of Edinburgh Castle. Performances went ahead regardless of inclement weather. We had to be bussed from Redford Barracks well before members of the audience arrived, because the only way into the castle was through the arena and over the drawbridge. Once within the seclusion of the Castle grounds, we waited around endlessly, with nowhere to sit and only a NAAFI tea kiosk available for refreshment. Being away from barracks, no food was available from late afternoon to nearly midnight, so some form of packed food was required for us. It took the form of a brown paper bag with sandwiches, a pork pie, etc., and perhaps a piece of fruit. It is not surprising that during the long

74

periods of enforced confinement within the castle, with nothing better to occupy the mind, plots were sometimes hatched as a way of making those up on the battlements in distant authority aware of general feelings of discord.

Things came to a head on one evening in 1957 when the word was passed around the Royal Marines massed bands that no one was to eat the orange that had been provided in the bag-meal. Instead, they were to keep it tucked underneath their arm until, at a designated point in the music, once all the performers were over the drawbridge and marching down the raked esplanade, the oranges were to be dropped. The only people who didn't know about this scheme were the Drum Majors marching at the front, the first they knew about it was when they were overtaken by a sea of rolling oranges. It was a great way of venting the bubbling anger of the many frustrated, wet and bored performers, and was probably recognised as such for no formal retribution was meted out. It must also have been great fun for the audience to witness!

Back in the 1950s and early 1960s, standards were not as high as they are now, when true professionalism is the order of the day. Lots of beer was drunk at every available opportunity and rough *scrumpy* cider was both cheap and popular. Urinating when full of liquid, was sometimes not restricted to designated urinals. One evening I was standing in the rear rank of clarinettists on the darkened esplanade of Edinburgh Castle, whilst in the darkness, the lone piper played his mournful lament from the ramparts, where he was picked out by a spotlight. In the cold and damp night air of Scotland, I became aware of a sound not unlike that sometimes produced in my childhood by the milkman's horse when outside my home!

One of the bass instrumentalists had decided that this dark interlude was an ideal time for him to relieve himself and this he was doing. It became very funny indeed and we all hoped that the lights would come back on before he had completed his task. This was not to be the case. He was lucky. However, the frothy stream that made its way down the esplanade was a dead give-away to those behind as to the culprit's identity. I was sorry for the young Scots piper who had stood alongside him during the lament whose cry of: "He's p'ssed all over ma' spats!" was only barely less audible than the Drum Major's order for us all to "Quick March!"

An angry Vivian Dunn

The musical nonsense that had occurred at Deal during Drill Field rehearsals for the 1960 Horse Guards Beat Retreat Ceremony had repercussions a short time later during the last night's performance of that year's Royal Tournament at Earls Court in London. The full display, including finale, had been concluded with General, later Field Marshal, Montgomery of Alamein taking the salute from the royal box. Lt. Colonel Dunn raised his baton and gave the downbeat for the scheduled march off. The massed bands should then have played *A Life on the Ocean Wave* followed by *Sarie Marais,* but a plot had been hatched to annoy Lt. Colonel Dunn by playing the regimental march as usual, and then for all to break into *Colonel Bogey* as loudly as possible instead of *Sarie Marais.* Everyone knew the words sung by servicemen to *Colonel Bogey* (*"Bollocks, and the same to you")* and the inference was obvious. That was the plan, but it went awry! On the downbeat some people played the regimental march while others played *Colonel Bogey*! The cacophony that ensued was unbelievable until eventually everyone was playing *Colonel Bogey* as loudly as they could.

In the meantime, Lt. Colonel Dunn, absolutely beside himself, dashed from the royal box area to the main exit doors and stopped the half of the Royal Marines massed band that were marching from the arena. He was in a total rage and ordered the Drum Major to get all those who had gone out of the opposite end of the performing area – and were now heading up to their accommodation in Warwick Hall – back down to join their compatriots. As it was the Royal Tournament's final night, some were already half out of uniform and into their civilian clothes, preparing to return to units across the country when the message reached them. Eventually they were all rounded up and brought down in full ceremonial uniform carrying their instruments.

Bugle Major John Wagstaff asked if the Corps of Drums, who had taken no part in the musical mutiny, could fall out. He was told to be silent and then the Colonel ordered one of the Drums Major to get a table for him to stand on to address the massed bands. He launched into a huge verbal lashing with various threats such as "I'll have you marching up and down the car park until you drop" etc., etc. He eventually ran out of steam and changed tack, saying things like "In all my time in the Royal Marines ... proud to lead them ..." and so on. It went on for ages until he came out with the real pearl for, in total despair, he shouted – "And Not Only That, You Played Colonel Bogey In The Wrong Bloody Key!"

This very clever and timely comment de-fused the situation and the bands were fallen out and dispersed to their various locations. It took a very long time for the Colonel's anger and embarrassment to subside, but once again a way had been found to get the message across to him that all was not well 'down below'.

Gigging

As I was based in Plymouth, travel to band engagements around the West Country meant many hours on a coach, returning to barracks during the night once the concert was finished. I was pleased to be accepted as a saxophone player in the dance band under the leadership of Band Sergeant Les Brown, who often used his Jaguar car to get us band members to and from the engagement. These private engagements were a great way of earning a little extra to supplement the meagre service pay of that era. A major problem was experienced time and time again when we were engaged to play at functions over the water in Cornwall. The road bridge across the River Tamar from Plymouth had not yet been built, and the last ferry back to Plymouth from Torpoint in Cornwall was at about 1am. We would virtually fly back across the moor to get to the ferry on time, because failure to do so meant a long looping detour across Dartmoor before we could get home.

I quickly became one of the *gigging* fraternity and used to play in civilian dance bands whenever possible. I was in the resident band of the Embassy Ballroom in Devonport. The line-up was trumpet, played by the band-leader Jimmy Warren, piano, bass, drums, with me on alto saxophone and clarinet. I took every opportunity to emulate the sound that the American saxophonist Dick Johnson with his quartet produced. I was one of the first to buy – and still have and listen to – his *Music for Swinging Moderns* album, released in 1956.

Personal transport now became a necessity, so I bought myself a 197cc Francis-Barnett motorcycle. It was totally devoid of springing except for the front forks and saddle. The actual frame, and pillion seat, was of rigid construction and every bump in the road was a worry – not for me but for my saxophone, tied to the pillion seat behind me.

I eventually was able to go one better and to change the bike for a Bond minicar. It had three small wheels: one in front and two trailing, and aluminium bodywork. The 250cc 2-stroke engine was just ahead of the front wheel and resembled the back half of a small motor bike. When the steering wheel was turned the wheel *and* engine turned completely to the left or right within the engine bay. This meant that the vehicle would turn in the road within its own length - which was useful as, like the motor bike from which it derived, it had no means of reversing! A push-pull lever on the dashboard changed the three gears as required. With such a small engine it was hardly exciting but, hey!, this was 1957. I could afford it and I was out of the rain. The biggest problem was experienced whenever a bus came alongside because, with my vehicle's wheels being only 14 inches in diameter and the bottom of my drivers' seat only 9 inches off the road, my eyes were about level with the bus hubcaps!

The routine following band engagements was that the returning coach would take a preordained route through the city centre so that the married men could alight where necessary to go to their homes. When the coach eventually reached Durnford Street Barracks, only those who lived in barrack rooms were left on board. It was their job to safely return all the instruments and stores to the band room, and to secure the room safely. As an *inlier* I always took my clarinet back to my barrack-room with me after this chore was completed, but one occasion, having placed it on a nearby windowsill whilst the unloading was done, I forgot to do so. Sadly, it disappeared, presumed to be stolen, before I could get back to pick it up. I was charged for its loss and had to pay for a replacement. I mention this episode because later in my story this particular instrument makes a significant and memorable reappearance.

Promotion courses

In 1958 I attended Part 1 of a course for promotion to Band Corporal. The course focused on developing military skills and leadership. It was open to all eligible Royal Marines candidates and was held at Plymouth. General Duty marines as well as band service personnel were on the course and assessed together. My long period of apprenticeship at Deal must have been worthwhile for, at the final examination at the end of this course for Junior NCO, I came out top - ahead of all the General Duty marines as well as my band service colleagues. As a mere Musician, I found myself commanding the final Passing-Out Parade under the eagle-eye of the Adjutant, Captain Alastair Donald. He was to go on to become a highly respected Military Historian in the Corps and a life-long friend.

Part 2 of the promotion course was undertaken at the Royal Marines School of Music in Deal. Another member of the Plymouth Band, Rex Ayling, was selected to attend and together we set off in his car for the long journey to Kent. His parents lived near Winchester and his intention was to drop off Christmas presents there on the way through Hampshire.

Rex's car, heavily laden with all our necessary kit and instruments, was probably not very stable. On the A303, and passing Stonehenge, an attractive girl overtook us in a sports car. This was like a red rag to a bull for my friend Rex, who put his foot down and attempted to catch up. Sadly, he had not realised that we were approaching a sharp right-hand bend. We didn't make it: the car flew off the road, rolled over several times in the mud and ended upside-down in a field.

I remember nothing further until I woke having my head stitched in Salisbury hospital. We had been taken there in an ambulance that had been called by an AA man, whose road-side box, in which he had been sitting, we had just missed as we hurtled past it into the field. When well enough to travel, Rex and I had to make our way, with all the kit, etc., by train to Deal. The car had been written off.

Despite missing the first part of the promotion course we both passed the final exam. Returning to the band at Plymouth, I was then promoted to Band Corporal. Many years later Rex was to take his own life following marital difficulties, but this was not before we had been members together of another band, that of Her Majesty's Yacht *Britannia*.

Madison Square Garden

Every third year, it was the Royal Navy's turn to 'lead' in the Royal Tournament, and this meant that the Royal Marines

Bands were well to the fore on these occasions. After one very successful year in London, arrangements were made for the show to be taken to New York City. On arrival in the United States, we were taken to the US army base on Governor's Island where we were to be accommodated for the duration of the visit. The venue for the British Military Tattoo, as it was called, was Madison Square Garden – not the modern Madison Square Garden at 4 Pennsylvania Plaza, but an older Madison Square Garden, situated about a mile away on 8th Avenue between 49th and 50th Street.

This grand venue, accommodating some 18,000 spectators, was demolished in 1968 but is memorable for me on two counts. The first was when I stood with the band in the arena after marching the Royal Marines Combat Display Team into position and watching in horror as its Commanding Officer, Captain Mike Easterbrook, fell 86 feet to his death from the underneath the roof. A 'death-slide' stunt was part of the show, and he had performed it safely many times before, but this time, the clip with which he was attached to the rope failed as his weight was put upon it. As he had crashed down without a sound, the audience thought it had been a staged joke using a dummy. It was a tragic and disturbing moment. Following that incident, Carabineer clips were universally modified to include a locking device.

The second memorable thing about the show was that during the Massed Bands display, involving musicians from the Army, Royal Air force and Royal Marines, eight of us from the Royal Marines Band were required to leave the formation and position ourselves at the front of the massed bands. Under microphones lowered from the roof, these eight gave a jazz 'combo' performance of *The Saints Go Marching In,* before being joined by the whole of the assembled massed bands. I was standing in the queue for lunch after the first rehearsal when an RAF musician standing behind me said to his chum, "Did you hear that super clarinet player from the Marines?" Unknown to him, I was that young clarinettist, and I glowed with inner pride. My lunch tasted extra special that day.

Nigeria

In 1960, the Plymouth Band was selected to partake in Nigerian Independence Celebrations. This entailed a long flight to Lagos where we lived in very poor conditions on a Nigerian army base. The food was so bad that we elected to fend for ourselves if they would give us rations. Thankfully, our Bugle Major was a first-class chef. We were so pleased that we had him with us. Political intrigue was rife, we could see only dark days ahead for the country. Military dictatorship loomed large and corruption seemed a way of life. At least fifty new luxury vehicles, painted in the Nigerian colour of bright green, had been obtained for the use of VIPs on Independence Day, 1st October. On 2nd October, they were all allegedly taken as personal trophies by individual members of the government's ruling party.

On the West Coast of Africa at that time, tropical diseases were commonplace. We had been immunised against malaria and yellow fever, etc., but concerns remained over the possibility of sexually transmitted diseases. With this in mind, and as a newly promoted corporal, I was provided with a box containing 1000 condoms and told to distribute them to individuals if any member of the band asked for any. Nobody did over the time we were in Nigeria, so at the end of our stay I wondered what I could do with my 'store' of these interesting items. Under a tree in a nearby clearing, I came across a local trader selling his wares. His stall contained all sorts of interesting native items. Cutting a long story short, we did a swap and I ended up bringing home a three-foot long stuffed crocodile, while he went off around the nearby village trying to sell balloons with funny ends on them!

At that time in Britain, people frequently put 'mascots' in the shape of furry animals, 'nodding' dogs, etc., inside the back windows of their cars. I modified the trend and, having done so, considered my unattended vehicle fairly safe with a three-foot crocodile in full view to any intending thief! Once, when visiting my brother, then living at Didcot, I put the crocodile in some grass near his front gate for him to find before I knew that he had been diagnosed with a heart condition. It didn't help!

CHAPTER 5

THEORETICAL TUITION AND HMS HERMES
1961 - 1964

In 1961, after serving with the Plymouth Staff Band for over five years, I was recalled to the School of Music at Deal and provided with a brand-new Married Quarter in Deal. On arrival, I learned that I was one of three young Band Corporals specially selected to study for a year to obtain the prestigious civilian Licentiate Diploma from the Royal Academy of Music in London. This was an entirely new concept and part of the forward-looking plans of the Principal Director of Music, Lt. Colonel Vivian Dunn.

There was one major snag that had not been properly thought through, which was to have a devastating effect on the success, or otherwise, of the whole project. It was this: higher musical training for those attempting the annual service examination for Bandmaster was overseen by a civilian 'Professor of Musical Theory'. This course for Bandmaster, much sought after by ambitious Band Sergeants, was of twelve months duration. The Professor's time was entirely taken up with the curriculum for his eight nominated students who were in competition with one another.

When we three young Band Corporals were nominated for the year's study for the civilian LRAM diploma, holders of which could bypass the Service course for Bandmaster, we were highly unpopular. It was not difficult to see why for, if successful, we would very likely take precedence in selection for subsequent promotion over those in the next room attending that year's Bandmasters' course!

The situation we three students were in deteriorated when we were told that we would study in a room next to the classroom wherein the Bandmasters' class was being taught, but that we would not be permitted to attend any of their tuition. We just had to get on with teaching ourselves the various subjects from textbooks as best we could, with the Professor being asked to mark our written work only when he could find the time. The subjects needed for the LRAM examination were not identical to those needed for a pass in the Bandmasters' examination, so the two courses were not entirely compatible.

The final nail in the coffin of our attempt to progress was when Lt. Colonel Dunn suddenly decided at the end of the year that my two colleagues and I should sit the imminent R.M. Bandmasters' Examination anyway, "for experience." Martin Blogg, the only one of our number to pass, was shortly to purchase his discharge from the Corps in order to pursue an academic career, to which he was entirely suited. He subsequently trained as a music teacher before reading divinity at Ridley Hall, Cambridge, and later became a teacher of Dance and Drama, setting up *Springs*, his own successful ballet company in 1979. As an academic, Martin was an excellent student, while my colleague Terry Williams and I struggled. Without adequate instruction, we two were never going to pass – and we didn't.

Aboard HMS Hermes

Our failure to pass the examination that had been unfairly foisted on us at virtually no notice had a further significance, for in those days only one attempt to qualify for Bandmaster was permitted. Having sat the examination, at which I had failed one subject, I thought that I was now ineligible for promotion beyond that of Band Sergeant, to which rank I had only just been promoted. Not only that, but I was also sent with only a few weeks' notice to serve at sea on board the aircraft carrier *HMS Hermes*. This meant giving up my married quarter at Deal and in its stead renting accommodation for my wife and young family in Fareham, nine miles from Portsmouth where *HMS Hermes* would be based when in UK waters.

HMS Hermes began her second commission on 24th April 1962 having been launched by Winston Churchill's wife, Clementine, at Barrow on 16th February 1953. After sea trials, the ship's aeroplanes were embarked. These consisted of 803 Squadron with its Scimitars, 892 Squadron with its Sea Vixens, 849 Squadron with its Gannets, and 814 Squadron with new Wessex helicopters.

At the end of May 1962 we sailed for the Mediterranean, with Gibraltar the first port of call. After leaving Gibraltar and carrying out replenishment at sea, the squadrons carried out day and night flying exercises off Sardinia before we entered Grand Harbour in Malta. After a brief self-maintenance period, the ship sailed for the North African coast and the El-Adem bombing range, where we were joined at sea by the submarine *HMS Tiptoe*.

The ship then paid an official visit to Beirut. I was lucky to have this opportunity, for at that time the city of Beirut was a cosmopolitan mixture of cultures, Armenian, Turkish, French and Arabic with modern blocks of offices, flats, shops and markets. This was well before the onset of a devastating Civil War.

Intensive flying followed off Cyprus, Crete and Malta before we returned to Gibraltar for more self-maintenance. It was around this time that one of our Scimitar pilots, Lieutenant Tristram, had an experience that he would never forget. Returning to the ship after a bombing exercise, his aircraft flew into a large seabird. The speed at which his plane met the bird caused it to impact into his windshield with such force that the toughened glass in front of his face shattered, and it imploded into his face.

Virtually blinded by the impact, he was 'talked back' to the ship by the pilot of his number two aircraft flying closely behind on his port side. Unbelievably, listening only to his opposite number in the other aeroplane, the injured pilot brought his Scimitar down to a scary landing on the pitching deck of the aircraft carrier, following which he was deservedly awarded the Queen's Commendation for Valuable Service in the Air.

HMS Hermes left Gibraltar in company with *HMS Centaur* and many escort ships to meet the American and French force comprising the Atlantic Strike Fleet. Towards the end of the subsequent exercise, cross-operations were undertaken with aircraft from *USS Forrestal* and the mighty nuclear-powered *USS Enterprise*. Further exercises followed with *HMS Centaur* and the French aircraft carrier *Clemenceau* before we were able to enjoy a spell of shore leave in Palma, Majorca.

The Royal Marines Bandmaster of the *HMS Hermes* band for this 1962/64 commission was a fine musician but he had an uncontrolled drinking habit that started at 'tot-time' each day. There was always a surfeit of rum available in the large Chief Petty Officers' Mess in which he lived, for his colleagues were all Fleet Air Arm personnel whose duties often prevented them from consuming their tots of rum with their colleagues at midday.

As the Band Sergeant, it was often necessary for me to cover for his failure to function when overcome with alcohol, a task I could carry out with relative ease during the early months on board. But one night, after a particularly sordid bout of drinking, he was seen to get up from his bed and urinate inside the private kit-locker of the Chief Petty Officer living beside him. This resulted in him being placed on Captain's Report. At the subsequent investigation, further misdemeanours were uncovered and the Captain had no option but to dismiss him from the ship with an accompanying Severe Reprimand.

When the School of Music at Deal learned of this, they hastened to arrange for a replacement Bandmaster to be sent out to join the ship. Knowing that this would be the case, the

Captain sent a signal to say he would be perfectly happy if his embarked Band Sergeant could be promoted to Acting Bandmaster and requested authority for him to continue on board in that capacity. This was agreed and I was duly promoted.

That Captain's name was W. D. O'Brien. He went on to have a highly distinguished career, retiring eventually as Admiral of the Fleet Sir William O'Brien - with whom I was privileged to serve again when Director of Music during the latter years of my time in the Royal Marines. Having, in *HMS Hermes*, placed one of my feet back on the ladder of success, he was able later to witness how important to me that initial move had been.

Some thirty years after this incident occurred, I was contacted by the Bandmaster whose duties I had taken over for the duration of the commission. As a civilian and long retired from the Corps, he asked me to accept his profuse apologies for his behaviour when Bandmaster of *HMS Hermes* in the 1960s. Not knowing that I had gone on to benefit from his shameful conduct, he said that he hoped I could forgive him. I was delighted to assure him that the waters had long ago passed under that particular bridge and with his apology fully accepted, we were able to part on the best of terms.

The ship returned from the Mediterranean in October 1962 for planned maintenance in Portsmouth Dockyard. In November, a 20-year Anniversary Dinner, at which my orchestra played, was held in the ship's hanger to commemorate the wartime Taranto Raid that had featured Naval Swordfish aircraft. It was hosted by the Flag Officer Aircraft Carriers with the First Sea Lord, Admiral of the Fleet Sir Caspar John, as guest of honour.

Once at sea again, *Hermes* carried out what is believed to be the last launch of a Swordfish aircraft from an aircraft carrier at sea.

The ships compliment of 2100 then headed for the Suez Canal for Christmas away from home in Singapore. After Christmas, a passage to Subic Bay in the Philippines preceded busy cross-deck operations with the *USS Ranger* - a truly enormous vessel: the first American aircraft carrier to be laid down with an angled-deck. She was some 319m long, with a crew of 3826. The *Hermes* flight deck, just 226m long, was terrifyingly small in comparison to the giant US ship, and the 'touch and go' landing attempts by US pilots strengthened their view that the British were 'nuts' to try to land on such a small area of pitching metal.

Passage north to Hong Kong for Chinese New Year was followed by an exercise where the ship was honoured by the presence of The Duke of Kent. As Bandmaster, on his ceremonial arrival I did manage to catch a glimpse of the Duke, but he had a packed schedule and was quickly out of sight.

Hermes then returned to Singapore Naval Base for a dry-docking period with the pleasant prospect of many of the crew living ashore for a few weeks. Prior to reaching harbour, the squadrons were flown off to temporary shore-side airfields. Scimitars went to Butterworth to spend time with the Royal Australian Air Force, whilst Vixens and Gannets went off to be with the RAF at Tengah and Seleta. A combined fly-past over Singapore Island was carried out before each squadron went its own way, leaving *Hermes* to enter harbour and make its way into dry dock. It is quite an experience to go down and to look up at the vast bulk of a ship in dry dock, and I shall never forget how insignificant I felt when doing just that during the time this ship was in refit.

Being off the ship was nice because the facilities of Singapore Naval Base were at our disposal. We soon learned to avoid the monsoon rains that seemed to arrive at 4pm every afternoon. Rushing torrents of water filled the deep storm-drains along every road in a matter of minutes. An hour later, the rains would stop and unpleasant, stultifying humidity would swiftly take its place. My memories seem to centre on the sticky heat and heavy rains of Singapore and the chilled *Tiger beer* that was consumed in large amounts by just about everyone when off duty.

During the refit, a spare propeller was fitted to replace one that was found to be damaged. The spare had three blades instead of four, but the Captain was assured that this wouldn't make any appreciable difference. The bottom of the ship, the sides and flight-deck were painted and, after frenetic activity both ashore and on board, the ship was taken out of dry dock and secured for sea. A post-docking replenishment-at-sea of fuel and stores was carried out and the squadrons returned to begin Exercise Sea Serpent. With all aircraft recovered and parked neatly down in the hanger, or on the flight-deck, we made our way towards Manila.

During some bad weather during this passage the ship's 'jumbo' crane, on the flight deck, broke free of its moorings and nearly pushed one of the Sea Vixens over the side! *Hermes* eventually anchored in Manila Bay with a combined SEATO fleet of 57 ships, and we were proud to learn that in one year,

Hermes had flown more sorties than had been managed during the ship's entire previous commission.

A second visit to Hong Kong on this deployment coincided with a heatwave and severe water shortages ashore. I arranged for my dance band to play in a city night-club on many of the evenings that we were in port. They fed us well, and it was a good way of earning extra money. I suspected that most of the ladies that frequented the club were also there for personal remuneration, but the services they offered would have differed somewhat from ours! Many years later, in England, I was shown an up-to-date publicity brochure for the club - still showing a photograph of my band and I playing in it. I guess the management got its money's worth out of us.

Enter the Urinecorn

The *Hermes* band was very popular on board the ship. I was always looking for things to brighten up performances and one idea I had would become part of Band Service 'folk-lore'. The post horn has always been a favourite instrumental feature. Endless repetition can get a bit boring, however, and attempts have been made to make these performances more memorable – visually as well as musically.

The post horn is a very simply constructed instrument, being just a brass tube about 26 inches long with a cup mouthpiece at one end and a small, flared bell at the other. Like a bugle, it can only produce the basic notes of its harmonic series, which are quite high in pitch because of the shortness of the tube.

The length of the post horn does not differ too much from the barrel of a rifle, so solos have been played using a rifle with just a mouthpiece inserted into the barrel. It was a gimmick that amused but allowed for little musical finesse as a rifle has no rounded bell to help deliver the sound.

I realised that provided a tube was of suitable diameter and the length of a post horn, it could be decorated in any number of amusing ways and remain playable. My first idea was to adapt the Captain's tubular chair from the ship's bridge but then, living in the same mess as the ship's plumber, I had a brainwave.

Ray Alberry, my trumpet soloist and I met the ship's plumber in his workshop, where we selected a length of copper pipe and attached it to the trumpet mouthpiece. Ray blew a note. I was looking for a concert 'A', the key in which the orchestral parts to '*The Post Horn Gallop*' is written. The first note produced was too low, so the plumber reduced the length of the tube by sawing a bit off and kept doing this until the tube produced notes of the correct pitch. All we then had to do was decorate it.

The plumber was responsible for the stowage of a range of new sanitary-ware items in the ship, and was able to produce for me a splendid, and fortunately brand new, 'corner-unit' urinal. This formed the bell of my new instrument. The plumber fixed the bent piece of copper tube to the base of the urinal with a rubber joint and fitted a mouthpiece at the other end. With the 'instrument' in the crook of the right arm and the mouthpiece held to the lips with the left hand, Ray was able to produce the notes of *The Post Horn Gallop* in the correct key. The

Urinecorn's debut performance featured a solo which was billed as *The Passionate Plumber*. With orchestral accompaniment, it was a riotous success when played at the end of an Officer's Mess dinner in HMS Hermes' Wardroom.

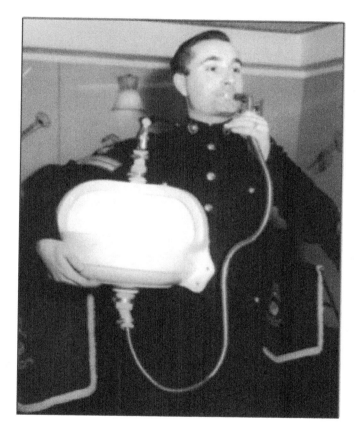

The prototype Urinecorn played by B/Cpl Ray Alberry

We couldn't decide whether to call it a 'Pisstolion' or a 'Urinecorn' but eventually the latter name was adopted as the least embarrassing, and news of the instrument's availability as a substitute for a hackneyed old post horn soon became

common knowledge. Its tone was superb – possibly aided by
the subtle effect of the grill in the bottom of the porcelain
bowl! *Blue Band*, the magazine of the Royal Marines Band
Service carried the following 'spoof' article, written by me, in
its Easter 1963 edition:

*It is rare these days to come across a musical instrument that is different
in every way from the normal types to be found in orchestras and bands
the world over. Therefore it gives me great pleasure to be able to introduce
you to the newest in a rare family that is neither string, brass nor woodwind
but rather, porcelain. To be known as the Urinecorn it is an interesting
combination of the art of plumber and musician. Pitched in 'A' it has the
bright tone of the Post Horn, yet it combines a subtle muted texture
produced by allowing the sound to pass through a surprisingly effective grill
in the base of the porcelain bell. This bell has a very cleverly designed anti-
splash rim, which, while allowing the sound to be projected forward towards
the audience, contains any excess moisture pushed through the instrument
by an over-exuberant player.*

*One entirely new aspect, built into this family of Urinecorns, is the
provision for the sound to be produced from underneath the right arm.
With the bell in this position it allows the player to effectively control his
intonation. (It is noted that a left-handed model is produced for those
unfortunately deaf in their right ears.) Attached to the upper rim of the
bell will be seen a length of tubing with a valve attachment. This is purely
decorative on the present instrument, but later models will have provision
at this point for a tuning slide that will allow the player to produce several
'shakes' that are at present considered impossible. Following along behind
this prototype Urinecorn in 'A' will be several others of varying sizes. In
observance of the policy of restraint, at present being exercised by the
Government with regard to excess spending of public money on new musical
instruments, these Urinecorns will not yet be made generally available to*

Service musicians. This is to be regretted, but progress cannot be delayed. All in possession of the ordinary Mk.1 Post Horn are advised to seriously consider the advisability of disposing of it in favour of this new improved Urinecorn once its acceptance by the Admiralty has been approved. Its effectiveness and interesting dual purpose cannot be denied!

Mishaps at sea

At the end of 1963, *Hermes* sailed for Osaka in Japan, which was expected to be the highlight of the commission. Regrettably, this was not to be so, for a major flight deck catapult fault was discovered as we neared Japan and our visit was cancelled. All we saw of Japan was the misty outline of Osaka whilst the ship's postman was ashore collecting mail. Without a catapult, we were un-operational and had to retrace our course back to Singapore Dockyard for emergency repairs. With the catapult out of order, aircraft were disembarked ignominiously by crane on arrival and taken by road to an airfield. Back in harbour, a defect was also discovered in the starboard shaft to the propeller from the ship's main engines. This meant another ten hot days in dry dock, during which time the ship's old four-bladed propeller, now restored, was replaced. Despite assurances, we had found that with the three-bladed propellor, the ship was prone to damaging vibration, so we were glad to have the original back.

During the next flying period, a Wessex helicopter suffered what is known in the trade as 'ground resonance,' providing flight deck personnel with more entertainment than they normally bargained for. As it prepared for take-off, it became jerkily unstable, and the rotor blades made holes in two nearby Sea Vixens. Luckily no one was hurt.

More bad news was to follow. Whilst at sea, it was decided to remove the large 'dustbin' shaped radar fitting from the top of the ship's mast. An initial attempt, using a Wessex helicopter, was not successful because the pilot started the lift before the radar's securing bolts had been fully removed. Not surprisingly, for an aircraft carrier is itself rather heavy to lift, the pilot only succeeded in ruining his helicopter's winch mechanism. After this the 'search and rescue helicopter' had a go and successfully removed the radar. The re-installation of the unit went more smoothly a few days later, but it was a pity that such enterprise should then prove fruitless, as that particular radar refused to work properly ever again!

Mombasa

Following a further replenishment-at-sea, *Hermes* set off for Mombasa on the East coast of Africa. Whilst at anchor at Mombasa, I took a safari through the Tsavo National Game Reserve. We had to set off very early in the morning to witness the animals beginning their day by finding watering-holes and food. The old bus we travelled in managed to get a puncture right out in the bush. Not the best place to have to change a wheel, so we let the local Kenyan driver do it whilst we climbed onto the roof of the bus to keep a look out for lions!

At the end of the safari, we came upon a 'tame' rhino that had a liking for jelly-baby sweets. Placing a sweet on ones left hand and offering it to the animal, while taking a photograph with the other hand as it advanced, produced a close-up showing what appeared to be staggering bravery - but it was entirely fake.

Leaving Mombasa, everyone on board looked fitter. Only a few hours short of our arrival at Suez, instructions were received for us to wait until being relieved on station by *HMS Victorious*. This meant a ten-day delay before we could transit the canal and return home to be reunited with our families at Portsmouth. Then, after only a brief spell in harbour, it was time to return to sea to await an onslaught of VIP's that would come to watch Exercise Unison, where the naval heads of Commonwealth armed forces met to discuss defence matters of mutual interest.

More mishaps and a funeral at sea

Just before the onset of the exercise, the Mirror Control Officer was blown off the flight deck and into the sea by the exhaust gases of a taxiing Sea Vixen. He survived the experience and was rescued by the search and rescue helicopter hovering on the port side, whose pilot had seen the incident happening right before his eyes. Following the exercise, the ship went back to the Mediterranean for a month. This period is best remembered for the runaway Scimitar aircraft that reared up and over its chocks on deck before going on to charge into a stationary Sea Vixen!

I have not given details of losses of men and equipment during the commission, but it must be realised that Naval Aircrew are a special breed of brave souls who take daily risks that are far beyond those that apply elsewhere, and that warships are dangerous places to work. In the two years I was on board *HMS Hermes*, when there wasn't even a war on, we lost eleven aircraft with eleven aircrew killed.

A Chief Petty Officer had a heart attack and died while playing volleyball in the lift-well, whereupon we were required to bury him at sea. Following navy tradition, his body was sewn into a canvas shroud by the ship's sailmaker, who ensured that a heavy weight was secured between the legs. The shrouded body was then placed on a raised metal slider at the edge of the deck and covered with a Union Flag. A funeral service, conducted by the Chaplain and attended by members of the ships company, was held, and we in the band played suitably solemn music. At an appropriate time, the slider was raised on the inboard end and the shrouded body slid off into the sea leaving the flag lying limply in place. The body sank out of sight immediately and after a few moments of reflection, the ship and its crew resumed normal duties. Having had the onerous task of sewing his shipmate into the shroud - 'last one through the nose!' - the Petty Officer Sailmaker – who was a member of my Mess – then consumed his traditional extra tot of rum.

As the ship's Acting Bandmaster during this commission, I had gained invaluable experience. Often thousands of miles from home, I had led a great team of talented musicians, entertained widely and, at distance, had even glimpsed the Duke of Kent. Now aged 29, it would soon be time for me to return home and take on another role in addition to my Service obligations – that of a loving husband and father to my young family.

Our full commission finally ended at Devonport in Plymouth, where the ship was de-ammunitioned and de-stored ready for a refit. The refit was to last until 1966, when *HMS Hermes* was re-commissioned as the Fleet's first 'all-missile' ship with upgraded equipment to meet the conditions then prevailing in Naval warfare.

I had one thing to do before I could return with my band to The Royal Marines School of Music at Deal. When I had left to join *Hermes*, it had not been under the best of circumstances. I had failed to measure up to expectations and I considered my promotion prospects to be at an end. Now, after two years as his Acting Bandmaster, I placed myself in front of Captain O'Brien and requested, or rather insisted, that he revert my rank to the Band Sergeant I had been on joining his ship. There was no way in which I was going to reappear in Deal wearing a rank for which I was unqualified. I thus ensured that I returned with my dignity intact!

GOLD ON BLUE

CHAPTER 6

DEAL, PORTSMOUTH & HMY BRITANNIA
1964 - 1968

My return to Deal coincided with my nomination to be an instructor of violin and clarinet within the Junior Training Wing of the RM School of Music. I soon learned that during my absence abroad, the rules that would have decimated my promising career had been changed. Students who had failed a subject in their attempt at the Bandmasters' Examination could now take that subject again. This I now did, having been busily teaching myself from textbooks throughout my time in the Far East and, despite not having the benefit of much formal instruction, I passed.

I enjoyed my time as an Instrumental Instructor and, as well as teaching violin and clarinet, became responsible for all aural training for Junior Musicians. I formed a student choir and did my best to enthuse the youngsters in their cultivation of a musical ear. Wednesday afternoons were set aside for recreational training - but in order, I suspect, to keep the civilian Professors gainfully employed, each was able to give tutorials to selected students who thus didn't have to go to the sports fields. Three periods were written into the curriculum for Wednesday afternoons. Instrumental instructors oversaw the practice of two of their students, whilst the third student was with his Professor.

Dealing with a bully

One afternoon Band Corporal Greenwood, a fellow instructor, came to me to tell me he was concerned about the deteriorating physical and mental condition of one of his students. I listened to what he had to say and then went to interview the boy in question. It quickly became obvious that he had been the victim of sustained bullying and when asked to do so, he showed me his backside that was badly bruised.

I immediately went to find someone to whom I could report this matter, for I was not going to allow any time to pass before it was addressed. The boy had told me that a senior lad in his barrack-room regularly assaulted him with a particular implement. I went to North Barracks, found his room empty, searched the locker of the lad who had been accused and found inside the implement that had been described to me.

I immediately went to inform the Company Sergeant Major or one of the Company Officers, but their offices were empty as it was the afternoon for sports. Accordingly, I considered I had no alternative but to immediately report the incident further up the chain of command. I went to the Administration Block in South Barracks, where the only office occupied was that of the Commanding Officer.

I had come too far now to give up, so I knocked on his door and, on being admitted, told him what had just been brought to my attention. A full investigation began and eventually the lad received the punishment he deserved, but I too was criticised because I had gone to the C.O. before letting others lower down the chain of command know of the problem! I did what I had to do. I was a newly-promoted Band Sergeant, and for me that carried responsibilities that had to be discharged faithfully.

The 1964 Royal Tournament

1964 was celebrated as the Tercentenary of the foundation of the Corps formed as 'The Duke of York and Albany's Maritime Regiment of Foot' three hundred years before in the reign of King Charles II. Celebrations were conducted throughout the Corps. At that year's Royal Tournament, held as always in London's Earls Court Arena, Lt. Colonel Dunn brought his considerable imagination to bear and decided to show all aspects of Royal Marines music-making during the show. From his available musicians he featured a full symphony orchestra, large dance band, ceremonial marching band and Corps of Drummers and Buglers to great effect.

Staging the event in what was predominantly a dirt-floored arena, more suited to horses and show jumping was problematic. This was resolved using mobile platforms with tiered seating and music stands bolted to the floor. In the darkness, and with performers seated in position on them, several platforms were drawn through the main doors into the arena where, positioned next to each other, they formed a tiered concert stage. Whilst the orchestra was performing at its end of the arena, two other platforms carrying the dance band were drawn into position at the opposite end. When the orchestral items were finished, the audience's attention turned to the newly positioned dance band. As this group was playing, the staged orchestra departed where, beyond the doors and out of sight, the performers swapped their orchestral instruments for their military band instruments and donned their helmets, ready to re-enter the arena as a ceremonial marching band. It was all clever stuff and a remarkable advertisement for the unique musicianship pertaining at that time only to the Royal Marines.

I was the lead alto saxophone player of the dance band that was conducted by Bandmaster 'Dougie' Drake, with whom I had previously served in the band aboard *HMS Sheffield*. His exciting band arrangements, compiled specially for the event, were well ahead of their time and our performance was one of the highlights of the show.

Portsmouth & the Royal Yacht

I was promoted to the rank of Bandmaster in 1965 and, to my great surprise, was told that I was to join the Staff Band of the Royal Marines at Eastney Barracks in Portsmouth. The Director of Music, Captain Paul Neville, had chosen me from a shortlist of available Bandmasters after an unfortunate incident involving his current bandmaster who learned that his conduct was considered unacceptable for anyone associated with the Royal Yacht *Britannia*.

Once again, the misdemeanour of another was to be to my benefit. The band to which I was now sent was recognised as the finest in the Corps, and from it musicians had been selected for service aboard Royal Yachts for over a century. Not only was I now to be a Bandmaster with the Portsmouth Staff Band, but also deputy conductor and player of violin, clarinet and saxophone on board the Royal Yacht *Britannia* for all Royal tours over the next four years!

My mother and father were still living just nine miles up the road at Fareham, and for many years they treasured the card I sent to them telling them of my appointment. What joy (and relief) they must have had to see a renaissance in my fortunes after the disappointments of a couple of years earlier.

Joining the band at Eastney Barracks, I soon learned that among the eighty musicians, there were nine Senior Non-Commissioned Officers, they were all older than me and vastly more experienced! It was to my great joy that I was able to work closely with the band's Drum Major, Colin Bowden, (no relation with Charles Bowden, who has featured earlier in my story) with whom I was able to bond. The two of us trusted each other implicitly and we became great friends. Under the auspices of the Barracks Adjutant he was the disciplinarian, leaving Captain Neville and me to devote our attentions to musical matters. When he retired from the Corps, Colin became an Officer in the Royal Navy & Royal Marines Careers Service.

Trouble on parade

The Portsmouth band was often to be found carrying out ceremonial duties in London both for the Royal Navy and the Corps. They didn't always proceed as planned. On one occasion, Drum Major Colin Bowden and I took the band to London to mark the relocation of the Headquarters of the Royal Marines Reserve to new premises at White City. We marched at the head of a column of Reservists under the command of a Royal Marines Major. It was a Saturday afternoon, and after leaving Shepherd's Bush the route took us past a busy pub on the approach to White City, where some boisterous activity was in full swing. As we marched past the pub, two drunken men fell out of the door. Both were wearing only underpants, having at some stage had a considerable amount of beer poured over them. They blurredly surveyed the scene as we passed by before one of them decided to join in with the band.

From my Bandmaster's position, marching three paces behind the band, I saw the miscreant stumble along the pavement to the nearest musician and, grabbing the upper part of his saxophone, started trying to 'honk' into it. Without thinking of any consequences, I immediately crossed to the scene and forced him to release his grip on the saxophone, whereupon the musician continued marching along the road with his colleagues, leaving me to deal with this half naked person. His eyes sparkled as he saw his chance to enjoy his afternoon even further and he went for me with all the tenacity of an angry polecat.

I was somewhat limited in what I could do, dressed as I was in full ceremonial uniform with my music baton clamped under my left arm. With my free right hand, I pushed the chap onto the bonnet of a parked car and thrust the scabbard of my sword against his groin area. This caused him to get quite excited. He wrestled with the scabbard of my sword, eventually lifting its end upwards causing the weapon to slide out onto the ground, hilt first. Sword dancing has never really been my 'thing,' and I knew that with the band fast getting out of sight along the road, I was in a rather difficult situation.

At this moment, the marching column of Marines reached the scene and, with the utmost panache, the Major in command of them appeared at my side. Without a word to me, and without even losing his step, he used the hilt of his drawn sword to bash the skull of my antagonist who, not surprisingly, suddenly lost all interest in the proceedings and in fact went very quiet indeed!

Retrieving my own sword from the ground, I hastily caught up with the band, whilst at the same time endeavouring to get the sword back into its scabbard from behind my back. Time was of the essence, because on arrival at the new RMR Headquarters just around the next corner, I would have to mount a rostrum to immediately conduct music for the inauguration ceremony. I just made it in time, and no one in the band was the slightest bit aware of what had been happening behind them.

I was grateful to be in the safety of the Headquarters area and thought that I would never see that miscreant again. Imagine then my anxiety as a police car swept through the gate, in the back of which I could see two beer-sodden, bedraggled and half naked angry men, one of whom was pointing his grubby finger at me! The police wanted me to demand that some action be taken against him, while this scoundrel was more than keen to complain that I had assaulted him. However, my concern was that we were in London on a publicity exercise and the last thing my superiors would want would be for it to be overshadowed by anything salacious appearing in next day's Sunday newspapers.

I foresaw the headlines, possibly with pictures of me in ceremonial uniform grappling with this half-naked thug and realised that there was no way the Royal Marines would come out of the situation smelling of roses. At my insistence, the police took no further action against the pair, and whole episode was quietly forgotten about.

Britannia's barber

Prior to embarking for the first time in the Royal Yacht for a Royal Tour, I was invited onboard to meet the Executive Officer in order that he could brief me on what he expected from embarked musicians. I was intrigued to learn that it had always been the case that the band would provide a barber from within its number. Not entirely surprising, because musicians often involved themselves with money-making activities on board ships. They could not play their instruments in the afternoon because this is when middle watchmen would be sleeping. Assuming that his request would be no problem, I readily agreed that a barber would again be provided.

Back at Eastney Barracks, I asked which of the nominated musicians was the barber. I was told that that he was no longer with the band. Band Sergeant Barry Baker immediately volunteered to be the embarked barber and I thought no more about it. On the first evening after sailing from Portsmouth harbour, Sgt Baker set up a tall stool in one of the passageways on board and a queue formed for his tonsorial attention. Within a very short space of time those in the queue, seeing how poorly the first chap's hair was being cut, disappeared! It was then that we realised that Band Sergeant Baker had never cut hair in his life!

It was my first trip on the Royal Yacht *Britannia* and I had promised that a barber would be provided so, in the absence of any other member of the band being prepared to volunteer, I took over Barry's set of barbering tools myself. My pride, however, would not allow me to go touting for business on the lower deck and I restricted my haircutting services to Officers and Chief Petty Officers. I managed to pick up some sort of technique and was kept fairly busy.

On one occasion with the Royal Staff embarked, the Queen's Chef came one evening to 'F' (the "friendly") cabin in which I lived with three other Chief Petty Officers. He asked me to give him a trim. I agreed and when the job was done he got up, said "Thank you" and disappeared aft into the Royal Apartments. Five minutes later, he arrived back at the cabin with a carafe of 'champagne and brandy cocktail' and some succulent breasts of pheasant that had featured on the menu for that evening's royal dinner. This 'payment in kind' was a whole lot better than the half-crown I normally received for a haircut! And, more welcome than the can of beer that the Admiral had offered me for cutting his hair!

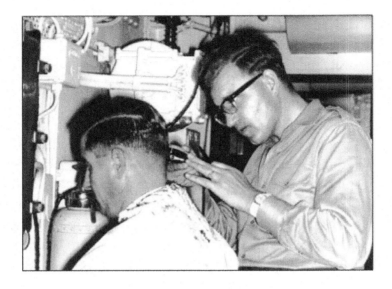

Britannia's barber, 1965

On Board Britannia

Life on board *Britannia* was cramped. It only had a small area
in which its detachment of Royal Marines lived and, when
embarked, there was no formally designated area for the
musicians to sleep. As Bandmaster, I lived with members of
the Chief Petty Officers Mess, and the Band Sergeants were
accommodated with their equivalent Petty Officers in their
Mess. The only available space for the rank-and-file musicians
and buglers to sleep was in the Yachtsmen's 'unwinding room'
that was really a NAAFI bar area.

Playing for the Yachtsmen in the unwinding room gave an
opportunity for the band to demonstrate individual
musicianship. I formed a seven-piece traditional jazz group
that became very popular. It was at the time when Mr. 'Acker
Bilk' was a well-known performer. Emulating him, I wore a

bowler hat, colourful waistcoat and a beard made by sewing individual strands from a frayed rope's end onto the toe of a stocking. Before each performance, I stuck the beard onto my chin with clear glue – which isn't as uncomfortable as it sounds. What I then needed was a name, so I became Mr. 'Utter Bilge'.

Mr Utter Bilge, 1967

After playing as an orchestra every night in the Royal Apartments whilst the royal family dined, the musicians would take their individual camp-beds, brought from Eastney

Barracks, and wait in the passageway for the nightly film show to end in the 'unwinding room' right up in the bow, before going into the room to find a space to put their bed. This nightly ritual only ended thirty years after the yacht was built when, during a refit, bunk accommodation for embarked musicians was arranged.

It is likely that the reason for the accommodation problems was this: in the previous Royal Yacht *Victoria & Albert III*, just some sixteen musicians were embarked at any one time. The *V&A* never went on long overseas royal tours. The Service record of Band Corporal 'Nippy' Read, who was leader of the orchestra at Portsmouth from 1931-39, shows that the longest trip he did lasted just fifteen days!

Britannia's maiden voyage was in 1954, carrying Prince Charles and Princess Anne from Portsmouth to Grand Harbour Malta, to meet the Queen and the Duke of Edinburgh at the end of the Royal couple's commonwealth tour on board *SS Gothic*. The Queen and the Duke of Edinburgh embarked on *Britannia* for the first time at Tobruk on 1 May 1954.

When *SS Gothic*, with a band of thirty embarked, rendezvoused with *Britannia*, just seventeen members of the band transferred over to the Yacht with the Royal party. The remaining twelve remained with *SS Gothic* for the trip back to UK, and eventually disembarked in London. In addition to the 17 musicians, the small Royal Marines Detachment in *Britannia* consisted of six Marines and two Buglers, which was very odd for bugle calls were not part of the ship's daily on-board routine, where silence is generally maintained. The Buglers did perform with the band whenever embarked, but otherwise they were employed alongside their General Duty colleagues.

The band personnel who transferred from *SS Gothic* to the brand-new *Britannia* in 1954 were shocked at the level of accommodation they found. They had come from a liner in which they had enjoyed a spacious air-conditioned mess, good sized lockers, plenty of hanging space for uniforms, ample stowage areas for instruments, proper beds and, for Senior Non-Commissioned Officer's, two berth cabins. The Sergeants' Mess in the Yacht had space for just four SNCO's, so the remaining thirteen members of the band had to live in the cramped conditions afforded by the Marines Mess on board and they naturally spilled over into the 'Unwinding room.'

A few months after returning to UK, musicians under the direction of Captain Kenneth McLean embarked in the Yacht for Cowes Week. After Cowes Week, *Britannia* sailed for Canada, where Prince Philip joined it. At Quebec, unusually for those times, a Beat Retreat had been scheduled, so Drum Major Knox and two Buglers joined the band that had been on board for Cowes Week.

This increase in band personnel raised eyebrows with the Royal Yachtsmen, for space on board was always at a premium and the extras embarked made things worse. No one in authority seemed keen to put their heads above the parapet over this matter and certainly Captain McLean didn't. Eventually, to ease the situation that continued until a major refit of the Royal Yacht in 1979, three Band Corporals would be promoted to Acting Band Sergeants for the duration of deployments. This arrangement allowed those selected to live in the Sergeants' Mess, where there was adequate room. This slightly eased the strain for'wd in the Marines barracks at a time when voyages were routinely becoming much longer than before.

Occasionally, to ease matters, the Drum Major and the four Buglers would be disembarked, if not required for further deployment duty on board, to return to Eastney Barracks in advance of *Britannia's* return to Portsmouth. Just a little greater insight of accommodation requirements at the design stage of the Royal Yacht's life would have negated a problem that went on for many years. The designers had found room to accommodate a royal Rolls Royce on board, so why not all the musicians in the band, who would always be embarked when a member of the Royal Family was onboard? Today, with *Britannia* open for public viewing at Leith in Scotland, visitors find it hard to believe that so many men lived in such cramped conditions and yet were able, always, to appear dressed immaculately.

The unwinding room was right up in the bow of the ship, where the deck rose and fell by many feet in even moderate sea conditions. In bad weather it was awful and sea-sickness was a major problem, for this space was where morning musical orchestral rehearsals took place in readiness for the evening's requirement to play during royal dinner in the royal apartments. I was a particularly poor sailor but was not at all alone in my misery. One musician, John (Bert) Kingston, suffered more than most. He could not keep food his down and regularly, on embarking for a royal tour, brought from his home a box full of tinned chicken supreme. It was all his system could tolerate and even then – not always for long!

With my violin under my arm I was waiting to play aft in the royal apartments one evening when a young Prince Charles came hurrying down the main staircase. Dashing to one of the nearby bedrooms he rapped on the door, opened it and shouted, "Grandmama, you are going to be late for dinner!" He then went swiftly back up to the next level. In response to the call, Prince Philip's mother - for it was she who was late - shuffled out of the cabin into the passageway. Princess Alice was very old, and was dressed, as always, as a Greek Orthodox nun. She stood in front of the lift and waited for a Royal Marines sentry to help her into it. He then closed the doors, pressed the necessary button and waited for the lift to disappear. As the lift rose, he dashed up the staircase to be in position as the lift reached its destination and to open the doors to allow the lady to go forward to where the other diners were waiting. She must have looked at him rather strangely, no doubt wondering if he had a twin on the deck below!

Also, each evening, small pairs of shoes belonging to the royal children were placed outside of their bedrooms, ready for a servant to gather them up for cleaning. Life above, and below, stairs continued as it had done for hundreds of years in stately homes. As a violinist with the royal dinner orchestra, I too was now part of this history wearing a uniform not unlike that of a royal 'flunkey', for the Royal Yacht tunic carried no buttons or Royal Marines insignia, just lots of gold braid.

World Cup Final 1966

Captain Peter Sumner eventually succeeded Paul Neville as Director of Music in Portsmouth and did so in time to direct

the Royal Marines Band at Wembley Stadium for the 1966
World Cup Final.

My grandchildren do not fully believe me when I tell them that,
as a member of the band, I 'played' on the turf at Wembley
that afternoon. Prior to the final whistle, I had also waited in
the royal tunnel with many of the biggest names in British
football as the seconds ticked towards the victory that England
achieved. Marching onto the pitch after the final whistle into
that cauldron of sound to play the National Anthem was an
experience like no other. In position on the pitch, we followed
the movement of Peter Sumner's baton but could not hear the
notes we were playing. Later we got into our coach and
followed that of the English team as, with a police escort, we
made our way through the excited crowds to the Royal Garden
Hotel in Kensington, where we were to play as an orchestra
for the celebration dinner, before arriving back in Portsmouth
in the early hours of the next morning. It had been a day few
will forget.

Peter Sumner departs

Peter Sumner was prone to sea-sickness more than most and
sadly was eventually unable to retain his appointment to attend
the Queen aboard *Britannia* on overseas deployments. Things
came to a head when, with him embarked, we met some very
bad weather in the Atlantic en-route to the Caribbean. At that
time, the cabin of the Director of Music was next to that of the
Senior Medical Officer, so when he became very ill, Peter
Sumner was unable to hide his condition from the Doctor.
Because of the inclement weather conditions, the yacht
eventually berthed at Madeira in Portugal, although we had

been heading for a re-fuelling stop in the Azores! Peter Sumner left the ship and was flown back to UK and I, as Bandmaster, took over his duties on board, swapping my violin bow for a baton.

After our arrival in the West Indies, Peter Sumner accompanied the Queen when she and her Staff flew out from Heathrow and, having re-joined the *Royal Yacht*, was able to resume his position as Director of Music. He returned to UK by air with the Queen when the royal tour ended. His last duties were performed in Barbados where the local Police band was under the command of Inspector Bill Greasley, a former Royal Marines Band Officer whom we all knew. Bill had retired from the Corps during the time I had been an Instructor at Deal, and I remember going to his farewell party arranged at the Swingate Inn on the Dover Road. He had just taken part in an annual Sergeants' Mess pantomime in the barracks at Deal, where his character had been that of a native witch doctor. In his farewell speech, he told us all that having been 'a black man in a white pantomime' he was looking forward to going to Barbados to be 'a white man in a black pantomime!' Such sentiments would not be expressed today.

Peter Sumner was taken by his senior Non-Commissioned Officers to a night club in Barbados for his farewell run ashore. It turned out to be a memorable evening. We were met at the top of some steps by the owner of the night-club, who proceeded to regale us with his knowledge of Shakespearian verse. Things went downhill from then on. The entertainers were local young ladies who felt the need to be naked on and off the mattress they had placed on the floor. Eventually, Peter was invited to dance with one of them and, on accepting the challenge, his hand went down onto her bottom, for which indiscretion he received a swipe across the face that quite ruined his evening: "Lookers, no touchers," she hissed!

With the Director of Music now again off the *Royal Yacht*, his duties were given back to me, and Britannia sailed through the Caribbean to transit the Panama Canal before entering the Pacific Ocean. I carried out Director of Music duties until we reached Fiji, where the Queen Mother was to join us for a lengthy tour of Australasia. Just prior to her arrival, Captain Paul Neville arrived, having flown across the world to become *Britannia's* Director of Music, in place of Peter Sumner. Having completed the Royal Tour that included Fiji, New Zealand and Australia, Paul Neville joined the Royal party and returned by air with the Queen Mother to the UK, leaving me with responsibility for the musicians in the *Royal Yacht* for the journey home by sea. Six weeks later, we arrived back in Portsmouth. Disembarking from *Britannia* and merging again with our colleagues at Eastney Barracks, we began again to make records, give concerts, and be featured on BBC radio and television programmes.

Portsmouth

In 1968, changes to the rank structure within the Royal Marines were brought in and a new rank of Staff Bandmaster (Quarter Master Sergeant) introduced for the Band Service. This was another point at which my career seemed to 'wobble' for I quickly realised that one of the newly promoted Staff Bandmasters would be sent to the Staff Band at Portsmouth and he would take over my job! The man nominated had served in the past as the Bandmaster at Eastney Barracks and therefore knew all there was to know – including Royal Yacht duties.

I was on a hiding to nothing when, on arrival, Staff Bandmaster John Masters took over my duties. He, rather than I, accompanied Peter Sumner's long-term relief, Captain Tom Lambert, the new Director of Music on board *Britannia* when the Queen went to carry out an Official Visit to Brazil and Chile in South America. I found myself gently, but completely, sidelined.

There was only one Bandmaster's job, and John Masters had moved into it with all the confidence of a senior man who had held the position at Portsmouth before. In the absence of both the Director of Music and the new Bandmaster on Royal Duty it fell to me, together with the non-Royal Yacht musicians still at Eastney Barracks, to provide music locally and indeed nationally as the need presented itself.

In 1968, with the introduction of WO2 Staff Bandmaster rank, it was decided to do away with an old-style appointment arm badge that had been in use within the Royal Marines Bands of the three Royal Marines Divisions (Portsmouth, Chatham and Plymouth) for many years. Directors of these bands would select a Senior Band Sergeant to act as his deputy. He would remain an instrumentalist within the band but would be available as deputy conductor if required. The individual selected would remove his Sergeant's chevrons from the upper part of his uniform's right sleeve, before reversing them and sewing them on the lower part of the sleeve with the musical lyre immediately above. This was an appointment rather than a rank. I was the last to wear this insignia and when I was later

commissioned, my tunic carrying it became an exhibit in the
Royal Marines Corps Museum".

My tunic with its Divisional Bandmaster Badge, 1968

Milton Glee Club

The band cultivated a strong relationship with the Milton Glee
Club, a well-run choral society in Portsmouth. Regular
concerts involving the Royal Marines orchestra were given in
Portsmouth Guildhall, with specially invited guest artists from
the world of entertainment. To be in regular professional
contact with such people and to support them musically on
stage was an extremely useful experience. I first met the
founder and conductor of the Glee Club, Stanley Mortimore,
in 1965 when I went to his office in the Dockyard Naval Base
to discuss programme details and soloists for his up-coming

concerts. Rehearsals with the choir were held in our band room at the barracks in a warm and friendly atmosphere.

Sir Alec Rose

Circumnavigations of the globe by sailing yacht have become almost regular occurrences now, but in the 1960s this was not so. In 1966, Francis Chichester was the first sailor to sail the 'clipper route' in *Gypsy Moth IV* single-handed, as did Alec Rose in *Lively Lady* the following year. Both received knighthoods for their achievements.

Alec Rose was a well-known local Portsmouth greengrocer, and his circumnavigation really caught the interest of people from the city. On his return to UK, he was awarded the Freedom of the City of Portsmouth in a memorable ceremony held in the city's Guildhall. The stage had been transformed into the Council Chamber for the day, with flowers everywhere all in the colours of the city emblem and, by coincidence, those of the ceremonial uniforms of my musicians, who were seated as an orchestra at the base of the stage.

As a local boy myself, it was a thrilling and joyous moment to conduct the music of *'Rose of England'*, a score I had searched for and eventually found in time for the event, as 'Sir' Alec Rose entered the Guildhall. He was greeted with tumultuous applause and responded with great humility when presented with his Freedom Scroll in its oaken and jewelled casket. Here was a city steeped in nautical history that knew bravery when they saw it and were glad to honour a man who had carried forward the best traditions of his home city. By sailing single-handedly around the world, in his own little boat and at his own expense while his wife looked after the family's local greengrocery shop, Alec Rose had demonstrated all the attributes that had, over the years, made Britain 'Great'.

LRAM lessons

Prior to the changes that had taken place following the formation of the new hierarchy of the band at Eastney Barracks, and spurred by the need not to give up, I studied in my own time for a second attempt at obtaining a civilian Licentiate Diploma from the Royal Academy of Music. An LRAM was an essential requisite for any aspiring candidate for Royal Marines Director of Music, and I was beginning to set my sights high!

During my time in Deal as a Non-Commissioned Officer Instrumental Instructor, I had regularly visited the seafront apartment of Clarinet Professor Ken Mettyear for evening aural music lessons. Now, from Portsmouth, I began a correspondence course with a former Royal Marines Director of Music, 'Pop' Talling, an examiner for London's Trinity College of Music, and paid him to mark the harmony and counterpoint exercises I sent to him through the post. I practised my violin and clarinet to soloist standard and prepared the pieces I would be required to perform on both instruments as part of my examination at the Royal Academy of Music. Another part of my examination would be to conduct a prepared work performed by a Guards Band at its London Headquarters, followed by a sight-reading piece in front of a Board of RAM Examiners. At the appropriate time I applied to take the examination, paid my fees and, on the day bidden, went to London with my accompanist.

When *Britannia* sailed for South America, I had been left with the larger part of the Staff Band at Eastney Barracks to carry out normal day-to-day duties as required. I decided to give the yacht a rousing send-off as it left Portsmouth harbour.

Naval shore establishments on either side of the harbour in turn carried out due deference to the Royal Yacht as it left its moorings, with salutes that involved the blowing of bosun's pipes and bugles as *Britannia* headed towards the sea. This was all very polished and appropriate behaviour for those times. The last Naval establishment to carry out this ceremonial procedure was always the submarine base, HMS Dolphin, on the starboard side as a ship leaves the harbour, and all on board Britannia stood to attention facing that way.

Immediately to port, I had gathered on the sea wall ten of my colleagues in civilian clothes, none of whom could play brass instruments, but each carried a bugle. On a given signal, a ten second fanfare of the most awful uncoordinated sound blasted from this group that caused the Admiral and his officers to dash to the side of *Britannia* nearest to us in an attempt to locate the source of such a hideous noise. By the time they had crossed the deck, my team had hidden down behind the sea wall and all that was visible was a large sign held aloft by unseen hands. It read "Bon Voyage – from 'B' band". Mission accomplished, we returned to barracks.

Over the weeks that the Royal Yacht was away, we learned that the South American trip was not all that it should have been and was not greatly enjoyed. When *Britannia* eventually returned to Portsmouth, I decided that it should be uniquely welcomed home. As it negotiated the narrow entrance to the harbour, the Royal Yacht was greeted by a fully visible fourteen-piece Royal Marines fanfare team of silver trumpets with banners on that same sea wall - and this time the sound from shore was sparkling and majestic. My pension was (hopefully) secured!

Before leaving Eastney Barracks to conduct the fanfare team on that morning, I had taken delivery of a letter that bore the insignia of the Royal Academy of Music. Knowing that the envelope must contain the result of my recent LRAM examination, I didn't want to open it until the business of welcoming *Britannia* home had been completed. Now, on the sea wall with the sound of the trumpets still ringing in my ears, I took the envelope from my pocket and broke the seal to learn that I had been successful. The news that I now had an LRAM diploma was so important to me, and so crucial to my career hopes, that I had to sit alone for a while on the sea wall to compose myself.

Interview for promotion to Officer

Within weeks, I was accepted for interview with two other candidates for a vacant Special Duties promotion to Lieutenant Royal Marines. The interview was held in the office of the Major General at Eastney Barracks. Two other candidates, Bandmasters Ben Finney and Terry Freestone - both older and more experienced than me - came from the Royal Marines School of Music at Deal for their interviews. They arrived at the General's Office by car after a long journey and a very early start.

Remembering how individual it had been to have chromium plated metal bits on my service belt when a band-boy, I had thought ahead and searched every shop in Portsmouth to find the whitest shirt available. It was a 'Double 2 White Light' shirt, with which I was to wear a Corps tie. I bought a new suit from C&A and new shoes to go with it. I even placed a tiny silver emblem in the lapel of my jacket that glistened every time I moved. I intended to stand out in this interview procedure.

On arrival at the General's office, we three candidates were required to write an essay and were later challenged to solve verbal problems as a team, before being interviewed separately by the General and his board of assembled officers. It was a probing interview, and it was necessary to be entirely honest in answering questions about my personal history. Much research had already taken place into the candidates' backgrounds and we had each achieved a 'positive security vetting' before being invited for interview.

I admitted to the board that I had not come from a privileged background. As far as I knew, no one in my family had ever been to university. Indeed, I told them that there was every possibility that my father's ancestors had been smugglers on the beaches of Dorset before switching to being Revenue Men and eventually Admiralty Policemen! The many positive things that had occurred in my life up to this point must have outweighed the negative ones, for I left the interview feeling that I at least had a chance of being selected. All I could do now was await the arrival of a signal (naval telegram) from the Royal Marines Commandant General's Office in London with the decision as to my future.

The decision reached me when I answered the doorbell of the house in which I and my family were living at Cosham to find my chum, Drum Major Colin Bowden, standing there. In one outstretched hand there was a bottle of champagne and in the other a copy of a signal that had just been sent to the Barracks from London.

His smile said it all, neither of us could speak, and I am still emotional at the memory of that moment when I knew that after nineteen years on the 'lower deck', I was to be commissioned as a Royal Marines Officer.

In 1968 this was momentous, for it changed perceptions of life at every level, from the way people viewed you to the way you viewed them, in a way that is now long gone, and perhaps rightly so.

I was promoted to the rank of Lieutenant Royal Marines on Christmas Day 1968, the day after Lt. Colonel Vivian Dunn retired from the Corps. Prior to going on Christmas leave the Sergeants' Mess, of which I had been a member since joining Eastney Barracks, was invited to the Officers' Mess for lunchtime drinks in time-honoured fashion. The Regimental Sergeant Major asked me to accompany him across to the Officers' Mess. As we ascended the imposing stairway up to the front entrance I could see and hear the band playing *'Congratulations'*. Having at school failed my 11 plus, and never having had the benefit of a course of instruction beyond that for Band Corporal, I now found myself welcomed into an Officers' Mess. I would serve as a Royal Marines Officer for the next twenty-one years!

CHAPTER 7

ROYAL ACADEMY OF MUSIC, SCOTLAND & THE QE2
1968 - 1974

My old uniforms had now to be discarded and new Officer pattern ones obtained. I was presented with a list specifying what Officers wore in temperate and tropical climates. I was shocked to learn how much most of it cost. Fortunately, I didn't have to pay for it all myself. I received a grant from the exchequer which enabled Messrs Gieves & Hawkes, military tailors in London's Saville Row, to supply some made-to-measure garments.

I was issued with a ceremonial Band Cape and was told that it had belonged to recently retired Lt. Colonel Vivian Dunn. When I protested that I expected to be issued with a new rather than a second-hand cape, I was told that I should be grateful, for if I were to set out to walk across the water to France whilst wearing this cape, I would make it! "Our Father which art in Deal" was the term used by all during his lengthy tenure!

I bought a sword from a retiring officer and saw a metal helmet box from a previous era for sale in an outlet specialising in such items. Having bought it, I found within it an officers' pattern white helmet with helmet plate badge, both of the highest quality. I had been very fortunate indeed.

My first appointment as a Commissioned Officer was to the Royal Marines School of Music at Deal, but this was for administrative purposes only whilst I attended a year-long course of musical study at the Royal Academy of Music in London.

A bad accident

Whilst in Deal, I became involved with the local church at Sholden. The graveyard surrounding the church was very overgrown, with many old tombs obscured by tangled shrubs. One sunny afternoon, I gathered up a few tools and went to clear some of the shrubs. After about half an hour of cutting grass and clipping undergrowth, I came across the raised tomb of a Vice Admiral of the White, who must have been an important man in these parts at the time of his death in the early 1800s. The tomb was surrounded by iron railings, through which some hefty branches were poking. They were part of an old bush that had grown between the tomb and the iron work. Clearing it away, I made the mistake of bending one of the stronger branches down as I chopped at its base. Without warning it sprang up into my face and I knew I had sustained a nasty injury.

Holding a handkerchief to my mouth where the greatest damage seemed to be, I retraced my steps to my home nearby.

Once inside the house, I looked in a mirror to discover that a branch had struck me and penetrated beneath my lower lip. Furthermore I had somehow managed to bite almost completely through my tongue, which was hanging by a thread and bleeding profusely. I was alone and I knew that I had to get myself to the local hospital, a mile and a half away. Folding my tongue back into my mouth, I walked to the hospital's casualty department. When I got there I was feeling pretty rough and, of course, was unable to speak. By gesture and grunts through a bloodied handkerchief I got some sort of message across. A surgeon, Dr. John Pond, was quickly on hand. He was in fact a family friend and, as conductor of the local Handelian Society, a professional colleague. He set to work with needle and thread and sewed my tongue back together, something I would never have thought possible.

Back at home, and after the anaesthetic had worn off, I realised that the nerves in the tongue had been severed and that I couldn't feel the forward part of my mouth at all. It felt as though all my front teeth had gone. For a week or so I had to exist on a liquid diet that Margaret decided to brighten up for me one Sunday tea-time. She gave me some custard that I sucked through a straw but, unfortunately, she had put some rhubarb juice in it! As I was scraping myself off the ceiling, we realised that this acidic concoction hadn't helped my recovery process.

Later, I quietly thanked providence for the fact that I was no longer an instrumentalist because, without adequate feeling in the mouth, surely any ideas of again playing a clarinet or saxophone for a living were misplaced. As a Director of Music

I would instead conduct, and I knew that my ability to do this was still intact.

Then I had a devastating thought: 'How am I going to engage with an audience if I cannot speak properly?' This heralded another point in my life, where fortune seemed to shine on me after all, for some time after the surface of the tongue had healed I could tell that the nerves within it were slowly growing back together. I began to feel my front teeth again as I passed my tongue over them and any words I spoke were becoming more intelligible. The lump beneath the healed skin beneath my lower lip remained inflamed, however, and I could feel something hard within it. On investigation, I found that a piece of the branch that had struck me was still embedded in my face several weeks after the accident. Hooking it out with a pin in front of a mirror, I was left with just a raised scar as a keepsake.

A robbery

Before leaving Eastney Barracks in Portsmouth, I had been presented with a pig-skin leather briefcase by my fellow Senior Non-Commissioned Officers to mark my promotion. In it I put my most valued and important papers and documents, including everything pertaining to my career thus far. During a visit to a colleague who oversaw the Royal Navy and Royal Marines Careers Office in Canterbury, the briefcase was stolen. I lost everything, including my vellum Royal Marines Service Certificate (recently given to me for safe keeping!), pay book, cheque book, passport, education certificates, birth and marriage certificates and car logbook.

Fortunately some of the documents were able to be replaced in time, but my Service Certificate, showing that throughout the whole of my time on the lower deck I had never received an annual assessment less than 'VG Superior', had gone forever. From the day of the robbery, I have been unable to provide any certification demonstrating that I had passed any examinations. I felt bereaved.

The Royal Academy of Music

Since the early 1950s, each year a Royal Marines candidate would be nominated to attend a Conducting Course offered by the Royal Academy of Music. This had been suggested by Sir Vivian Dunn, who had been knighted on his retirement. Sir Vivian had been a former RAM violin student, as well as holding a Fellowship from that august body and was a member of the RAM Club. Although the course was limited to eight international students and lasted two years, the Royal Marines candidate attended only the final year.

I attended lectures on the study of harmony, orchestration, musical history and form, aural training and conducting. My course was overseen by Maurice Miles, Professor of Conducting at the Academy. He was a delightful man whose sensitivity and charm was apparent for all to see. He could conduct with just the movement of an eyebrow – and often did!

During the year, I had several opportunities to conduct the Student Orchestra and much enjoyed doing so. This orchestra sometimes gave performances away from the Academy, and one such was arranged in the nearby St Marylebone Parish

Church. When the coach arrived to take the performers and all their equipment to the venue, I knew from experience that there was no was that the timpani were going to fit into the boot of the coach, nor through the doorway of the vehicle itself. Together with two of the percussionists, we manhandled the timpani out of the Academy and down the steps and then briskly set off for the church. We got there before the coach arrived and had the percussion instruments all set up by the time they did. It was just as well, for the concert had to open with a piece featuring the timpani and this would not have been possible had we not taken matters into our own hands. Maurice Miles was delighted to know that some common sense had prevailed, and everyone learned the lesson not just to assume that everything will always go into the boot of a coach!

I managed to fit all the course lectures into three successive days in each week and was therefore able to spend just those days in London and away from home. At the end of the course we sat final examinations in each subject and conducted the student orchestra. Even though, at the age of thirty-four, I was a decade older than my fellow students, they each had the benefit of advanced general education and musical scholarship. I hardly expected to do well and was therefore delighted to learn that I had been successful and was awarded the RAM's Advanced Certificate in Conducting, the Italian Ricordi Prize, together with a set of bound scores of all nine of the Beethoven symphonies. These were presented to me by The Duchess of Kent, who presided over my graduation ceremony.

Bill Greasley, the former RM Band Officer who had gone to command the Barbados Police Band, had now returned to UK to become the Stage Manager at the Royal Academy of Music.

After the graduation ceremony, Bill asked me to see him in his flat at York Gate as he had something he wanted to give me as a keepsake. It was a score, annotated throughout in blue chinagraph pencil by Sir Henry Wood and carrying his signature. This was presented to me, together with one of Sir Henry's unique wooden batons. Both items have excellent provenance and must also have some considerable value. I later offered them to the Royal Marines Corps Museum, but the Curator showed no interest in them at all because, he said, Sir Henry had not actually been a Royal Marine! They remain in my possession together with other collected treasures, including a bass drum, saved from a skip, that may well have gone around the world with the Queen in *SS Gothic* on her 1954 commonwealth tour, after her coronation the previous year.

Items that the Corps Museum did accept from me for display include a superb Broadwood upright piano, hand-painted with scenes of Victorian England and carrying candle sconces, from the Victoria & Albert III. At some stage it had been transferred from the yacht to the band room at Eastney Barracks, and for many years was used daily for rehearsals. With a new piano available from the School of Music in Deal, I considered that the ancient V&A instrument deserved preservation, so I offered it to the Corps Museum.

Arbroath

Back in Deal, I learnt that I was to become the Director of Music of the Royal Marines Band based at HMS Condor at Arbroath in Scotland – considered then by some to be the Band Service Penal Colony! I arranged for a removal firm to collect my family's furniture and effects at Deal on a Friday for delivery to a married quarter in Arbroath on the following Monday. By this time, I would be there to meet it. The removal van got to Arbroath on the Sunday and the driver decided to look for the delivery address so that he would know exactly where to go on the next day. On parking outside of the house the next-door neighbour appeared and, unbidden, insisted that the driver unload the contents there and then into the vacant property.

The neighbour was in fact Lieutenant 'Dougie' Haigh, the Director of Music that I was to take over from. The forcefulness of his character was demonstrated that day, for not only did he unlock the married quarter to allow the delivery to take place, but he insisted that the contents of the tea-chests be placed in whatever room he thought appropriate.

When I arrived the next day, our things were spread in piles throughout the house and, with the packing cases gone, it was total chaos! Mrs. Haigh then appeared and said that she didn't know why I had been sent to relieve her husband, because they both loved being in Scotland and didn't want to return to Deal. "Go back where you came from" she said as she firmly closed her door!

The next day Lt. Haigh and I had to travel 66 miles south to Rosyth in order that I could meet Admiral Dunbar-Nasmith, Flag Officer Scotland & Northern Ireland. He was a charming man whose father had been a highly decorated wartime submarine Commander. He welcomed me in the way I had hoped Dougie Haigh would have done. Returning to *HMS Condor*, a Naval Air Station that was about to become a base for 45 Royal Marines Commando, I met the band personnel and carried out the prescribed 'hand-over' procedure. Signatures were required for all manner of items of equipment once counted and checked, and I insisted on looking carefully at everything I was signing for.

Casting my eye over a pair of double basses lined up against a wall, I thought that the neck of one looked slightly odd. I touched it and the scroll part fell off, taking the four strings with it. Had I signed for that instrument, broken before my arrival and was known to have been by the man I was replacing, I would likely have had to pay for the repair.

I was quite pleased that my powers of observation had paid dividends and I thought I was now safe. However, on my first morning behind my new desk, Bugler Coad came to me with a pile of forms for me to sign. He told me that they were the Band Standing Orders and each had been reprinted because of the change of command from my predecessor to me. He told me that it was just a matter of me signing my name at the bottom of each form. Without fully checking each one I did just that and then, on his way out of the door, he turned to thank me profusely for what I had done. When asked why he was so pleased when I had merely done what was considered necessary, he put on a beaming smile and told me that one of the forms he had included was an Adoption Certificate in respect of his wife and himself! I had un-knowingly signed as guarantor for a baby they were about to adopt. I was so bowled over by the absolute cheek of the man that I decided to allow it to go ahead.

Bugler Coad was one of the real characters of the Corps. Stories about him now abound and most of them are, I suspect, true. He was brought before me as a defaulter on one occasion that I particularly remember. It was a simple offence, he was guilty and I gave him a real roasting before determining his punishment. I was sure that he would never even want to look at me again. The Drum Major repeated to him the punishment I had awarded, turned him about and marched him out of my office. Within seconds there was a knock on my door and Coad's head appeared around it: "I'm going fishing tonight, Sir. Can I drop a nice one around to your house if I catch any?"

On another occasion, as Duty Bugler, he was going to be late on parade where he needed to sound the *Fall In* at 8am. He sounded it on time, but did so whilst on his bike, approaching the parade ground at a rate of knots!

HMS Condor had been a Naval Air Station for many years and was under the command of Captain John Mott Royal Navy when I joined it. A decision had been taken that this establishment would be transferred to the Royal Marines to become Condor Barracks and that it would become the home of 45 Commando Royal Marines. Responsibility for the 'hand-over' was given to Captain Mott's Executive Commander 'Jumbo' Merrin, Royal Navy, who took over command as Captain Mott came to the end of his career and retired. I remained in contact with John Mott, for in retirement he became resident custodian of the National Trust's Culzean Castle on the coast of Ayeshire. I was occasionally able to take my orchestra to entertain guests and visitors within the castle and to carry out Beat Retreat ceremonies on the outer lawned areas of this delightful venue.

Travelling to the castle each time was a memorable experience, as it entailed the band coach navigating an unusual road which boasted an 'Electric Brae'. Quite simply when going up what appears to be a distinct incline the coach needed no throttle at all whilst going down the other side of the 'hill', the driver had to accelerate to keep moving. It is a very strange phenomenon to experience but is actually just an optical illusion.

When 45 Commando arrived at Arbroath they brought with them a black dog named 'Oscar'. It had been with the Unit during recent operations in Aden and, for its bravery, had been adopted as the Commando's mascot. It was a real Arab gutter-hound, yet marched on parade with its handler as if it was one of the Queen's corgis. Once on parade, it was a total embarrassment as a mascot, for someone had taught it to howl loudly whenever a bugle was sounded. The Handover parade from the Royal Navy to the Royal Marines had to be *heard* to be believed. The dog commanded considerable attention on that day - probably as much as it had commanded the previous evening, when it had attacked and killed the *HMS Condor* WREN's cat!

Rosyth

With the transfer of the governance of the establishment from the Royal Navy to the Royal Marines, my Admiral decided that his band should move from Arbroath to be near his headquarters at Rosyth, some 15 miles from Edinburgh. This entailed considerable planning, for as well as moving all the musicians and their equipment, their families had to be re-housed in married quarters in the new area as well.

I was charged to find somewhere that could become our band-room and rehearsal facility. I was able to take over a building in Rosyth dockyard that had originally been a naval chapel. It was ideal in the circumstances and served us well. My office now had a real nautical flavour too, because it contained a wooden binnacle from a sailing ship converted for use as a font. A super brass diver's helmet formed a lid under which was hidden a receptacle for holy water. It was 1970, and the daily rum issue in the Royal Navy had just been abolished. This was a shame, for had it not been, my binnacle could have been very useful!

The Port Admiral at the time was Rear Admiral Terence Ridley, a much respected royal naval officer who had specialised in engineering and who received the Freedom of Dunfermline during his tenure, an honour only held by one other person at the time, Her Majesty The Queen Mother. A delightfully individual character, he was well known for wearing a monocle rather than spectacles. Earlier in his career he was once confronted with the sight of a group of naval engineering students all wearing monocles, at which time he tossed his into the air and caught it in his eye. He then invited the class to emulate that feat. There were no takers. When we took over the chapel in his dockyard as our band rehearsal facility, we named it 'Ridley Hall' in his honour."

Once fully settled into our new environment at Rosyth in 1972, I was anxious to publicise our presence. After considerable thought, I arranged what was advertised as a *Royal Marines Band Spectacular* in Dunfermline's Pittencrief Pavilion. I involved my orchestra, concert band, dance band, a local choir and a professional vocalist. The show ended with a finale involving the Drum Major and the Buglers and Drummers of the band. All proceeds were donated to a Scottish War-blinded charity. It was a very successful evening, so I was bitterly disappointed to find it virtually ignored by the local newspaper.

I wrote privately to the Editor, whom I knew personally for he was an honorary member of my Wardroom Mess at HMS Cochrane and explained how I had hoped that this public relations opportunity for the Royal Navy would have been adequately covered. Some days later, I received a telephone call from the Admiral's Secretary telling me to be at the Admiral's office, five miles away, in twenty minutes!

On arrival, he thrust a copy of a just published local paper and told me to read certain sections of it. To my consternation, I found that my personal letter to my 'friend' had been printed as a letter to the Editor under a banner headline, *Royal Marines Director Complains!* Not only that, but the Editor's *Weekly Comment* column was entirely devoted to my remarks.

Suffice to say, the Admiral was not entirely pleased, and I was mortified. It is difficult to be a publicist for anything without being seen to be 'showing off,' for an invisible line divides the two. I had been seen to cross it! Fortunately, I was in my first job as a commissioned officer and therefore survived this baptism by fire. It was a lesson learned in the hardest fashion. I trod a very lonely path for some weeks after that episode, for as I was in trouble even my Wardroom 'friends' seem to keep a respectable distance lest, perhaps, they become tainted by association.

There were many Royal Naval Establishments in Scotland at this time, and it was my job to ensure that each received musical support as often as possible. From my band, I was able to field several small combinations of musicians at the same time, so that important occasions such as Trafalgar Night Dinners on 21st October each year could be catered for. When the diary allowed, I took the band around Scotland and elsewhere to perform at various civilian venues.

The Royal Marines Band is an ideal public relations vehicle for the Royal Navy, which otherwise finds it difficult to 'wave the flag' effectively. Unlike the other two Services, most of what the Navy does is done offshore and out of sight. Parading the White Ensign deep inland is a bonus indeed. In particular, I realised that entertaining youngsters in schools would be really worthwhile.

Our performances were not recruiting exercises, for almost all the schools that we visited were Infant or Junior Schools. But it was a way for the band to get 'out on the road,' and a week-long schools tour also enabled us to be in a particular area for long enough to undertake public concerts – some of which would be paid engagements! We kept getting invited back to the schools we had visited and were even able to travel as far as North Wales each year for one of these 'schools tours'. The children adored our presentations. The tuba player performed solo items on an American sousaphone with a large pair of red paper lips glued to its large forward-facing bell. Some children were selected to conduct the band as it played a simple piece, while their classmates in the audience were given all manner of percussion instruments to play. All joined in the fun of music-making.

Being the only Royal Marines Band based north of London made us autonomous. So long as we were fulfilling our role in fully supporting the Naval Service throughout Scotland, I was able to manage the band diary with little interference. For many Scots, and others with links to that country, membership of the band was highly sought after, and leaving it at the end of a term of service was always marked effectively as can be seen from the photograph of a presentation to Band Sergeant Jack Malpass of a desecrated trombone with tartan accoutrements.

Band Sgt Malpass is presented with a brass player's version of a set of bagpipes, 1972

Time was also set aside for sport and recreation, and we took full advantage of the nearby Royal Navy sports fields at Rosyth. On one occasion, the band organised a charity walk that was very popular and a successful fund-raiser. Someone had the bright idea that we should use the walkways on either side of the Forth Road Bridge for this event. With check points at each end, participants walked across on one side, under the carriageway and through a second check point before making the return crossing to North Queensferry - and, if they wanted, repeating the procedure. A surprising number of people kept this up all day.

Aboard the Queen Elizabeth 2

In 1973, the band was selected to cruise for eight days on board the fabulous Cunard liner *Queen Elizabeth 2* for an international body known as the *Young Presidents' Organisation*. It had privately chartered the ship for the Organisation's use for a week in May of that year, turning it into a floating university by day and a place of tremendously varied entertainment at night. Holidaying in Scotland, a senior YPO executive had seen my band perform and was impressed by the variety of what he saw. After a lengthy discussion, and a visit to Falkirk to attend one of my concerts, our selection was confirmed.

To qualify for membership of the *Young Presidents' Organisation,* individuals had to be under forty-nine years of age and President of a company which had a large minimum annual turnover. All on board *QE2* for this cruise were in an income bracket that most can only dream about and had travelled from all over the world to join the ship at Southampton for an eight-day trip that was to take in Tangiers, Palma, Gibraltar and Lisbon.

Thirty-two members of my band accompanied me from Scotland to join the *QE2* in Southampton. Amid great enthusiasm, and totally incognito - for it was a condition of the contract that the presence of Royal Marines musicians was kept secret - we boarded the ship on the evening before departure. On the jetty next day, a 200 strong Welsh choir and the full Regimental Band of the Royal Artillery entertained us as the great ship nosed its way towards the open sea and the first port of call, Tangiers.

YPO 'Odyssey of Knowledge' Brochure 1973

We had been promised that, as entertainers, we would be treated exactly the same as everyone else on board because this was to be a 'one-class' voyage. Even so, we were overwhelmed to discover that our cabins were all first class with en-suite facilities. Fixed to each cabin door was a temporary sign saying, 'Captains Quarters – PRIVATE'. This was obviously going to be a trip with a difference. Inside each cabin there were masses of fresh flowers, presented as a gift from the Chairman of YPO. The final touch was added by Cunard officers themselves who had delivered to every cabin, with their compliments, a bottle of vintage champagne and glasses. All this and we had not yet cleared Southampton Water!

One of the main objects of the cruise was to provide constant daytime educational facilities ensuring thereby that all costs for the trip could be legitimately expensed. To this end, university dons and expert speakers were on hand to deliver a compelling programme of seminars. The ship's many plush and intimate lounges were ideally suited to this. Distinguished speakers included the President of General Motors, George Romney (Governor of Michigan and US Cabinet Secretary), humourist Art Buchwald, novelist Arthur Hailey; The Duke and Duchess of Bedford, portrait photographer Yousef Karsh, Lord Montague of Beaulieu, the BBC's Sheridan Morley, and finally, King of Swing Artie Shaw! It is not therefore surprising that this cruise was termed YPO's 'Odyssey of Knowledge'.

Lunch was the first meal of the trip. We were offered a menu of staggering proportions. Ten courses for lunch were a bit much, even for our young enthusiasts. What a way to start a week's work! We truly felt like the multi-millionaires with whom we were travelling. In our civilian clothes, we were asked to mingle with the guests and had an opportunity to meet for the first time some of our fellow entertainers, including Joe Loss and his orchestra, The Dutch Swing College Band, Trio Los Paraguayos, and The Hennesseys, one of Wales' foremost traditional folk music groups.

Luncheon

RMS Queen Elizabeth 2

Saturday 19 May 1973

Hors d'Oeuvres
Chilled Grapefruit, Marguerite – Asparagus Tips, Roquefort – Potted Shrimps
Mortadella and Salami Salad – Tomatoes Monegasque
Tomato, Grapefruit, Orange, V.8, Pineapple, Apple

Soups
Hot Chicken Bouillon – Chilled Cream of Asparagus
Cream of Mushroom

Fish
Fisherman's Platter *(Fried goujonettes of sole, prawns and scallops; served with Tartare sauce)*
Lobster and Celery Salad, Mayonnaise Sauce

Entrees
FRIED EGGS FARMER'S WIFE STYLE
(Eggs fried in butter with a slice of smoked ham, garnished and served with lionnaise potatoes and grilled tomatoes)
SWEETBREADS FINANCIERE

Grills (To order: 10 to 15 mins.)
CALF'S LIVER AND BACON, ONION SAUCE, HOT POTATO SALAD

Vegetables
Mashed Carrots and Turnips – Fried Egg Plant
Lyonnaise and Baked Jacket Potatoes

Cold Buffet
Roast Ribs and Sirloin of Beef, Raifort – Roast Lamb, Mint Jelly
Roast Chicken with Saratogas – Roast Duckling with Orange Sauce
Rolled Ox Tongue – Roast Vermont Turkey, Cranberry Sauce

Salads
Lettuce and Tomato – Russe – Jamaican – Pear and Cottage Cheese

Dressings
Choice of French, Russian, Mayonnaise, Roquefort, Green Goddess
Thousand Islands and Ceasar

Desserts
Coconut Custard Pie – Bavarian Chocolate Cream Pie – Peach Havanaise Roll
Fruit Jelly – Raspberry Sherbet
Vanilla, Strawberry or Tutti-Frutti Ice Creams, Hot Caramel Sauce
Fresh Oranges, Apples, Pears, Grapes, Pineapple, Bananas

Cheeses
Cheddar – Cheshire – Port Salut – Wensleydale – Brie – Edam – Cottage
Camembert – Danish Blue – Pont l'Eveque – Stilton – Philadelphia
Caerphilly – Gorgonzola – K raft – Gouda

Beverages
Full Roast Coffee – Instant Coffee – Iced Tea or Coffee
Ceylon, China or Indian Tea
Hot Chocolate – Horlicks – Fresh Milk

QE2 *Lunch Menu, 19 May 1973*

Dinner

RMS Queen Elizabeth 2

Saturday 19 May 1973

Appetisers
Melonball Cocktail, Creme de Menthe – Seafood Cocktail, Russian Dressing
Sardines in Oil – Pate de Foie Gras – Bismarck Herrings
Smoked Salmon with Capers

Soups
Boston Clam Chowder – Potage Cressionaire
Cold: Boula Boula

Fish
Fried Fillets of Plaice, Tartare Sauce
Rainbow Trout Saute

Entree
Coq au Vin

Roast
Roast Duckling, Apple and Savoury Sauce

Grills
Entrecote Steak, Garni – Pork Chop, Chesapeake

Vegetables
Creamed Silverskin Onions – Baked Broccoli
French Fried and Roast Potatoes

Cold Meats
Roast Ribs and Sirloin of Beef, Raifort – Roast Lamb, Mint Jelly
Roast Chicken with Saratogas – Roast Duckling with Orange Sauce
Roast Vermont Turkey, Cranberry Sauce – Rolled Ox Tongue

Salads
Fresh Fruit – Tossed Lettuce and Tomato

Desserts
Souffle Arlequin – Cherries Jubilee – Fruit Compote, Chantilly
Grand Marnier Sorbet
Fresh Oranges, Apples, Pears, Grapes, Pineapple, Bananas

Cheeses
Cheddar – Cheshire – Port Salut – Wensleydale – Brie – Edam – Cottage
Camembert – Danish Blue – Pont l'Eveque – Stilton
Philadelphia – Caerphilly – Gorgonzola – Kraft – Gouda

Beverages
Full Roast Coffee – Instant Coffee – Iced Tea or Coffee
Ceylon, China or Indian Tea
Hot Chocolate – Horlicks – Fresh Milk

QE2 Dinner Menu, 19 May 1973

Our first commitment in this vast and quite remarkable ship
was to perform as a concert orchestra in the *Double-Down*
Room during the opening ceremony. We were then free until
the evening, when my orchestra divided to play during dinner
in the two first class restaurants. From then on into the night,

the ship was bubbling with nightlife. Every lounge had live entertainment of some sort or another from individual cabaret artistes to 'groups' and even an escapologist. The *Theatre Bar*, with the temporary décor of a seashore pub—nets and barrels, etc., —very soon became a popular haunt and was throbbing well into the night – every night, with us performing splendidly enthusiastic Scottish reels.

The second night at sea as *QE2* continued her passage to Tangiers was designated *British Night*. For this the whole decor of the principal rooms was altered. We volunteered to assist with the transformation team and worked valiantly to assemble the vast array of prefabricated items that had been secretly brought on board. These included life-size depictions of a London double-decker bus, various styles of taxi and scenes of British life. Festooned with hundreds of flags and balloons, the ship was transformed by nightfall when festivities began. First came various cocktail parties, invitations for which had been thrust under all cabin doors. Next, dinner, with another mind-boggling menu wrapped for the occasion in printed *Union Jack* covers.

Each table setting had a costume doll for ladies and a bowler hat and copy of the Financial Times for the men. Again, my two orchestras performed in the restaurants before diners were invited to join Joe Loss and his orchestra and dance in the *Double-Down* room. As midnight approached, Joe Loss introduced the climax of the *British Night* festivities. On his cue, the Band of HM Royal Marines and I marched on to the dance floor and carried out a carefully choreographed display culminating with the ceremony of Beat Retreat. Until this moment, no one knew that we were on board, for up to this point we had not been seen in uniform. The sudden appearance of the white helmets and precision marching in the ballroom of the *QE2* off the coast of Portugal was a rare moment for all to savour.

I had originally planned to further enhance the appearance of the drummers during the actual display of 'Beat Retreat' by using Ultraviolet lighting. Before leaving Scotland, I carried out a rehearsal to see the effect of a UV light source on the white equipment, helmets, and drumsticks of the Corps of Drummers and Buglers. Some stage performers used this form of lighting, and I knew that it picked out white clothing worn by dancers in discos. I thought that I could utilise this effect on the dance floor of the QE2, but I was wrong. Under UV light, only things that had been washed in detergent were picked out. Anything painted with white emulsion paint - in our case all ceremonial kit from the helmets down - was reduced to an uninteresting khaki colour. Even though the painted kit wasn't picked out by the UV light, we could possibly have gone ahead with the UV concept because the cotton gloves of each performer, having been washed in detergent, would have looked truly spectacular when the main lighting was extinguished. I decided not to reduce the colourful visual impact of my band, though, so my UV plan was shelved.

Back now to my cabin to change, to find a bottle of whisky on the table with a card inscribed: 'From the Queen, with love, God Bless Her'. Thinking that mine was the only cabin to be so lucky I kept quiet but learned later that every member of the band had also been given a bottle!

Tangier in Morocco was reached next day in unusually inclement weather. A 'shore adventure' had been organised for a local beach where everyone had been invited: *"to dine on pillows under striped tents on Moroccan sands topped off with a wild camel ride."* Rain caused the venue to be changed to the local caves, but the excitement was no less vivid - tribesmen on camels thrust past the cave entrances in a demonstration of savagery that I am convinced was calculated to cause coronaries. Here was one good reason why members of YPO had to be under the age of 49.

On leaving Tangiers and before reaching Majorca, the *QE2* rendezvoused with the US Sixth Fleet in the Mediterranean. Steaming alongside the nuclear aircraft carrier *USS John F. Kennedy* at more than thirty knots, we stood in awe at a display of impressive naval firepower. It is rare to have such a close view of an aircraft carrier catapulting its aircraft into the air. Once launched, the aircraft proceeded to demonstrate their supersonic and aerobatic capabilities whilst a running commentary was given by the Commander, US Naval Forces in Europe, Admiral William F Bringle. He had been transferred to QE2 by helicopter from his ship for this purpose.

After lengthy demonstrations that left the onlooker breathless, each aircraft was recovered on board *John F. Kennedy*, still only a few hundred yards off to our starboard side. Rarely has a fighting unit had the opportunity to display itself to such superb effect, and it was with considerable pride that we, in our ceremonial uniforms, formed as a band to play a musical salute to the Admiral and then the United States and British National Anthems. *QE2* then broke away to head for the island of Majorca.

On arrival at Palma, as the gangways were lowered, local dancers and musicians greeted us and a most unusual sight met our eyes. On the jetty were some 250 donkeys, all saddled up and looking just about as interested as only a donkey can. The plan was for all the guests to select a donkey and ride it for half a mile, where motor transport was waiting to take them to the Plaza De Toros bullring. Here, the famous matador Henry Higgins took an awfully long time to dispatch a couple of bulls in the only private encounter anyone could remember.

On completion of this unsavoury spectacle, we were all whisked off to the estate of a Spanish nobleman for a Fiesta. Suckling pigs were roasting in the open air over wood fires, while rows of chicken were cooking gently on banks of turning spits in the huge kitchen of this old fortress. The garden and grounds were lined with tables laden with food. 'Serving wenches' drew ewers of wine from the hogsheads placed around the square. The coloured lights that were strung throughout the trees of the estate gave a suitably fairy-tale effect. Medieval jousting was staged with horses, armour, lances, swords, heraldic shields and shrill fanfares. Together with the usual traditional flamenco dancing that followed, this was a night to remember. It is not surprising that *QE2* was a little late that night gathering up her flock and getting to sea again.

Heading for Gibraltar, the weather again deteriorated badly. *QE2's* service speed is 28.6 knots, and a bad sea can still cause considerable discomfort. We were due to berth at Gibraltar for only six hours, during which time a special concert was to be given in St. Michael's Cave by the resident Army Band. To follow this, I had been asked to plan something along the lines of a British Military Tattoo. An aircraft had been chartered to fly out from Heathrow the Army's famous 'White Helmets' motor-cycle display team, and the military band, pipes drums and dancers of the Royal Scots. These, together with the Band of the Royal Regiment of Fusiliers based in Gibraltar and my own Royal Marines Band disembarked from the *QE2*, made for a very impressive show that was given live television coverage. The motor cyclists were returned to the UK by air in time for a long-standing engagement in Worcester the next day. All of this had occurred during our six-hour stop in Gibraltar!

Once again, we headed for the open sea, this time for Lisbon in Portugal. Each hour of the day was filled with activity and interest. Preview screening of films took place, including the epic Jesus Christ Superstar, whose Director and Producer, Norman Jewison, were on board as guests of YPO. The tennis deck was a big attraction, featuring exhibition matches by tennis legends Lew Hoad, Ken Rosewall and Virginia Wade. The two outdoor swimming pools drew the bikini-clad YPO wives and girlfriends, who in turn drew the interest of my musicians.

Leaving Lisbon, we headed northwards towards Southampton. It was Sunday, where normally at sea, the Captain of a ship officiates at a church service at 11am. Today, it was advanced to 9.30am and taken by the Very Reverend Martin Sullivan, Dean of St. Paul's Cathedral, who had been embarked throughout the week for this sole purpose.

I produced an orchestra, and the service was held in the *Queen's Room*. Hymns included the coronation setting of *All People that on Earth do Dwell* and the voluntaries were Elgar's *Idyll* before the service and Haydn-Wood's *Elizabeth of England* to follow. During the afternoon, the YPO's official Closing Ceremony was held in the *Double-Down* room. For this, the Joe Loss band was on one side of the platform, my Royal Marines Band was on the other, while above, on a balcony, was the Dutch Swing College Band. The ceremony ended with Joe Loss conducting the combined bands in a rousing rendition of *When the Saints go Marching In*. It was quite an occasion.

For the last night on board, all entertainers before boarding at Southampton had been asked to wear fancy dress and to vary the content of their acts for their final performance. We were ready with our *piece de resistance,* appearing as a Negro spiritual choir complete with hired animal costumes and jungle-book masks etc. Inappropriate today, but all those years ago this behaviour was perfectly acceptable. We even had our own 'blacked-up' Al Jolson!

Everyone entered into the spirit of the evening. The Dutch Swing College Band appeared as buskers, with clogs and banners. My drummers, who had at various times in the week appeared playing trumpet fanfares dressed in authentic 1664 and 1805 Royal Marines uniforms, now appeared in the full regalia of Tower of London *Beefeater* Warders. The note of magic with which this cruise had begun was continued until the very end. *Annabel's* night-club throbbed to the sounds of The London Four and the subtle artistry of the Trio Los Paraguayos well into the early hours. Many people did not go to bed that night. The experience was so precious and no one wanted the bubble to burst.

On Monday, our arrival back at Southampton at 8.30am marked the end of an extremely successful venture. We were able to 'show the flag' and demonstrate the versatility of Royal Marines musicians to a captive audience of some of the most influential people in the world, ashore and afloat, orchestrally, vocally and ceremonially. When it was all over, there was to be the difficult task of explaining it all to our nearest and dearest - and perhaps convincing ourselves that it had all happened.

Fortunately, I didn't need to explain. Together with the wives of Joe Loss and Peter Schilperoot, leader of the Dutch Swing College Band, my wife Margaret had been invited along for the cruise as a guest of the Young Presidents' Organization. Engagements like this must come only rarely. We were each presented with an Italian marble paperweight with gold and enamel inscription, and I also received an engraved silver salver from the YPO. Yes, sometimes life in a Royal Marines uniform can leave indelible memories.

Not long after all this excitement, I was told that I would be returning to Deal for another appointment and that I was to be relieved as Director of Music in Scotland by Lieutenant Keith Sharpe. We had served together as young musicians in the 1950s in the Plymouth Group Band, and I knew him to be an oboe player of distinction. As oboes are not used in a marching band, oboe players are required to play cymbals or perform as bass drummers when on parade. I recall that Keith had been *Master Bass Drummer* on many high-profile occasions in his earlier career.

My farewell dinner was held on a Burns' Night in the Scottish Wardroom at *HMS Cochrane* in Rosyth. What a memorable event that turned out to be. A different brand of whisky was served with each course. I travelled south next day on an ebb tide of scotch whisky!

CHAPTER 8

DEAL, KIEL & THE NIGERIAN STUDENTS
1974 -1978

To vary careers and to give Directors of Music wide-ranging experience, Officers are regularly moved around between administrative and musical posts. Indeed, this is how I came to be in Scotland in the first place. After three and a half years, I learned that my tenure in Scotland was to end and that I would return to the School of Music at Deal to become Assistant to Lt. Colonel Paul Neville, Principal Director of Music Royal Marines. His band at the Royal Marines School of Music was used as a vehicle for the training of Bandmasters and music students and undertook numerous public and ceremonial engagements throughout Great Britain and abroad. My duties would be largely administrative, but I needed to be ready at any time to deputise for Paul Neville in the event of his attention being diverted elsewhere.

My arrival back in Deal was memorable. Having 'marched out' of my married quarter in Rosyth, I had arranged to move my family back into our own home in Deal. Margaret and the

children travelled independently from Scotland by train whilst
I undertook a final band engagement in Wales with the
Scotland band. By the time they arrived in Deal, I had expected
to have taken back our home from the civilian Married
Quarters Officer in the barracks, who had allocated it as a
married quarter during our absence. Our household goods and
effects were also due to be delivered to our home that day.
When I reached my house I was devastated, as I could see
through the windows that the renter of the property had not
moved his family out as instructed. The renter, who was a
musician in the band of which I was now the Assistant
Director of Music, was in the USA on a scheduled band tour
and, in his absence, his wife and children had locked the door
and had gone away somewhere.

We were homeless, with all our furniture and belongings about
to arrive on the drive of a house we couldn't get into. The
Married Quarters Officer, who had considerable responsibility
for this hiatus, was unable to offer any immediate practical
help.

Fortunately, our plight was recognised by a sympathetic
neighbour who allowed us to temporarily store our possessions
in his unused garage. Margaret, the children, a cat and I then
sallied forth to find somewhere to spend the night. Money was
tight and I didn't have a credit card. Being a bank holiday – it
just had to be, didn't it – we couldn't find anywhere that would
take us except the imposing (and expensive) Queen's Hotel,
next to Deal Castle on the seafront. During a brief stay at the
hotel we managed to contact other local friends, one of whom
offered us the use of their home as they were going away for a
few days, but I couldn't expect my family to continue to put

up with such a nomadic lifestyle. I was eventually told that I could move my family into a vacant married quarter. It had been empty for over a year and it took us two days to clean it and make it habitable.

After thoroughly cleaning it, I was visited by the ashen faced Married Quarters Officer who explained that I had to vacate the property because of a regulation pertaining to the payment of removal expenses covering our move from Scotland. If I remained in the married quarter, I would lose a considerable amount of the generous relocation grant to which I was entitled because I had not moved directly into my own property, as had been my plan. I could ill afford to lose any of the relocation grant.

I arranged to meet with the Officer outside of our home in Deal, where he made a forced entry into the property to assess the situation. As the renter's family were evidently not living there, he advised me that I was at liberty to remove all their possessions from my home. After attempting to remove clothes from two drawers in a bedroom, I realised that I couldn't do this and was left with no other course but to await the musician's arrival back from America with the band.

When he returned, I 'had a few words with him' but it still took many days for him to get his wife and children back to Deal and for them to vacate my home. He vehemently denied all knowledge of my impending return and insisted that he had not received my letters or those from the barracks MQO. At first I believed him, for surely no one would be stupid enough to get into this sort of difficulty, particularly when it involved the man who was to be his boss. However, my faith in him evaporated when I found the letters in question, opened and discarded in an outside refuse-bin among maggot-infested rubbish at the rear of my house.

These letters were used as evidence when charges were raised against the musician. He was required to reimburse me for the costs I had incurred when my family was denied access to our own home. When it was all over, the barracks MQO arrived at our door with a bouquet of flowers for Margaret. He was so grateful to her for not making an official complaint that could well have cost him his job. For years afterwards, whenever Margaret or I met him in Deal, he expressed his thanks for the way we had accepted the awful situation in which we had been placed.

The galloping Major

Major Roger Brind, who early in his career had qualified as a Physical Training Officer within the Corps, was the Second in Command at Deal Barracks. His daughter, Bryony Brind, would later become the poster girl for British Ballet in the 1980s after Rudolph Nureyev had selected her to become his partner at Covent Garden. Major Brind, together with the Adjutant, rode horses on parade whenever circumstances permitted. On one occasion, a church parade concluded with a march past of troops in South Barracks. The band, having led the parade through the town and into Jubilee Gate from the Dover Road, wheeled left onto the grass behind a saluting dais on which the Town Mayor and Commanding Officer were standing, ready to return the salute of the Royal Marines as they marched past the dais and up towards the Officer's Mess. Major Brind, with drawn sword in his right hand and mounted on his charger, was proudly leading the column of marching troops.

Just as he drew level with the dais, the now stationary band began heavy linking drum rolls into the Regimental March, *A Life on the Ocean Wave*. The horse didn't take kindly to this and, without warning, took fright and charged off to the right across the grass towards the Sergeants' Mess with the Major clinging on with his only free hand. It looked like the charge of the Light Brigade. The spectators' humour quickly turned to concern as the horse reached the edge of the grassed area and found itself on tarmac. Slipping and sliding it eventually came to a halt, but not before the Major had utilised every aspect of his horsemanship to remain in the saddle. He maintained his dignity as he completed an unexpectedly lonely ride back to the stables in North Barracks before, I suspect, putting his charger on a restricted diet! Then, no doubt, he would have had to explain to his Commanding Officer why he had left the parade halfway through and without permission!

Musical administration

Being Assistant to the Principal Director of Music gave me an insight into the administrative workings of the School of Music, as well as an opportunity to become involved with key people in the music profession. It also brought me back into contact with the Royal Academy of Music and, in particular, Maurice Miles, its Professor of Conducting and my former tutor. He visited Deal each year to oversee the Bandmasters' Examination and any examinations for Director of Music that were necessary.

I learned much about tri-Service procedures, the Army School of Music at Kneller Hall and the Headquarters of the RAF Music Services at Uxbridge. Rumours of establishing a combined Services Music School were spreading at this time, and the idea would continue to simmer for several years. There would come a time when the rumour would become an issue with which I would be required to grapple for many long hours, but this would all be in the future.

Shirley Bassey plays Bandmaster George Simpson's violin on board HMS Belfast in the Pool of London, 1975

Kiel Week

In 1975, the Band of the Royal Marines (Fleet), based in Chatham, was due to undertake a prestigious engagement in Germany, where they were to play a prominent part in that year's *Kielewoche* celebrations, an event when tall traditionally-rigged sailing ships of all nations are brought together. The

Band's Director of Music, Captain Peter Sumner, became ill and I was sent to direct the band in his place. I joined the band at Dover when they arrived for the ferry trip to France, from where we were to be transported by touring coach to Kiel. When on board our ferry and just prior to its departure, I was told that the navy truck containing all our instruments, personal belongings and equipment was too tall to be loaded, and that it would not be able to cross to Belgium until a larger ship was available, which would be many hours later.

There was nothing I could do to alter the situation, so we continued our own journey across the channel. On our arrival in Belgium, I looked out for the "luxury" touring coach we had been promised, but there wasn't one. On the far side of the vehicle park were two ancient khaki painted British Army of the Rhine 'hard-assed' Bedford busses. They had small tell-tale union-jack flags painted on the back and my heart sank. Yes - they were for us, and in them we were to embark on a nine-hundred-mile journey through Belgium and onwards to Kiel on Germany's Baltic Sea coast.

Because of the distance involved, it had been agreed that we should break our journey at the NATO Headquarters at Mons in Belgium. On arrival at Mons, the bandsmen went directly to their accommodation block and I was taken to the Officers' Quarters and shown to a room. I then received a telephone call from a senior Royal Naval officer, who explained that he would pick me up in half an hour to entertain me at his residence. After dinner and at the end of a convivial evening he took me back to the Officers' Quarters and, in the dark, I found my way to what I took to be my room.

Finding that the key wouldn't turn in the lock, I realised that I had yet another problem. Suddenly, the door was swiftly opened from inside and I found myself staring into the barrel of a handgun being held by an angry Eastern Bloc officer in his underpants. He spoke no English and I spoke no Serbo-Croat, so the situation was not without some immediate concern for both of us!

I accepted that I must be outside the wrong room, even though the number on the door corresponded exactly with the one on my key fob. After apologies conducted entirely by gesture, I made my way back to the entrance to the Officers' Quarters, only to find that there were several accommodation blocks in line, and all were identical. There was nothing for it - I had to try my luck in another of them. Fortunately at my first attempt it was the correct one, and the door opened to my key.

I had just got to bed when the telephone rang. I found myself talking to the driver of the truck that had been delayed at Dover earlier that day. He told me that he had reached Belgium but was now being refused permission to travel on to Kiel because of a discrepancy in the paperwork provided by the Royal Navy authorities in the UK.

Without our kit we could do nothing in Kiel - or anywhere else, for that matter – so despite it being in the middle of the night, I contacted the duty officer at the British Embassy in Belgium, explained the situation and requested their assistance. The impounded vehicle was swiftly released and it reached Mons by dawn, in time for the musicians to collect their overnight bags containing their toiletries before they went to breakfast. Given the circumstances, I thought a difficult situation had been well handled - until the wrath of the MOD bureaucracy later descended on my head for involving British Embassy staff outside normal working hours and without prior permission. Tough!

Continuing our journey to Kiel in our dismal busses after breakfast the following day, I was informed that one of the musicians travelling in the second vehicle had been suffering with 'piles,' an ailment not helped by the lack of comfort provided by the Bedford seating. He had sensibly reported to the NATO hospital after arriving in Mons the previous day and was seen by a doctor who, after a quick examination, had provided the patient with a rubber cushion with a large hole cut in the centre! After sitting on it for a couple of hours, he found that gravity was doing things to the area of his distress that was almost worse than the squashing effect of before. He asked that we call at a clothes shop en-route to Kiel to see if a clothes stand was available. He thought that by hanging on it by his shoulder-straps as it stood in the back of the bus, he may have devised a more comfortable way to travel!

My first official task in Kiel involved meeting the local Mayor at the *Kieler Rathous*, for which I had to wear my full ceremonial uniform with helmet, boots, sword, etc. I was informed that a staff car and driver would arrive to take me to the City Hall at 10am. It did - but instead of the smart staff car I had expected would arrive, it was a small German Army khaki Volkswagen 'Beetle', with only two doors. I headed for the front passenger seat, next to the driver, but he quickly barred the way, pushed the back of the front seat forward and, ramrod stiff, looked straight at me and declared: "Admirals in 'ze back!" I shall not forget the difficulty with which, taking care not to bend my ceremonial sword scabbard, I climbed into and eventually out of, that vehicle.

Before leaving UK I had been required to signal my height, weight and age to Naval Headquarters "for social reasons." I thought this a bit odd but did so anyway. All was revealed on the final night of *Kielwoche* when I attended the spectacular Celebration Dinner to mark the closing of the week's festivities. It was held in a salubrious venue to which the Captains of the tall ships and many civic dignitaries had been bidden. The seating for the meal was in tables of four. The seating plan indicated at which table I should sit and when I reached my place I saw sitting opposite a lady of the same height, weight and age as myself.

Another of the chairs was occupied by a young Swedish tall-ship Captain with long blonde hair who was both handsome and debonair. His English language skills were exceptional and included much waving of arms and hands. Tall slender wine glasses were in place on the table, and it wasn't long before he sent one of them crashing to the floor with a particularly demonstrative gesture. If it had been me, I would have quietly summoned a waiter, apologised and asked if the debris could be removed. But not him. He made a great fuss of asking for the General Manager and on his arrival, pointed disdainfully at the shattered crystal on the carpet and said loudly: "'Dere is glass!" As always with this sort of person, he won the day. The broken glass was quickly cleared up and a replacement wine glass was provided for him on the table. His companion was visibly proud of him, and she gave him smiling encouragement throughout.

I was further embarrassed at the end of the evening as it was expected that the principal guests, who had transport provided for them, would give lifts home to those that had been selected to be their companions at the dinner. My companion, waiting in line for our car to arrive, visibly wilted when she saw, in the line of smart waiting limousines, a grubby khaki Volkswagen beetle, and realised it was for us. I guess she drew the short straw that night and has probably 'dined-out' on the story ever since!

News of how we had travelled to Kiel was greeted with great sympathy by our German Navy hosts, who were quite ashamed that we had been subjected to such an awful experience. When I explained that we would face the same conditions on our return passage to the UK, some senior German officers stepped in to help and arranged for us to be transported back by air, together with all our equipment. German Air Force *Nor-Atlas* twin-boomed transport aircraft took us to RAF Northolt. Thanks to our new German friends, two days of travelling in considerable discomfort was avoided.

Not everyone was grateful that our hosts had been so thoughtful. I received another 'short back and sides' for having dared to change the plan for our return, and no one thanked me for carrying through to fruition a prestigious international engagement that had had all the signs of imminent disaster throughout.

April Fool's Day 1976

At about midday on 1st April 1976, when everyone in barracks was leaving to commence their Easter leave, I was told that the

Commandant of the Royal Marines School of Music wished to see me urgently in his office. I went along, to be told that he had just received a telephone call from the Royal Marines Headquarters in London to say that my promotion to Captain Royal Marines had been approved and that it was to take effect from that very day!

This was news to everyone and unbelievable to me, for it had always been the case that at least six months' notice of promotion was given. The Commandant was smiling, as well he might, and I thought that I was the victim of an April Fool's Day prank. I told him so too and by way of reply he said: "Well there is my telephone. Ring your wife and tell her the news!" Looking him straight in the eye I rang Margaret at home and at no time did he attempt to stop me. It was then that I realised that it must be true.

Margaret came to join me in the Officers' Mess for a small celebration with the few people who had not yet gone on leave. I had come to work that day as a Lieutenant and by lunchtime was wearing the rank of Captain. Weird!

Later, I would learn that this circumstance had come about because, well into the future, I was being considered as a possible candidate for Principal Director of Music. To be eligible, though, I would need to have to have completed a range of jobs including running a standard band (for me, the FOSNI band in Scotland), having an administrative position (for me, Assistant to the Principal Director of Music) and leading a Royal Marines Staff Band for five years. Time was of the essence, so it had been decided to give me immediate promotion to Captain, thereby ensuring my eligibility, with others, for selection to the highest office in the Band service.

Elevation to Captain Royal Marines meant another change of job, and I became Director of Music Training at the School. This meant that I was responsible for the recruitment and maintenance of civilian professional teaching staff, the training of all instrumental music students and the running of training courses for promotion through the ranks for all uniformed personnel.

Captain Hoskins, 1976

Training musicians for Nigeria

The staff at the School of Music comprised seventeen civilian Professors and a full complement of Non-Commissioned Officer instructors. As well as for Royal Marines musicians, training was also available for foreign and Commonwealth students. Life became very interesting when we were told that a batch of Nigerian students would shortly be arriving to begin a basic musicianship course. The School of Music was to train a complete band for the Nigerian Navy, the first (and only) time a task of such magnitude was attempted for an overseas organisation.

On their arrival, it was immediately obvious that no thought had been given to the sailors' individual suitability as potential instrumentalists. They were just Nigerian sailors that had been taken from their naval duties on ships and told that they were to be trained to perform as musicians in a band that would be formed on their return to Nigeria! Despite my misgivings, I was advised that acceptance of these 'students' was non-negotiable. Likeable as they were as individuals, the success of the venture appeared to be bleak. At the end of their course, each student was presented with a certificate of attendance, although it wasn't clear to me just how much they had learnt!

In due course, the Military Attaché to the Nigerian Embassy asked to make a visit to Deal to inspect his men. As part of the visit, a Regimental Lunch in the Officers' Mess was held in this Brigadier's honour, and I was anxious that this went well. Fortunately, one of the Honorary Members of the Mess, Sir Rex Niven, had been a British diplomat in Nigeria, and had at one stage of his career been the Speaker of the Nigerian

Parliament. Sir Rex was invited to the lunch and was seated next to the Brigadier, where he was not only able to discuss Nigerian matters in a knowledgeable way but did so in the very dialect of the province from which the Brigadier had come. Brilliant!

The Nigerian authorities paid little concern to their students' welfare throughout the time they were with us. They arrived in Deal wearing just the thin uniforms they had been issued while serving in Africa, so we kitted them out with thick blue Royal Naval trousers and woollen jumpers to combat the cold of a British winter. After being with us for some months, their Embassy allowed them to travel home for a short leave period. On their return, one of the students told me that he had arrived back in in Nigeria to learn that his wife had died in childbirth many weeks before, and he had not even been told of the tragedy.

Not long after the Nigerian students had returned, one of their number, who was a Chief in his village, came to my office to explain that he and his men wanted to make a presentation to me and my wife. He had been instructed by his 'Elders' to make us honorary members of his village. It seemed to be something of an honour so, on a specified day, we went to the Barracks tailor's shop as instructed, where we found that a set of colourful robes had been made for each of us.

Wearing them, we presented ourselves for the 'ceremony' at which all the Nigerian students were present. A local press photographer took photographs as I was presented with a heavy *Head of an Oba of Benin*. I was told that it was made of bronze and had been brought from the Chief's village, where it had been from ancient times. At home, I placed the artefact on a small coffee table where it could be admired. During the first night, our cat must have jumped onto the table, causing the 'bronze' to crash to the floor. Dashing downstairs to investigate the noise, I found the 'Oba' shattered into pieces. But far from being made of bronze, it had been constructed from a brittle glass-like and bronze-coloured material and filled with wet sand to give it its weight. All was not what it had seemed.

Presentation by the Nigerian students, 1976

Conscious of the possibility that the Chief who had arranged the presentation had himself been taken in by his colleagues in Nigeria, I resolved to say nothing about what had happened to save him embarrassment. Some years later, when the Nigerian students had long returned to Lagos, I recounted this story to guests at a dinner party at my home. Two of the guests were the proprietors of an exclusive art and china shop in Deal. "Oh!" said one, "How interesting. Those Nigerians bought that thing from our shop!"

Freeman of the City of London

1977 was the year of the Queen's Jubilee. Many celebrations were arranged across the country, and I was fortunate to be able to take the Junior Band of the Royal Marines for the first of these celebrations to be held in the City of London itself. The occasion involved a marching display and Beat Retreat at London's Guildhall. Later, in conversation with City Aldermen, I was told that I had been proposed for appointment as a Freeman of the City of London. Events moved on apace and it was not long before a date had been set for Margaret and me to attend an installation ceremony at Guildhall, followed by luncheon in the presence of the Lord Mayor and Court of Aldermen, where I was introduced as the "Youngest Freeman". This, I suspect should be interpreted as the 'most recent'.

An intruder at Coldblow

Although, to the Royal Marines musician, their military role is of secondary importance, it demands thorough and intensive training each year. For junior musicians under training, time was set aside for this within the general syllabus. One military training exercise involved the young musicians being required to provide security around a sports complex at Coldblow, near Deal, and for them to react to various security 'situations' that were programmed to arise over the weekend. Clad in camouflaged uniforms and carrying rifles, they set about their task with considerable enthusiasm, but I suspected that boredom could soon prevail.

Although I was not due to be personally involved in this training exercise, I decided to enact a little charade of my own to lighten the proceedings. Late on the Saturday evening, I drove into the countryside and parked within half a mile of where the youngsters were patrolling inside the perimeter wire of the sports complex. I then walked the rest of the way towards them. I had dressed in camouflaged combat kit, but was also wearing the black rubber gorilla head I had saved as a souvenir from the earlier Scotland Band QE2 trip. On my hands I wore hairy rubber gloves obtained from a joke shop. To complete this incongruous and ridiculous facade, I held in front of me the three-foot long stuffed crocodile, swapped for the box of condoms in Nigeria in 1960, as if it were a weapon!

As I got closer to my objective, I spotted a partly hidden Service land-rover. In it, I could just make out two Royal Marines Commando instructors. I didn't look their way and merely staggered past as I thought a gorilla might when armed with a crocodile. There was silence from the land-rover until I heard one of the men say, "Did you see that?" "See what?" said the other. "That was a bloody gorilla!" said his chum. Strangely, neither of them got out of their vehicle to check and I continued on my way unhindered.

Walking down a track by the side of the wire fence, I saw a couple of young trainee musicians looking my way. "Where's your officer?" the gorilla said in its best Irish accent only to be greeted with stunned silence. One of the lads then raised his rifle, pointed it at me, and I heard the click of the trigger on an empty chamber as fortunately the gun was not loaded with live ammunition. There then began a lot of shouting, as people realised that something unusual was happening that was definitely not on the list of events to be expected during the night.

I got as far as the main entrance to the sports complex, whereupon I was unceremoniously grabbed and taken inside. At this point, I wondered whether my prank had not been a bit too foolhardy, for I was placed facing against a wall with legs and arms outstretched while a full body search was carried out. Finally removing the gorilla mask, the boys realised that they had 'captured' their Director of Music. They took great delight in making my life uncomfortable for an hour or so!

An interview on *Britannia*

Lt. Colonel Paul Neville retired from his position as Principal Director of Music in 1978 and Captain Jim Mason, Director of Music of the Portsmouth Band and Royal Yacht, was nominated to succeed him. I then found myself selected for interview by the Flag Officer Royal Yachts on board *Britannia* to replace Mason as Director of Music. The interview took place in the Admiral's Day-cabin. I made no reference to my past involvement with the Royal Yacht, for my new position would be a high priority Officer's appointment. I suspected that the Admiral was not fully aware of my past association, either.

In the decade since I had been the *Royal Yacht* Bandmaster the Admiral, Flag Officer Royal Yachts, had changed and I had not previously met the man who was now interviewing me. As he maintained an imperious dignity, surrounded as he was with paintings and decorative artefacts from previous Royal Yachts, I sat there intently aware that he obviously didn't know that I had been in this hallowed place before. On that earlier occasion, his predecessor had been sitting in the chair I now occupied whist I had stood behind him cutting his hair! Further, I knew that the polished satinwood cabinet to the right of his desk contained cans of beer because, all those years before, I had been offered one in payment for services rendered rather than the half-crown I had hoped for!

My controlled approach to the interview was successful. I was duly appointed and became the only *Royal Yacht* Director of Music to have previously served on board as the Bandmaster and as an instrumentalist.

CHAPTER 9

PORTSMOUTH & HMY BRITANNIA
1977 - 1981

Having worked with the band at Eastney Barracks a decade earlier, I felt quite prepared when I took over as its Director of Music My predecessor had arranged for a delightful private dinner party to be held on board *Britannia* prior to his departure, to which he invited past *Royal Yacht* Directors of Music together with their wives. Among those present were Sir Vivian and Lady Dunn, Paul and Anne Neville, Margaret and I and, of course, our hosts Jim and Alice Mason. We all signed a menu card. It is possibly the only document containing the signatures of the first four Royal Marines Band Service Principal Directors of Music. Serving in the *Royal Yacht* had been for each of us a cherished and extraordinary experience.

Menu card signed by the first four Royal Marines Band Service Principal Directors of Music, 1977

As Director of Music on the Staff of the Commander-in-Chief Naval Home Command, whose flagship is *HMS Victory* – the oldest ship in the world still in commission, it was also my duty to provide musical support onboard that famous ship. There were ceremonial occasions throughout the year that required the presence of a band or orchestra, culminating with events on 21st October, when Trafalgar Day was formally commemorated. Regular dinner parties on board were occasions of grandeur and often historic significance. During

178

my tenure, on one memorable occasion, Margaret and I were invited by the Admiral to join other guests and dine with him in the Great Cabin of *HMS Victory*. My memory of this colourful candlelit evening will never fade, when tradition, ceremonial dignity, exquisite food, wine and romance had been so beautifully intermingled.

Music for Royal Yachts

The building of the first *Royal Yacht* is attributed to King Charles II, and many have subsequently seen service over the years. They have grown in size since the 1600s as Royalty felt the need to embark on ocean journeys rather than local forays around the British coastline.

In the late 1600s, an elaborate ceremony took place whenever Royalty visited a ship. On the approach of the Royal Barge, the ship's *noise of trumpets* was to sound until the barge came within musket shot of the ship. As the trumpets ceased, all on board that carried whistles were to whistle and then the whole ship's company was to hail the barge with a joint shout. When this had been done, the trumpets were again to sound a welcome to the ship's side. The port side was to be used whenever possible and it was to be well-manned with the fittest and best fashioned men of the ship's company ready on both sides of the ladder.

The Captain of the ship was to receive the royal personage whilst on bended knee and then to take his royal visitor 'wheresoever' he wished to be taken before arriving at the Great Cabin. This cabin was to be furnished to the best degree, so that there the royal guest may rest and await such food as was available to be brought to him.

Being *ready for his meat,* the trumpets were again to sound at *the carrying of it up,* and musicians were to be at hand *to play when he is at it.* Meanwhile, all the guns of the ship were to be made ready, laden and primed so that the royal guest could *command what he 'pleaseth' of that nature.* Thus having been entertained and fully informed by the Captain in all his demands, he was to be waited upon at his departure as he was at his coming in. He was to be given a farewell salute with so many guns as the ship was able to give, providing that they were always of an odd number. When the barge had achieved a fair distance from the ship, the trumpets were to sound a *loath to depart.*

By the end of the 1800s it was customary for Royal Marines musicians to embark in Royal Yachts whenever Royalty was on board. Up to the end of 1903 these instrumentalists, able to play in orchestral as well as wind band combinations, were taken alternately from musicians serving with the Royal Marines Light Infantry based in Gosport and the Royal Marines Artillery based at Southsea in Portsmouth. In 1905, the complement of embarked musicians was increased to twenty, to be furnished on all occasions by musicians serving with the Royal Marines Artillery. At that time, King George V had born the cost of the musicians' musical instruments and had also provided the RMA band fund with an annual grant. This latter arrangement continued into Queen Elizabeth II's reign, though the amounts involved were not significant: some 25p per man/per day in the early 1980s. It was referred to as *green cloth money.*

HMY *Britannia*

The most recent Royal Yacht, the *Britannia*, built by John Brown's shipyard on the Clyde in the early 1950s, cost £2.1million to build and was based on the design of two north-sea ferries, the *TS Arnhem* and the *TS Amsterdam*. She was given a cruiser stern and an altered bow. Many ornate and historic fittings were taken from the previous Royal Yacht *Victoria & Albert III* and reused in *Britannia*. The wheel with which the coxswain steered the ship throughout its lifetime had been salvaged from an old 'J' Class racing yacht, also named *Britannia*, before she was taken out to Spithead and scuttled on the orders of King George V.

It was a real honour to serve on board *Britannia*. With the sole exception of the Royal Marines Director of Music, the Admiral would personally interview three candidates for each Officer vacancy as it arose. Young 'Seasonal Officers' were sometimes brought aboard and attached to the Royal Staff to cover certain busy periods. Occasionally, an Officer from a Commonwealth country to be visited by the Queen in the Royal Yacht would be seconded for the duration of such a visit. Normally in *Britannia*, Royal Naval Officers could expect to hold two-year appointments before returning to the fleet. The selection criteria was very strict. I once heard this report regarding an interviewee: "Although very well educated, and unmarried, this officer is not to be regarded as a contender for appointment to Her Majesty's Yacht. He is much too big, is apparently not very good at writing letters – and he would be very expensive to feed!"

Christian names for everyone, even the most junior Yachtsman, were used throughout *Britannia* by all senior personnel. Newly appointed Executive Officers with experience only of general service with the fleet found it a very odd practice, and several went to the lengths of banning it for a while until they realised that long-serving Yachtsmen were disciplined and 'different'. Such officers soon learned that service on board *Britannia* was a unique experience.

Britannia's home berth was offshore between two buoys in a relatively sheltered spot in the far reaches of the harbour at Portsmouth. Access on foot to the gangway of the ship was by 180 metres of linked floating catamarans, forming what was known as the 'walk ashore'. Each catamaran had swinging hand chains on each side, but there was nothing firm to hold onto if the sea was choppy. Stepping from one catamaran to the next was often a tricky business, especially if equipment and bulky musical instruments were being transferred to or from shore - which, of course, happened every time the band embarked or left the Royal Yacht to return to Eastney Barracks following Royal Duty.

In *Britannia,* the Royal Apartments were decorated with many artefacts and historic items, including the framed tattered white ensign found on Scot's sledge next to his body after his ill-fated trip to the South Pole. Many royal photographs were displayed, one of which - of King Edward VII wearing his uniform as Admiral of the Fleet - hung in a prominent position in the Wardroom. On his sleeves, the curl of gold lace over his rank faces the wrong direction. His medal ribbons were on his left breast, as they should be, so it cannot have been the case that a 'negative' photo image was accidentally printed. No! The

King's tailor got the King's uniform wrong, and no-one had the courage to point out the error. The photograph became an item of great interest to newly embarked Royal Yacht Officers - it proved that no one gets it right all the time!

A further anomaly on board *Britannia* occurred in 1977 when the Queen's Silver Jubilee medals were distributed to servicemen. The Flag Officer Royal Yachts did not include nominees from the embarked Royal Marines Band because he understood that they would be considered as members of their parent band based at Eastney Barracks. The Commanding Officer at Eastney Barracks considered that the opposite would be the case so, without nomination, no one received the medal. Early the next year the Queen, ever observant, noticed that none of the band on board was wearing the medal, and when told the reason she immediately decreed that four band members, whom she personally nominated, should be given the medal. I was required to arrange for the Silver Jubilee medals to be presented to Band Colour Sergeants Malcolm Kennard and Michael Howarth, Colour Sergeant Brian Peever, and Bugler Peter Law in accordance with the Queen's wishes.

The Morning Colours Ceremony

This historic ceremony, when the white ensign is raised, is held on board all Royal Navy ships every day at 8am when in harbour, both in the UK and abroad. In *Britannia*, however, the band paraded for the ceremony on the fo'c'stle rather than the quarterdeck as is normally the case. This was to ensure that whilst long-held Royal Naval traditions were adhered to, Queen Elizabeth, aft in her apartments, was not unduly disturbed – though she may well have been awake anyway. This ceremony was always conducted by the Bandmaster. I was not required to be with the band but, as Director of Music, I made it my business to always be present on the bridge-wing alongside the Commander and the Officer of the Day for the duration of the daily ceremony. Then, I would go below and have my breakfast!

This procedure was not written into the rules, but I always ensured that if the musicians were up and about then so was I. As the only Royal Marines Officer embarked, it was important for me to set standards and then to maintain them. I therefore ensured that during my tenure I never missed a single occasion when the band paraded for *Morning Colours*.

When abroad and disembarked on foreign soil, the National Anthem of the host country always preceded our own, but on board Her Majesty's ships, the British National Anthem is played first followed by that of the host country. When naval ships from other countries are in harbour, some or all of their National Anthems are also played whilst the Officers remain at the salute. When on the coast of South America this could take some time, for several of the anthems in that part of the world are more like overtures!

Entering & leaving harbour

The 'Entering and Leaving harbour' position for the band was always up on the Royal Deck. As this deck was immediately above the Queen's and Prince Philip's bedrooms, it was wise, if it was to be an early arrival, to play softly to begin with, and to increase the volume only gradually! For these events, the

Bandmaster assumed a playing role as the band was conducted by the Director of Music.

When Captain Peter Sumner was on board *Britannia* in 1966, we were in the West Indies for a tour of all the Islands loyal to the British Crown. It was the time of *Festival* or *Mardi Gras* in the Caribbean. As the Royal Yacht, with Her Majesty embarked, left each island at about midnight, Peter, having listened to the local steel band on the jetty playing its newly composed speciality, would return to his cabin and arrange that tune overnight so that we could play it as we arrived at daybreak at the next island. We produced authentic rhythmic sounds using an old brake-drum, beaten with a wind iron from the band store.

The layout of the twenty-four musicians (four across and six deep) when paraded on the Royal Deck was:

Clarinet	Clarinet	Clarinet	Clarinet
Piccolo	Bass Drum	Cymbals	Clarinet
Horn	Eb Saxophone	Bb Saxophone	Horn
Cornet	Cornet	Cornet	Cornet
Euphonium	Trombone	Trombone	Tuba
Side Drum	Side Drum	Side Drum	Side Drum
Drum Major			

The Silent signals

In keeping with the tradition that verbal orders were rarely given on board *Britannia,* the orders *Coming to Attention, Band Ready* and *Stand at Ease,* etc., were indicated by the Director of Music using his baton to give certain signals. The playing position of the band, aft on the Royal Deck and well away from the Admiral on the bridge, meant that hand signals from him were necessary for the band to be always within his overall control. On seeing his signals, appropriate action was taken. This meant that the bridge had control of when the band would play and when it wouldn't. When everyone had had enough, the Admiral would wipe the back of his thumb across his throat to indicate that we should cease entirely and go below. Easy!

The *Man Ship* drill

Many people remember *Britannia* dressed 'overall' with flags in a foreign port, awaiting the arrival or departure of the Queen. The Yachtsmen lined the side, often in their distinctive white tropical uniforms. The procedure for getting the Yachtsmen into their positions for *Man Ship*, as it was known, was achieved through hand signals from Officers on the bridge.

Prior to *Man Ship*, a cord was laid out along the length of the yacht's side on each of the decks that were visible from the shore. This cord had numbered pennants sewn to it at two metre intervals. The Yachtsmen would be fallen in on *Britannia's* disengaged (seaward) side, sized and numbered. Most had carried out this routine many times before, so they knew exactly where to stand. At a signal from the bridge, they would silently move aft marching in slow time, along the decks and keeping their eyes on the numbered pennants as they passed over them. On reaching the number they had been individually given, they would halt and remain facing aft. When everyone was correctly positioned, a Yachtsman on the bridge would press a button and quiet buzzers at deck level would

186

sound. At this signal, all Yachtsmen would turn to face outboard. If the Queen was not immediately ready to board or leave *Britannia*, the buzzer would sound three times to signal *Stand at Ease!* which we all did! Eventually, one long buzzer followed immediately by a short one would bring us all to *Attention!* again. All clever stuff!

The area set aside for the band for the *Man Ship* drill was along the side of the Royal Deck above the Royal Apartments. My position was at the head of the musicians and furthest aft. The first time I stood there as the Director of Music was an occasion when it was blowing a gale. The well-rehearsed routine went flawlessly, even though I was quite a distance from the nearest buzzer. After the Queen had boarded I began to feel strangely lonely and, bracing myself against the wind, I glanced carefully from beneath my helmet and realized that because of the strong wind, I had missed the buzzer signal to turn for'ard and march off. The bandsmen had heard it and had gone, leaving me alone! I then adopted a typically British *stiff-upper-lip* approach and pretended that it was always my routine to act independently. In my own good time, I turned for'ard, and made my way below – feeling very foolish, as you can imagine.

Britannia supported a lot of top weight, and with so many Yachtsmen lining one side of the ship during *Man Ship*, a considerable list to that side could be induced. In any other ship this would not have mattered, but in *Britannia* it mattered a lot. The angle at which the royal gangway met the jetty was always carefully calculated months in advance of our arrival in a port. The time of day, state of the local tide, etc., all had a bearing on the calculation, for no one wanted to see the Queen struggling up or down a gangway that was too steep. If the angle was likely to be extreme, a platform would be erected on the jetty before *Britannia's* arrival, to which the gangway from the ship would be lowered. All these careful arrangements would be of no avail if the yacht were allowed to list towards the jetty when the crew *Manned Ship*. The cunning solution, always adhered to, was simple. The Royal Barge and the boats on the disengaged side were partly lowered on their davits out of sight of dignitaries and onlookers on the jetty. This counterweight kept *Britannia* upright, with no one on the shore-side any the wiser.

The *Scandalizing* drill

How does *Britannia* pass under a low bridge? This problem first arose when Royal visits to Canada were planned, as the voyage would have to include transiting the St. Laurence Seaway to the Great Lakes. The problem was that *Britannia's* mainmast was too tall to allow the Royal Yacht to pass under some of the road bridges spanning the Seaway. It was known that these bridges would be crowded with sightseers anxious to get a view of the ship as it passed beneath them, so a drill needed to be carried out to reduce the height of the mast for a short time and it had to be performed with panache.

The solution was achieved by placing a hinge well below the top of the mainmast that allowed a drill known as *Scandalizing* to be carried out as *Britannia* approached low bridges. A Chief Petty Officer was first hauled aloft in a bosun's chair to undo a bolt that secured the mast some fifteen feet from the top. The upper portion of the mast could then be eased backwards on the hinge by Yachtsmen hauling on a rope from the quarterdeck. The considerable weight of the mast was taken by another team of yachtsmen for'ard, who only allowed the movement to be taken slowly. After passing through the bridge, the mast was returned to its upright position so that the Chief Petty Officer could replace the bolt before being himself lowered to the deck.

Before the main mast could be shortened, the flag flying from it, in this case the Royal Standard, had to be lowered so the mast was 'undressed' (hence the term *Scandalizing*). Protocol demanded that the Royal Standard was flown at all times when the Queen was on board, so as it was lowered from the mainmast, a duplicate was broken from the mizzen. As all three Royal Yacht masts had flags flying constantly – that of the Lord High Admiral (the Queen) at the fore, the Royal Standard at the main and the White Ensign at the mizzen – quite a complicated procedure ensued during *Scandalizing*.

Another foreseen problem regarding passage through the St. Laurence Seaway was the likelihood of bumping the side in some of the very narrow sections of the Seaway. This problem was overcome before *Britannia* left the UK by fitting a rubbing strake along the length of the ship at the waterline. This eight-inch wide, and twelve inch deep, projection from the hull meant that damage from any slight contact with an obstruction was likely to be only cosmetic and could easily be painted over. The strake remained in place throughout the Royal Yacht's lifetime.

The uniforms

Musicians embarked in *Britannia* wore a special ceremonial tunic that resembled those worn by circus lion-tamers. It had hooks and eyes at the front to draw the leading edges of the tunic together. It was embellished with gold braid but carried no Royal Marines insignia whatsoever. There were no buttons anywhere and the red, gold braided, collar was devoid of further decoration. Badges of rank worn on the arms were gold on blue, rather than the normal gold on red worn by Royal Marines ashore.

When paraded for Royal Duty, the band was to all intents and purposes visually an extension of the civilian domestic staff of the royal household. Ceremonial belts were not worn and the difference between indoor and outdoor ceremonial wear was merely the addition of white-buff music pouches and a white pith helmet.

The helmet badge was the brass Brunswick Star, with laurel leaves surrounding the globe, surmounted by the royal crown and lion. This design is worn by all Royal Marines, but for all members of the Portsmouth Band, not just those specifically embarked in *Britannia*, there were further embellishments. The cypher of King George V, in silver, was positioned below the globe, whilst above it just below the royal crown the combined cyphers of Queen Elizabeth II and Prince Philip, also in silver, were fixed. Thus, the band had the unique privilege of wearing the badges of two monarchs at the same time. The King's cypher had been his personal award to the band after their involvement in his visit to India for the Delhi Durbar in 1911. On her accession to the throne, Queen Elizabeth II decreed that the King's cypher should continue to be worn but superimposed by the cypher of her own reign.

In 1912, King George V issued an order requiring bandsmen serving at Eastney Barracks to wear a special cap badge:

His Majesty The King has been graciously pleased to confer on the Band of the Royal Marine Artillery a distinctive badge to commemorate their having accompanied His Majesty to India in the 'MEDINA'. The badge consisting of a gilt grenade, on which is mounted the Royal Cypher G.R.V. and Crown in silver, surrounded by a gilt laurel wreath, will be worn on the forage cap by all non-commissioned officers and men of the Royal Marine Artillery band at all times in lieu of the present grenade.

The Cypher G.R.V. in silver will also be mounted on the Helmet Plate of the Royal Marine Artillery Band (all ranks) over the Anchor and below the Globe.

During my time in the Band Service, this order remained in force. Directors of Music of the band at Portsmouth did not wear the badge in their caps, as their officer rank excluded them from the scope of the order, although their Brunswick Star helmet plates did conform with this requirement.

Another cap and helmet badge honour was bestowed on the Portsmouth Band in 1955 by the following declaration:

Her Majesty The Queen has expressed a wish that members of the Portsmouth Group Band should wear the combined Cyphers of Her Majesty and His Royal Highness the Duke of Edinburgh on their forage caps and helmet badges.

This Honour is in recognition of the attendance on Her Majesty The Queen by the Band during Her Majesty's Commonwealth Tour in 1953-54.

The Band will wear the new badge in the manner indicated below:

1.   *Caps. The combined Cyphers (surmounted by the St. Edward's Crown) in silver, is to be worn above the existing cap badge as a separate device secured through the cloth of the cap by a vertical pin attachment.*
2.   *Helmets. The combined Cyphers (without Crown) in silver to be affixed by a screw attachment to the base of the Crown which forms part of the existing plate. The Royal Cypher G.R.V. is similarly to be affixed to the lower part of the existing helmet plate.*

In my time, the rig worn by the band *below deck* was an open-necked lovat shirt and trousers and a green beret where necessary. Corps-coloured canvas belts were worn at the waist. Footwear was restricted to white plimsoles without socks. Plimsoles were accepted by the yacht laundry on a regular basis so they were always immaculate and, perhaps more importantly, sweet smelling. The laundering service was available twice weekly. Run by a highly efficient group of Royal Yachtsmen under the command of a Petty Officer, the laundry could be used by everyone on board, including the Royal Household.

Uniforms for use in the tropics were made of white cotton. After use, the laundry washed and starched each suit before returning it on a clothes hanger. Normal Royal Marines badges and buttons were used, but these had to be inserted as required and retained in position with split-rings. When *Britannia's* Bandmaster, I had sewn each of my badges of rank and Royal Yacht shoulder flashes onto holed thin copper sheeting. This, cut to the shape of each badge had eyes from cap badges soldered to the back. My accoutrements were thus secured to the white tunic. The badges were quite heavy and not entirely comfortable when only wearing a T-shirt beneath, but this did not present a problem.

Each year, Royal Marines musicians seconded from the band at Eastney Barracks for service in the Royal Yacht were given an extra issue of new items of kit. Included were *gold on blue* badges for all uniforms, a pair of best blue striped trousers, plimsoles and specially designed kid-leather non-toecapped sea service boots. These items were issued whether they were really needed or not! Often, the issue from the previous year had not been over-worn, and there was a ready market among non-seconded friends for any unwanted items!

Throughout my time as Director of Music in *Britannia*, I wore the blue uniform of a Royal Marines officer with collar and tie whenever I was embarked. On relaxed occasions, when sweaters were substituted for jackets, I wore a blue sweater in the same pattern as my Royal Naval colleagues. Where, on the shoulders, they wore gold lace to depict their rank I wore the stars of a Royal Marines Captain.

The rig for Royal Yacht officers during the annual visit to the Isle of Wight for Cowes Week comprised of white leather shoes, white cotton trousers, blue uniform jacket, white open-necked shirts with a black-silk cravat. I complied with this also.

Accommodation on *Britannia*

Back onboard *Britannia* after ten years, I was relieved to find that each of my twenty-four onboarded musicians could now be comfortably accommodated in a redesigned Royal Marine Barracks. No longer was it necessary for anyone to queue with camp-beds outside the *unwinding room* right up for'ard, waiting for a film to end. The nightly embarrassment of earlier years was no more. My own cabin was also adequate and comfortable. My neighbour was Lieutenant Timothy Lawrence, *Britannia's* Assistant Navigating Officer. On completion of his term of duty on board, Tim became an equerry at Buckingham Palace. He would eventually marry Anne, the Princess Royal and reach the rank of Vice Admiral.

Musical rehearsals on *Britannia*

Musical rehearsals had to be carried out in the *unwinding room* right up for'ard underneath the forecastle deck. Because of its shape, it was quite the worst space possible for rehearsals, even in good weather. Being right in the bow area meant that the deck was rising and falling with each wave, and the rise and fall was determined by the severity of weather conditions. It felt never less than fifteen feet!

Imagine being in the *Britannia's* central passageway, right up in the bow. To your left there is a compartment which is some twelve feet across on the left-hand side, narrowing to a virtual point on the right as the bow section of the ship narrows. Any form of instrumental seating arrangement was unsatisfactory, but it was all we had. Being so far forward meant that the sea-state could result in a totally inadequate morning's rehearsal.

This was a real problem, because the orchestra was required to play in the royal apartments every evening, and the chosen printed (and often dated) music programme was daily placed on the royal dining table next to the menu card. Substituting easier pieces for those more difficult, and therefore requiring more rehearsal, was not an option.

Music for royal dinners & State Visits

The choice of music to be taken on board for royal tours was decided by the Director of Music well before embarkation for a period of Royal Duty. I was always advised of particularly notable dinners or other occasions when the music would add significance to the event. In Bremerhaven, for instance, for a Banquet during the Queen's State visit to the Federal Republic of Germany in May 1978, I ensured that the music to be played during dinner was appropriate for this Teutonic occasion, both visually and aurally. On leaving the Royal Yacht, guests would often take these cards as personal mementoes.

The Queen never at any time sought to influence my choice of music. My selections were forwarded to Buckingham Palace for approval and printing on specially tooled gold-edged cards. These cards, carrying the personal cypher of the senior member of the royal family to be embarked, were then brought from London in the royal baggage by the Royal Household and delivered to my cabin. Each day, following rehearsal, I ensured that an appropriate set of music cards was given to the Keeper & Steward of the Royal Apartments for placement on the Queen's dining table before the meal was served. Accompanying the cards for the music programme would be similarly sized printed menu cards, each decorated with a coloured vignette of HMY Britannia at Cowes, that were also placed on the dining table. When embarked in *Britannia*, menu cards for the Queen Mother were handwritten and always in French.

During more relaxed moments, such as the annual holiday cruise around the Western Isles of Scotland, other musical combinations were sometimes used during dinner instead of the formal orchestral group. A small dance/swing band was always popular, as was my Scottish ceilidh group.

The royal dinner orchestra always gathered in a passage two decks below the Royal Dining Room, prior to coming up to the level on which they were to play during dinner. At one end of the passage there was a damage-control door that would be activated from the bridge if required. It had a large warning bell above it that sounded if the water-tight door was about to close. When tapped with the wood of a violin bow, the cover of the bell gave a perfect *concert A*, to which the strings tuned whilst awaiting the signal for them to get into position two decks up.

The Queen and any guests would assemble in the Royal Drawing Room for pre-dinner drinks, before passing through the space where the orchestra would eventually play to enter the Royal Dining Room. We remained out of sight until the area was clear and the doors of the dining room had been closed.

Only fourteen of the embarked musicians formed the dinner orchestra each evening. The remaining ten musicians, termed the *chair party*, were first up the stairs armed with folding stools, music stands and folios of music. The folding stools had been made by the inmates of Her Majesty's Wormwood Scrubs Prison and the canvas top of each stool was marked recording this fact. Once these were in position, the piano cupboard was opened, several smart buckets and mops were put to one side and the instrument was lifted out.

Within three minutes of the Royal diners walking through the area, we were able to begin the first item on the music programme, as the Keeper & Steward of the Royal Apartments opened the doors to the Royal Dining Room to allow the orchestral music to be heard throughout the meal.

On a given signal at the end of the music programme, the orchestra left quietly, again with the help of the *chair party* and out of sight of those dining. It was my job to ensure that the end of the final musical item coincided with the serving of coffee. This was achieved by me closely monitoring the speed at which the courses were being consumed.

Musical *Extras*, played in ships and establishments as further entertainment for guests at the end of a dinner, never featured in the Royal Apartments in my time. Music tended to occupy a place between the soup and coffee! Once, however, the Queen Mother did ask the orchestra to re-site itself in the Royal Drawing Room after a particular dinner. She hoped we would select music from the shows she remembered from her youth. Fortunately, our music library on board had many such items, and we were able to provide her with a delightful, if somewhat dated, 'soiree musicale'.

Perhaps strangely, unless one considers that *Britannia* was a royal home, the National Anthem was not played in the Royal Apartments during social functions – not even prior to the drinking of the Loyal Toast. Even on occasions when the Queen was dining with her officers in their Wardroom, the officers would merely stand, contrary to naval tradition - for in ships of the fleet officers remain seated for the Loyal Toast, and the toast would be drunk in silence.

In the Wardroom, the normal naval routine for *Extras* to provide musical entertainment would follow. Wardroom dinners were held every Saturday evening whilst *Britannia* was at sea. At specific times members of the Royal Family were invited as guests to dine with the officers and on these occasions *Extras* featured as after dinner entertainment and looked forward to as such.

A particularly favoured musical item for the Queen was *The Post Horn Galop* and she never seemed to tire of it. Varying visual presentation of this piece exercised us all. Players of the post horn managed great dexterity but, at the end of the day, it was still just *The Post Horn Galop*!

On one memorable occasion my soloist, Band Colour Sergeant Alan Upton, produced a superbly entertaining rendition. The Queen was dining with her Officers in the wardroom – hence the availability of a musical *Extra* and Alan Upton was to enter from a side door on hearing the introductory three-note fanfare played by the orchestra. All was ready, the soloist was announced and the fanfare rang out ... and there was silence. The door to the Dining Room remained closed!

I smiled sweetly and, in some embarrassment, re-played the fanfare. This time, the door did slowly open, and the post horn was heard 'peeping' away like an emaciated animal. The soloist then appeared dressed from the waist upwards in his full scarlet mess-dress, black bow tie, cummerbund, etc., but from the waist down he wore khaki shorts, stockings and sandals like a soldier from the TV sit-com *It Ain't 'alf Hot Mum*. Alan entered astride a wooden hobbyhorse, with little wheels at the back that the carpenter had made for him. This, he struggled to ride around the dining table whilst maintaining the musical line. Unexpected and original, it was yet another demonstration of the ability of the embarked musicians to entertain over and above the call of duty.

The popularity of *Extras* comes from the time when, after a Service Dinner, the principal guest would be invited to select a piece to be played especially for him, or her, from a list of available musical items. The Bandmaster would be invited to sit next to the principal guest and partake of a glass of port whilst advising on the merits of each item on the list. Quite why it was traditional for the glass provided for the Bandmaster to be at least twice the size of a normal one (in the fleet as well as in the Royal Yacht) I have no idea. It may have been to get the Bandmaster sufficiently onside so that orchestra would play for longer than they would otherwise have hoped!

I have always viewed the musical contribution to service dinners as gentle entertainment to give *atmosphere* to the occasion. Even in the royal apartments, the music was little more than *aural wallpaper*. This does not in any way detract from the fact that the music had to be played well. It always was, and in the same league as everything else pertaining to British Royal Yachts over the years. *Britannia* maintained its reputation by always being recognisably better than any comparable vessel afloat.

When embarked in *Britannia* I was also able to entertain the Officers with several 'Soiree Musicales' in the Wardroom. The following programme of music is typical of these occasions:

1.	*Overture to 'The Marriage of Figaro'*	Mozart
2.	*Three Pieces from 'Suite in D Major'*	Bach
3.	*Concerto for Oboe & Orchestra*	Albinoni
4.	*Extracts from the opera 'Carmen'*	Bizet
5.	*Fantasia on 'Greensleeves'*	Vaughan Williams
6.	*Rustic Fiddle Dance for Strings*	Bizet
7.	*Divertissement 'Espagnole'*	Desormes
8.	*Themes from 'Porgy & Bess'*	Gershwin

Italy

Heading for Italy in 1980, where the Queen was to carry out a State Visit, one of my Band Sergeants became ill and his messmates were concerned at his increasingly erratic behaviour. He was the only cellist I had on board and, with a State Visit ahead, I couldn't afford to be without a player for this key instrument. *Britannia's* Medical Officer agreed that a replacement cellist should fly to Italy and join the Royal Yacht on our arrival at Naples. My Band Sergeant was then to be escorted by air back to the UK for an appointment at the Psychiatric Wing of the Royal Naval Hospital at Halsar in Gosport. At about this time, a brass instrument on board was found to be inexplicably damaged and in need of replacement, so the relief Band Sergeant was asked to bring one with him to Italy. I loved the signal request sent from *Britannia* to the Stores Officer Music at Deal: "Just One Cornetto!" it said.

I eventually learned that when my Band Sergeant presented himself for his appointment at the hospital, he found himself in the company of a man in a white coat who proceeded to interview him. It was only when a real psychiatrist entered the consulting room that my Band Sergeant realised he was being interviewed by another patient!

Leaving *Britannia* at Naples, my orchestra accompanied the Queen to Rome for the start of her State Visit. Our official duties were largely confined to performing at the British Embassy, for this part of the visit was very much in the hands of our Italian hosts. The situation altered when the Queen returned to *Britannia*, where she hosted a State Banquet on board for the Italian President. It ended in the usual way, with my band beating retreat alongside on the jetty.

Immediately after I returned on board, I was asked to report to the Admiral's Secretary, who told me that the Queen had expressed concern at my band's playing of the Italian national anthem. "What was all that bugling at the start?" she had apparently asked the Admiral. She intimated that she certainly hadn't heard any of that on the many occasions the anthem had been played in her presence while in Rome! I was made to feel that I had possibly caused a diplomatic gaffe and was instructed to present myself for an audience with the Queen in the Royal Apartments at 10am the next morning.

Armed with a copy of *National Anthems of the World,* published by the Blandford Press, I appeared as bidden in my ceremonial frock-coat. After listening to her concerns I was able, with the help of the printed score in the book, to show that we had indeed played the Italian anthem exactly as written. Composed in the nineteenth century, it has a twelve-bar fanfare which leads into the main theme, followed by a change of key for a second theme and it then repeats back to where the initial fanfare ended. The "bugling" had been the twelve-bar introductory cornet fanfare.

In Rome, evidently only the theme of the anthem had been played as a salute to the President, very much in the way that just the first six bars of the British national anthem are sometimes played as a salute to minor members of our royal family. With honour restored, I promised Her Majesty that I would listen intently to how the anthem was played when we reached our next destination, Tunisia.

On our arrival in Tunisia I paid particular attention to what I was about to hear. As the Tunisian Guard of Honour paraded on carpets laid out on the desert sand, the local band was so out of tune and awful that I am not sure that even they knew what they were playing. When the Queen returned on board, there were twinkling smiles all round. The Queen is most concerned that things should always be done properly, and she goes out of her way to determine whether they have been.

State gifts

During State Visits, each Head of State seemed anxious to outdo others when it came to the presentation of gifts to the

Queen. During an extended tour of Eastern Arabia, a Sheikh presented The Queen with a magnificent 14inch high centrepiece for the royal dining table, depicting camels in repose under palm trees on an onyx base in the shape of his Country. The fruits on the palms were precious stones and the remainder of the structure was solid gold. On the way back to UK, I was delighted to learn that the gift had actually been made in Bond Street, London! In return, the Queen gave the Sheikh a signed photograph of herself with Prince Philip, together with a ten-inch silver salver engraved to record the occasion. These were the standard gifts the Queen presented on State Visits, regardless of what she had received.

Beating Retreat on *Britannia*

The historic ceremony of *Beating Retreat* has its origins in an order given to the army of King James II in 1690, when soldiers were summoned back to their barracks by the beating of drums. Today, the format of the ceremony is well established. The band plays a quick march, a slow march, then the buglers perform a drum display before re-joining the band for another quick march. The finale comprises a solemn evening hymn, followed by the emotive rendition of *Sunset*, and ending with the playing of the National Anthem.

A *Beating Retreat* ceremony was always held to conclude Royal receptions, and frequently took place on shore alongside *Britannia* in a floodlight area laid out parallel to the Royal Yacht's side. Midway across the end section, at right angles to the yacht, two flag poles were erected: one bearing the flag of the country we were in and the other the white ensign. These flags were lowered by Yachtsmen as the band played the *Sunset* call.

Each flagpole was secured in an oil drum that was filled with water. The oil drums were painted with the same high gloss blue as *Britannia* itself, and the setting under the floodlights was perfect. Unrigging at the end of the ceremony was simply a matter of removing the poles from the oil drums and emptying out the water.

On the rare occasions when *Britannia* was not able to berth alongside a jetty, it was possible to carry out the *Beat Retreat* ceremony on board, utilising the relatively small veranda deck of the Royal Yacht. This required careful choreography because of the confined space. I incorporated aspects of funeral drill, where the band would *form lane* by moving into two single files on either side of the deck, thus freeing the central space for the buglers and drummers to carry out their routines.

In the UK on one memorable occasion, *Britannia* was berthed between two buoys in the river Dart. The Queen had that day carried out Lord High Admiral's Divisions at the nearby Britannia Naval College up on the hillside, and in the evening after a scheduled Royal Dinner Party on board, we carried out *Beat Retreat* on the veranda deck with the Queen's guests around us. It was a beautiful summer's evening. The sound of the band's music drifting across the water was all that could be heard until we finished. As I turned to salute the Queen, applause broke out from both sides of the river as the local population, watching from vantage points on the hillsides, registered their appreciation for what they had seen and heard.

We didn't realise that anyone other than the Queen and her guests were watching or listening until the applause erupted from all around. It was a special moment, and I was grateful that what the Royal Yacht does when far from home had been witnessed in UK at last.

On one occasion, I oversaw a floodlit *Beat Retreat* ceremony on the veranda deck of *Britannia* with a musician dressed in a Bugler's uniform who performed the complete drum-routine without rehearsal. This was necessary because of the sudden sickness of one of my four drummers and buglers. The musician who stood in for the absentee bugler was the leader of my orchestra, Corporal Christopher Davis, who later in his career would become the Principal Director of Music of the Royal Marines.

Beat Retreat ceremonies occasionally presented unusual challenges. For example, during an official visit to Kuwait in 1979, a huge arena had been cordoned off alongside *Britannia's* position. This, we were then told, was to allow crowds of onlookers to witness the ceremonial protocol and our floodlit *Beat Retreat*. I quickly realised that my band of just twenty-four musicians would appear totally inadequate in such a large space. It also worried Prince Philip, who sent for me and outlined his concerns. I was tasked with doing something about it. There was no way in which the size of the arena could be reduced at short notice, for platform seating had been built all around its three sides much like that at Horse Guards Parade in London for the annual *Trooping the Colour* ceremony.

I contacted the local army Commander and suggested that his large Regimental band might like to entertain the audience for half an hour immediately prior to the Royal Marines band disembarking to *Beat Retreat*. He was happy to accept, and all I asked in return was that on the completion of its performance, his band should remain on parade and occupy as much space as possible at one end of the arena, while we did our bit at the end nearest the Queen. This utilised a large chunk of the space I couldn't fill and made for a better presentation all round.

I faced a very different challenge in 1980, when the Queen paid a State Visit to Morocco and had invited King Hassan II of Morocco to attend a State Banquet on board *Britannia* as it was berthed alongside in Casablanca. Not only did the King arrive over an hour late, but he brought with him many family members who had not been specifically invited. This caused great consternation on board, for the food had been cooked to perfection for the agreed time by the royal chefs and would be much spoiled by any delay. Also, to seat King Hassan's unexpected extra family members, other lesser mortals had to be withdrawn at no notice from the seating plan, as the Royal dining table could only accommodate 56 people. The Royal Staff were most upset that their careful plans for the evening had been compromised.

Normally on these occasions, a reception for the dinner guests precedes dinner, and then another reception, to which many other guests were invited, followed when the dinner was over. The whole proceedings would be drawn to a dignified close by a performance of *Beat Retreat* on the jetty to be witnessed by all. During the State Banquet, and whilst conducting the orchestra, I received a message from the Queen informing me that because of the delay, she had revised her plans for the rest of the evening. Following the meal, my band was to go onto the jetty and be prepared to carry out the *Beat Retreat* ceremony without delay.

As soon as I could, I went to my cabin and changed from my Mess kit into my ceremonial uniform and joined my musicians on the jetty. I then realised that I had a considerable problem on my hands. The Queen herself always decided when the Beat Retreat should start by making her way to the side of the Veranda Deck and standing beneath a particular overhead lamp. This was her signal to me that the ceremony should begin.

Unfortunately, King Hassan had brought with him an armed guard of over a hundred, many of whom were aloft on their camels and had filled the floodlit area into which the band was to march. It was imperative that I move them all out of the way. Taking one look at the size of these white turbaned, scimitar-swinging tribesmen sitting on top of the ugliest camels I have ever seen, I realised that I could do with some help!

I sent for the Officer of the Watch to join me on the jetty, intending to give him the job of clearing the area. To my dismay, when I spotted him making his way along to the Royal Yacht's gangway he was the smallest officer on board and therefore unlikely to be even noticed by most of the King's guards.

Seeing the Queen getting closer and closer to the lamp she intended to stand under, I sensed that this was a situation that I had to deal with myself. I strode forward into the floodlit area and by gesture tried to force, cajole and otherwise make the mounted guards move away. As far as they were concerned it was their jetty, and they were close to *Britannia* to protect their King, who was out of their sight anyway. With only white gloves and a baton I was hardly equipped to deal effectively with these guards who didn't understand much English, so I became more than a little demonstrative with my gestures.

Eventually, they understood what was required and they reassembled some way back just in time to allow me to begin the ceremony as the Queen's tiara began to sparkle under the lamp on the Veranda Deck. Unknown to me, the saga had been recorded by a BBC television crew and had been broadcast back home as part of that evening's UK news bulletin. Evidently, Keith Graves, the BBC reporter covering the State Visit, explained that had it not been for the Royal Marines Director of Music, the evening would have ended in the same disastrous way in which it had begun. Someone somewhere must have been impressed, for as a result I found myself a few months later receiving an invitation to attend the annual *Man of the Year* luncheon in London. It was all a bit embarrassing to be on the top table, for I had only been trying to do what was necessary to retain my prospects for a timely retirement and pension!

At the end of each period of Royal Duty, Her Majesty was always graciously pleased to send a signal to the Flag Officer Royal Yachts collectively thanking everyone on board *Britannia* for their part in a successful Royal Visit. Only very rarely was any particular group or individual singled out, so it was a highly significant honour for us when, heading to Portsmouth, the signal specifically mentioned the Royal Marines Band with whom the Queen said she had been: "most impressed throughout." The signal, by tradition, concluded with the order: *Splice the Mainbrace!* a time-honoured instruction allowing all on board to enjoy an extra celebratory tot of naval rum. For the band, this one tasted better than most!

Dining with Royalty

Embarked for the first time in Britannia as its Director of Music, I received a telephone call to my cabin from the Admiral one morning, telling me that it was usual for Her Majesty to invite her newly joined officers to dine with her in the royal apartments and that I could expect such an invitation. Later the Admiral telephoned me again. "Forget dinner", he said. "It is to be lunch - TODAY!"

In some trepidation I decided to ask my colleague and friend Lt Cdr Nick Carter, Keeper & Steward of the Royal Apartments, for any advice regarding attending a royal luncheon. He said that I should see him in his cabin before the lunch because there were points I should be aware of. On arrival there and to put me at my ease he explained the routine surrounding lunch. On his desk I could see a place setting for dessert with a knife & fork beside a plate upon which there was a single banana. "Lunch finishes with dessert which today is fresh fruit," he said. He then proceeded to demonstrate how I should eat a banana using a knife and fork!

I thought he was joking, but he wasn't. Firmly securing the banana to the plate with the fork he used the knife to slice it in half lengthwise. He then placed the fork into the fruit near to the end of one half, pressed the knife blade across it and by pressing down it released the clutch of the peel and he was left with a bite-sized piece of fruit on the fork that he conveyed adroitly to his mouth. Easy peasy, I thought, but what a rigmarole! Suitably briefed, I made my way to the royal apartments.

The lunch table was set for six: the Queen, Prince Philip, the Admiral, the Queen's Private Secretary, a distinguished Lady-in-Waiting and me. Prince Philip was opposite the Queen and I was seated to his left. Nick Carter had given me a valuable tip which was that I should try to follow what Her Majesty did and aim to finish a dish at the same time as she did. This was because when the Queen placed her knife and fork together on her empty plate, servants removed it and everyone else's as well - finished or not! Wise words for me to follow. There was a chance I was going to enjoy this.

Sitting next to an ever-inquisitive Prince Philip was a daunting experience which I confess was something of a trial. However, I looked forward to demonstrating my expertise when it came to eating the banana that was to follow the main course. Dessert plates were put in front of each of us before a serving dish of fruit was offered over one's left shoulder. The Queen declined, as did the Admiral. Prince Philip, however, reached into the dish and took some fruit, so when the dish was offered over my shoulder I was ready. Shock! horror! There were no bananas, only fresh cherries on stalks! How was I to eat them with a knife and fork? I remembered Nick Carter's sage advice: "Watch what they do and do likewise."

Prince Philip seemed not to care where the bouncing cherry stones ended up, but I was a little more circumspect. Some stones remained tightly clasped in my left hand while possibly being under the watchful eye of Her Majesty across the table.

My mind was working overtime and I decided that if she were to ask me why I seemed to be saving cherry stones, I would have said that they would come in handy if my percussionist needed to re-seed his maracas! Fortunately, I wasn't asked. This was the first of many occasions where I was as a privileged guest at the Queen's table.

Britannia's church services

Royal Church Services were held on Sunday mornings in *Britannia's* Wardroom, or in the Royal Dining Room, laid out as for cinema performances, if royalty was embarked. Yachtsmen were always invited to attend the services and, as for royal cinema shows, they were able to sit in chairs behind the embarked members of the Royal Family.

The Queen entered the room from the front once the remainder of the congregation had assembled and, as she came in, she could see everyone standing in place before her. Traditionally, no punishments were carried out in *Britannia*. Any serious defaulter would be quickly transferred to the escorting Royal Naval guard ship, and his kit would follow him within thirty minutes! Minor misdemeanours, however, were left to the Coxswain of *Britannia* to sort out. His routine was simple. The defaulter would be required to accompany the Coxswain to Royal Church on Sunday and a little area at the back of the congregation, easily visible to the Queen as she entered, was set aside for them. On entering, the Queen knew that anyone alongside the Coxswain must have been a *naughty boy,* and the miscreant would also know that she was aware of the situation. In such a close-knit community, it was an exquisite form of retribution!

A small orchestra was always in position to accompany the service. Hymns were chosen by the Admiral's Secretary, often having earlier consulted the Master of the Household to ascertain any royal preference. With no Chaplain embarked, the service was always taken by the Admiral from a lectern at the front. Printed Orders of Service were made available. In-going and out-going voluntaries were always part of the proceedings, and music to accompany the psalms as well as the hymns was played.

A quite intricate technique was needed for the psalms. Some required one note to be occasionally repeated before moving on within the chant. The actual tune can also change completely at some point, and where these things happen was never indicated in the music scores that the musicians in the orchestra were reading.

My solution was to conduct with my baton in one hand while holding the Psalter in the other. Normal baton movements showed the bar-lines as they were reached. Bars were, however, often of differing lengths often needing pauses, etc. When a note was to be repeated before moving on, I indicated it with the cork heel of the baton instead of the point. When this was seen, the players automatically repeated the note they had just played. When it was necessary to change the actual tune, the signal was given by raising the Psalter in the non-baton hand without using my baton at all. I found it to be the only way that control was always in my hands for I was, of course, also leading the singing of the psalm whilst conducting it!

Once, I used a *recorder consort* rather than an orchestra for the whole of a service. It was a nice change, very baroque in sound and Queen Elizabeth seemed to greatly enjoy it. The consort produced a lovely sound and the occasion was quite memorable.

Britannia's cinema

The Royal Family enjoyed watching films as a way of relaxing after dinner, so their dining room was often converted into a cinema once the tables had been cleared and moved to the sides of the dining room after dinner. Armchairs for members of the Royal Family would form the front two rows, with dining chairs arranged behind them. Yachtsmen were invited to attend if they wished, so long as they wore relaxed, but properly laundered, evening uniform. Officers wore mess-kit every evening and would attend the films if not on duty. The male *royals* were always in black tie and Dinner Jackets, the ladies always wore exquisite evening gowns. It made going to the pictures a whole new experience!

A large screen was lowered at the after end of the royal dining room and the film would be shown from two synchronised Gaumont British hidden projectors, which were permanently installed over the top of the cool cabinet just beyond the bulkhead of the royal galley. The films came in huge cylindrical metal cans, each containing one spool of film – there were usually two cans for each film. One evening Prince Philip, who we understood was never too keen on watching films, asked the Chief Electrician, hidden away in the galley, ready to operate the projectors, how long that night's film was to be. "Oh! About four cans" came the reply. Prince Philip, with some annoyance, then asked how this could possibly be and the reply was: "Well Sir, by the time it is over, I'll have drunk about four cans of beer!"

Rest and recreation on board *Britannia*

During long sea passages, often without Royalty embarked, elaborate events were arranged on board in support of various charities. It could take six weeks get to and from Australia, and these weeks without the Royal Family embarked gave ample opportunity for recreation. Village fetes were held on the Royal and Veranda Decks with all manner of stalls, etc., in place. Among the Yachtsmen even a *vicar* and his *wife* were usually found to officially open the event and to present prizes at the end of the afternoon. Great fun was had by all.

Kite flying competitions were held when conditions allowed. Entries were judged by the Admiral prior to the start of any competition. He awarded prizes for best design and size, etc. I once won the award for the smallest kite, made from one of my music programme cards taken from the Royal Dining Room. My kite was only seven inches long and four inches across at its widest point. I stiffened it with a broken baton, gave it a tail, and used a nylon fishing line for its string. As *Britannia* sailed through the South Pacific Ocean, I lined up at the start of the competition with my kite sticking out of my shirt pocket, whilst other competitors needed help to carry theirs.

All I needed to do to keep it airborne was stand near the back end of the Royal Deck and let it ride in the slipstream created by *Britannia* as it moved steadily through the water. I tied the fishing line to my finger and just stood there reading a book, while everyone else fought battles to keep their kites aloft. In the end, it became obvious that I was likely to win the prize for the longest flight, so the Chief Petty Officers' Mess hatched a cunning plot to defeat me. They flew a black plastic refuse bag with a hoop of light wire around the neck to keep it open. The bag was fed out on the end of a line to where my little kite fluttered forlornly in the breeze. It was duly captured and hauled in. They won. I was defeated because the kite flying rules didn't allow for piracy on the high seas to be an excuse when my own kite's flight had been so abruptly curtailed!

Those with a penchant for fitness found many ways of exercising on the upper deck when not on Royal Duty, and sports competitions between the messes often took place. My favourite sport was a form of deck-tennis. A high volleyball net was erected on the Veranda Deck, where singles and doubles matches were played. No racquets were needed, for the 'ball' was in fact a quoit made from rope and covered with green baize cloth. It was tossed underhand over the net by the server, to be caught and returned, all in one movement, by the receiver. Throwing was not permitted, neither were overhand returns. The game often developed into a highly skilful contest.

Those whose fitness regimes went further than most took part in half-marathons. They would run circuits of the Royal Yacht, along the Upper Deck before crossing to the other side at the after end and would then head for the bow. When that point was reached, the runners would cross over to the side where they had started and do it again. They would keep it up all afternoon! I focussed my fitness routine on kite flying and deck tennis!

During one long trip, posters began to appear all over *Britannia* announcing; "The Flying Vellucci's are coming!" Nobody seemed to know what was meant by this, and nobody owned up to placing them. A week or more went by before a similar batch of posters appeared. It was all very strange and the phenomenon became the talk of the Yacht! Then, one Saturday morning, new posters proclaimed that the 'Vellucci's' would be arriving on the fo'c'stle at 2pm. By the appointed time everyone not on watch was up there waiting and, to a fanfare - and on the stroke of the hour - eight of the smallest members of my band came into view dressed in black tights, singlets and briefs.

They each sported false black handle-bar moustaches with curled ends and had with them an array of large 'weights' made of blackened cardboard, each marked with their supposed weight in kilos. It was hilarious as they tossed these things around in a mock trial of strength. The Flying Vellucci's were actually the nucleus of a band-mess team for a sports afternoon that had been arranged for all and would follow immediately on the Royal Deck. Everyone now realised that they were being drawn to it as if by a pied piper.

Horse racing on the fo'c'stle was another popular pastime. The course was laid out with galley food-trays full of water for jumps and up-turned broom heads for fences. Races would be contested by six wooden horses and riders that had been fashioned from blocks of wood, each about a foot long. A Yachtsman would move them as required. Two Yachtsmen had buckets with huge dice in them. The first would toss his dice to identify the number of the relevant horse, whilst the second would toss his dice to identify the number of moves forward that the horse could take. Each race was treated as seriously as the racing at Royal Ascot itself. Real bets were placed, fanfares were played at the start of each race and officers would often dress for the occasion wearing top hats!

Quiz nights on board were also very popular and were often held on Saturdays in the early evening. Each Mess listened to the twenty questions asked over the internal broadcast system and formulated their answers. After the final question had been asked, the answer papers would be taken to the Yacht's Radio Office to be checked to determine the winning Mess.

Royalty when embarked, always entered a team and, gathered in the after end of the Royal Yacht, would compete with the most junior Yachtsmen. Sometimes, questions such as: "Name the winner of the King George VI Steeplechase in 1980" seemed to be directed aft rather than for'ard, but mostly the questions were of general knowledge.

In the Officers' Wardroom there was a three-line whip for these events and competition, especially with the Chief Petty Officers Mess situated immediately below, was fierce. In the event of the Wardroom being the winners, the CPO Mess members would signify their displeasure by bashing their ceiling with wooden broomsticks. We felt their displeasure beneath our feet. A large dish of hot and salted chips was always available on the coffee table around which officers gathered during these quizzes. This was the only time that Royal Yacht Officers on board ever saw or ate chips, and it was a treat greatly looked forward to.

The concert parties

At sea when favourable conditions allowed, concert parties would be held on the fo'cstle for the entertainment of the Royal Family and the Yachtsmen.

In the South Pacific in 1977 a concert party was organised to entertain the Queen Mother, who was on passage from Fiji to New Zealand. I thought it about time that the Gentleman of the Royal Household became involved as entertainers rather than being themselves always entertained, so I formed a choir in which they joined with members of the Chief Petty Officers Mess to form one of the acts for the show. Having just left Fiji with the strains of the wonderful traditional Fijian farewell song *Isa Lei* ringing in our ears, I was keen to use this piece. Sadly, although I had the music for it in my library, I didn't have a copy of the words.

I mentioned this to members of the band and was delighted when one of them told me that he had them from a previous visit to Fiji. In no time at all, he produced the three verses for me that I then carefully and methodically rehearsed with the members of the Royal Household. I wrote out a four-part harmony for the song and then placed a copy, together with the words, on the bulkhead of each of the toilets in the after end of the Royal Yacht. It was my way of ensuring that none of them would be able to say that they had not had opportunities to rehearse their part.

Up on the fo'castle, the choir was greeted with loud applause at the end of their rendition during the concert, but I noticed that a Fijian dignitary sitting next to the Queen Mother was, to say the least, unimpressed. All became clear when later I was told that the Fijian words that I had been given, and that the choir has learned so assiduously, were absolute gibberish. I had been the butt of a band joke that had paid off handsomely! It is at such times that a personal sense of humour was useful.

The Queen made a State Visit to Eastern Arabia in 1979. During a lull in the busy programme of events, a Royal Yacht concert party was organised. The idea of a choir to balance the many humorous acts again came to my mind, but this time I decided to use only the ladies and gentlemen of the Royal Household - both. They chose to sing a simple arrangement of *Beer, beer, glorious Beer* but because we were in the Gulf the words were changed by the men, without even telling me, to *Oil, Oil, Glorious Oil*. The ladies, having that day been given burkas, yashmaks and hand jewellery by their Gulf hosts when on shore, decided to dress-up in them and were unrecognisable to the Queen, sitting just in front of them.

Right at the last minute, and after all rehearsals had been concluded, the gentlemen of the Royal Household decided to play another trick on the ladies. Unannounced, they began to sing *Jolly Fine Boating Weather*. There was total confusion and many sideways glances. When they got to the 'middle eight,' the men had their own words that were sung to the song's rhythm. They sang *Bum-titty, Bum-titty, Bum-titty, Bum ... Bum-titty, Bum-titty ... Titty-bum*. The ladies tried to join in, but were much disturbed when the men included actions by grasping each of the afore-mentioned body-parts as the words were sung. The confusion was obvious. The Queen was in hysterics.

Britannia carried as part of its complement a specialist Chief Petty Officer Sailmaker, who was also useful with his sewing machine whenever any tailoring was required. Like the ship's photographer he had a nice little earner built into his role. The Sailmaker's Shop, wherein he was always to be found, was a veritable treasure-trove, for it contained things made on board over several decades.

Whenever a particular item of clothing was needed for a Concert Party, one only had to speak nicely to *Sails* and the most elaborate costumes would be readily available. Anything from a judge's wig to a bridal dress could be obtained in no time at all. If asked before *Britannia* left its mooring at Whale Island in Portsmouth, even the most obscure items could usually be sourced, for there was a large Royal Yacht lay-apart store on the Island where such items were often available, awaiting such a call.

Back in the mid 1960s, one Chief Petty Officer Sailmaker liked the idea of dressing-up, or perhaps more to the point – cross-dressing! He had never fully allowed his tendencies to be widely known until the final evening of a royal tour to the West Indies at a concert party immediately prior to his retirement from Royal Yacht Service. His act left a deep impression on everyone. Ballet music was heard as he appeared from the hatch that connected his workshop below with the stage on the foc'stle, where the performance was being held. He wore a tutu, resplendent with gossamer wings attached to his back. Unfortunately, as he emerged, one of the wings caught on the rim of the hatch, and he had to perform his entire act holding the broken wing in position over one shoulder.

The Queen, sitting not two metres from his embarrassed and well-rouged face, was in stitches. His act was a riot for all the wrong reasons. He disappeared down his hatch as soon as he could – and was not seen again for several days.

Re-provisioning *Britannia* at sea

During long voyages, arrangements were made to re-provision and refuel *Britannia* at various stages of a trip. This was carried out by *Britannia* rendezvousing with a Royal Fleet Auxiliary vessel and transferring what was required by jack-stay transfer. When it was necessary to refuel, a long hosepipe was strung above the water between the ships. These replenishments at sea gave an opportunity for the band, if weather conditions allowed, to take the tedium out of what was often a lengthy process. The band was always grouped on the fo'c'stle to play. This kept them out of the way of the 'action' and provided aural and visual entertainment, not only for the Royal Yachtsmen involved but also for the RFA vessel that had met us. It was usual for the Bandmaster rather than the Director of Music to conduct the band on these occasions.

The Flag Officer Royal Yachts, at the time Rear Admiral Hugh Janion - later to become Rear Admiral Sir Hugh Janion KCVO - called me to the bridge one morning in 1980 whilst *Britannia* was re-fuelling from a Royal Fleet Auxiliary tanker in the Mediterranean. Both ships were in position steaming alongside each other, and fuel was being pumped across to us. I was taken to the side of the bridge and asked to observe the light line strung between the bows of both vessels. It showed the distance between the ships by means of numbered pennants along its length.

Having been briefed on the importance of keeping station during the re-fuelling evolution, the Admiral then asked if I had ever *conned* a ship. My negative reply induced him to say that it was now time to do so, and with that he took me to stand by a compass binnacle. He then made me aware of the yacht's course and speed, brought a duty Yachtsman over with the log to ensure that any alterations to course, etc., that I were to give were recorded, and then gave an instruction I shall never forget. "Director of Music, you have the Yacht!" With that he turned on his heel and left me and walked into the bridge housing closing the door behind him.

We were not on Royal Duty and I naturally thought I had been set-up and that *Britannia* was being conned from some emergency steering position somewhere, but this was not the case. Whenever I saw the distance-line sagging slightly or paying out I would give an instruction: *Steer one-nine-zero* or whatever, followed by *Midships*. The Coxswain, at the wheel down below in the steering compartment, would repeat what I had said and the Royal Yacht would answer to the changed rudder position.

I had control of *Britannia* for at least twenty minutes before the Admiral reappeared and with a broad smile said: "Thank you Director of Music, I now have the Yacht." I must have been effectively monitored from somewhere, but I know not where and it doesn't detract from the fact that I was allowed the privilege and responsibility of an experience of a lifetime. It had been brought about by an Admiral who expected Officers serving in the Royal Yacht to be capable in all situations. He appeared to think very little of it, but I was deeply grateful for his confidence and have remained so to this day.

Storing *Britannia's* beer

When *Britannia* was initially designed there had, not surprisingly, been little provision for something as mundane as a beer store – certainly not of the size likely to be needed! This concentrated the minds of many embarked personnel over the years. The Chief and Petty Officers arranged for their beer to be stowed deep down in the forepeak and took delivery of barrels of special *Export Ale* directly from the brewer. These barrels had to be stowed deep down in the forepeak – a space right up in the bow that was too awkwardly shaped to be of general use. To get it there, the barrels had to be carried along the main inner passageway between decks. This hard and heavy work had to be done by the Chief and Petty Officers themselves because they were going to be the beneficiaries. In Portsmouth, some days before *Britannia* sailed, they sweated through hours of real graft and were often the butt of many sour comments from junior Royal Yachtsmen looking on.

Officers did not drink beer in the Wardroom (the practice was deemed *unofficerlike behaviour*), so an invitation to visit the Chief Petty Officers' Mess during a period in the tropics was not to be missed! Having stowed all this nectar whilst *Britannia* was berthed between its buoys at Whale Island in Portsmouth, it had to be later retrieved from the forepeak with the empty barrels taking their place. In the tropics, this was hot sticky work that again had to be done by the Chief and Petty Officers in full view of grinning Yachtsmen.

The canned beer for the Junior Yachtsmen came aboard in cardboard cases. Stowage for these was something of a problem, only really resolved when it was decided that it was an unnecessary encumbrance to embark a royal Rolls Royce for every foreign trip, as most British embassies and consulates in the countries to be visited had one for Diplomatic use anyway.

Within the initial design for *Britannia* provision had, however, been made for such a vehicle, and a garage with up-and-over sliding doors had been provided amidships on the starboard side of the Boat Deck. Davits enabled the car to be hoisted inboard from the jetty and positioned *fore-and-aft* on the deck. As the garage was also positioned *fore-and-aft*, with the access door running along the car's length rather than at its end, there was a need to get the vehicle sideways into its allotted space within the garage. In *Britannia*, nothing was ever impossible, so the car would be gently lowered not onto the deck but onto a platform that had wheeled tracks beneath it, going sideways into the garage. *Handraulic* assistance from the outboard side was all that was required to store the car safely until required.

Once it had been determined that a Rolls Royce would never need to be embarked for a foreign trip, the garage space became an ideal place to store the Junior Yachtsmen's cases of beer. No excessive humping up or down ladders needed to be done. Beer always readily available and, best of all, was guarded by the Watch-on-Deck, who used the garage as their preferred location when on night watches during inclement weather. The cases of beer were ideal for sitting upon and the area was rather cosy for those playing 'uckers, or cards, whilst awaiting the call to deal with any unforeseen nautical emergency that may arise.

Uffa Fox

Before the annual Cowes Week yachting races, in which the male members of the Royal family loved to participate, it was usual for *Britannia's* Admiral to visit the Regatta's administrative offices on the Isle of Wight to sort out minor details of procedure. Uffa Fox, a remarkable old sea-dog and boat designer who had taught the young men of the royal family to sail, lived at Cowes. He once invited Prince Philip, the Admiral and several of *Britannia's* officers, including me, to take lunch with him in his home at Cowes.

The trip from Portsmouth to Cowes was in the Royal Barge that, on arrival, was berthed at a private jetty underneath Uffa's workshop. Upstairs, his apartment was beautifully laid out for lunch and we were all made very welcome. Uffa, ever the comedian, thought nothing of putting a whoopee cushion in an armchair before inviting his royal guest to sit in it! He did most of the entertaining after lunch himself, for he could sing a huge range of sea-shanties and liked nothing more than to do so in his broad Hampshire dialect.

He was known throughout his long life for drinking copious amounts of alcohol. Indeed, the story goes that at one time he would drink port from a tumbler. This might well be true, for in 1958 his friend and neighbour, the Australian-born composer Hubert Clifford, composed *The Cowes Suite* in his honour. This orchestral suite contains a section where the bass trombone is required to imitate the sounds of a ship's siren signalling: *I am turning to Port!*

Procedure for Officers leaving *Britannia*

In the 1950s and 60s it was customary for officers leaving the Royal Yacht to return to the fleet on completion of their tour of duty to present *Britannia's* Wardroom with a memento. This was often made of silver, but sometimes porcelain. With a considerable turnover of personnel (officers only did two-year tours except for the Flag Officer Royal Yachts, the Keeper and Steward of the Royal Cabins and the Director of Music, who could expect to serve for longer) a surfeit of donated items was becoming an unnecessary encumbrance in the Wardroom.

It was therefore decided to do away with this custom and, instead, officers leaving would each receive a framed photograph of *Britannia,* signed on the front by the Admiral. The reverse side, which would also be glazed, would contain the signatures of every officer with whom the leaver had served whilst on board.

When the time came to leave, it was always done with the leaver wearing civilian clothes. He would approach *Britannia's* gangway, where every member of the Wardroom was assembled in order of seniority. Going along the line, he would bid farewell to each in turn until the Admiral was reached. He would then be presented with his framed picture of *Britannia* and, with it safely tucked under his arm, would descend the gangway for the last time, never to return unless specifically invited to do so - and even then never whilst the Royal Yacht was on Royal Duty. When it was my turn to leave, the Admiral presented me with my framed picture and I swiftly marched out of sight. This I thought was a more dignified way of departing than I had witnessed on an earlier occasion, when a senior officer had descended the gangway and, mistakenly thinking he was out of sight, rode away on a rusty old bike!

Service in the Royal Yacht carried with it a great deal of personal responsibility, and competence at one's job was of paramount importance. In time, individual capability would become known and recognised throughout *Britannia*. Not surprisingly, when a really useful individual had to retire from Naval Service, he might well be approached with the offer of a role in the Queen's service ashore.

Rank and position in the Royal Navy didn't necessarily come into it. My steward, Yachtsman Simon Solari, worked for Prince Charles as a valet and for Diana, Princess of Wales as her chauffeur when he left *Britannia*, while a Chief Petty Officer became an executive at Ascot Racecourse. The Queen's Coxswain, known the world over as *Norrie*, became an important figure at Windsor Castle and *Sax* French, the Royal Navy's Chief Writer in the Royal Yacht, eventually became Comptroller of the Royal Staff at Sandringham. His is a particularly poignant story, for at the height of his successful second career, both he and his wife were diagnosed as having cancer.

In January 2003, having learned of his illness, I wrote to him at his grace and favour home in the grounds of the Sandringham estate. His reply said much about the regard that the Royal Family has for former *Yachties*: "Audrey and I have been very touched by the number of cards and messages we have received. After leaving hospital I was confined to bed and our first visitor was Her Majesty the Queen. The following week the Prince of Wales called in – not the sort of thing that can be

shared with (and believed) by anyone other than fellow
Yachties".

Not surprisingly, the de-commissioning of *Britannia* brought
into existence a thriving group calling itself the *Association of
Royal Yachtsmen*. It holds re-unions and dinners on a regular
basis. A member of the Royal Family often attends these
functions as Guest of Honour, and happily mingles with those
whose privilege it has been to serve in the Royal Yacht.

CHAPTER 10

LORD MOUNTBATTEN OF BURMA
1900 - 1979

The assassination of Admiral of the Fleet the Lord Mountbatten of Burma, Life Honorary Colonel Commandant of the Royal Marines, came as an immense shock to the Royal Marines – and to the country. A great-grandson of Queen Victoria, he was born on the morning of 25th June 1900 at Frogmore House in the grounds of Windsor Castle, and was assassinated soon after midday on 27th August 1979, holidaying in the waters of Donegal Bay in Mullochmore in the Republic of Ireland. Mountbatten's life was one of privilege, challenge, adventure and happiness. He shaped and witnessed great moments of history before his untimely death. He packed a great deal into his seventy-nine years.

Mountbatten was born into the Battenberg family, one of the oldest Protestant families in the world, which can trace its ancestry back to the reign of Charlemagne, Emperor of the Romans, from 800. He was to be given four Christian names, but at the request of Queen Victoria, the name Albert was added. He became Louis Francis Albert Victor Nicholas, but all his life people called him 'Dickie'. As Prince Louis of Battenberg, he joined the Royal Navy in true family tradition. With his father, the then First Sea Lord, he crossed the Solent on 8th May 1913 to present himself at the Royal Naval College, then at Osborne on the Isle of Wight. He was twelve years and ten months old.

His family adopted the name Mountbatten on 14th July 1917, just three days before the British Royal Family had changed its name to Windsor, due to rising anti-German sentiment amongst the British public during the First World War.

There were tens of thousands like Prince Louis who had been to sea or were about to in the approaching war. At that time, the Royal Navy was the pride of the nation with almost sixty battleships, fifty-five cruisers, seventy-eight destroyers and sixteen submarines.

Flying was only in its infancy and was an almost unknown and dangerous adventure. Mountbatten became one of the few to take to the air before the First World War when he was only eleven and his family was living at Admiralty House in Sheerness. He once said that he remembered a small grass airfield nearby, from which he was taken up in one of the early aircraft. The aeroplane looked like a *box-kite* with a small pusher engine in front and appeared to be held together by wires like a birdcage. He held on to the petrol tank as the pilot flew a couple of circuits before landing again. He had been very excited at his unrestricted view of the countryside below, which he considered to be a better view than was available from any modern-day cockpit.

The twenty-one years between the two World Wars were possibly the happiest of his life. With his cousin Edward, Prince of Wales, (later King Edward VIII) he travelled the globe. His was a world of diplomatic parties and pageantry, fast cars and pretty girls. In 1921 he travelled to India and on St Valentine's Day of that year he proposed to his girlfriend, the beautiful Edwina Ashley, one of the richest girls in the world. They were married five months later at St. Margaret's Church in the shadow of Westminster Abbey. King George V, Queen Mary and most of the members of the Royal Family attended; the Prince of Wales was the best man. They swiftly became one of the most glamorous and powerful couples in the British aristocracy. Part of their honeymoon was spent in Hollywood, and from then on, the world of films and show business were never far removed from Mountbatten's life.

On Valentine's Day 1924 he became a father, with the birth of his daughter Patricia. It was two years to the day since he had become engaged to Edwina, but he still managed to maintain his high-speed lifestyle. He owned a 40-knot speed boat and claimed to have driven his Rolls Royce from Park Lane to Portsmouth in an hour and thirty-two minutes – probably faster than it can be done now. He loved polo and became something of an authority within the sport, but he also developed a reputation as a man who worked very hard professionally.

Regarding his Service career, Mountbatten revolutionised the Radiocommunications Branch of the Royal Navy and commanded his ships with dash and flair. His first was *HMS Daring*. "Daring by name, daring by nature. That's us." he told the crew. His next command was *HMS Wishart* not, you may think, a name to conjure with but to Mountbatten it was the greatest name in the fleet. It was the one to which all sailors dedicated daily prayers. "Our Father," as he told them: "*Wishart* in Heaven."

There was sadness in the nineteen thirties when King George V died as did Mountbatten's brother, Georgie, the Second Marquess of Milford Haven. He was also deeply involved with the anguish of the Abdication. There was war with Germany again, and its declaration would re-unite Mountbatten with the former King Edward VIII, now Duke of Windsor. In September 1939, Winston Churchill asked him to take his new ship *HMS Kelly* to Cherbourg to collect the Duke and his American wife. Churchill was also keen that his only son Randolph should accompany the Royal party. Embarrassingly, Randolph reported to *HMS Kelly* in the full dress uniform of an Officer of the 4th Hussars, but wearing his spurs upside down and inside out. Randolph evidently didn't have a clue about riding, nor was he well acquainted with the 4th Hussars. He complained bitterly that Mountbatten had not pointed out his error before the Duke of Windsor noticed but was informed that they had all been very amused.

On arrival back in UK in the blackout, *HMS Kelly* came alongside South Railway Jetty at Portsmouth in total darkness. Only a couple of small blue lights indicated where Mountbatten was to berth his ship. A brow was then placed against the ship's side and the Duke disembarked. At the moment his foot touched again English soil, floodlights came on and he was greeted with a royal salute by a full Royal Marines Guard and Band paraded on the dockside. The lights were then extinguished, the Duke got into a car and was driven off.

HMS *Kelly* became one of the 'little ships' of the war alongside HMS *Amethyst*, *Ajax*, *Exeter* and *HMNZS Achilles*. Under Mountbatten, HMS *Kelly* symbolised the spirit of a defiant nation. On 8th May 1940, at night in a minefield in the North Sea during the Battle of Norway, *Kelly* was torpedoed by a German E-boat. There was a tremendous explosion and, as Mountbatten was desperately trying to control the situation, the E-boat came out of the mist and collided with his ship. It rode up out of the water and struck the pom-pom gun mounting on the upper deck before sliding off. The E-boat left a lot of its equipment behind, including its steering wheel. Mountbatten later commented that it was perhaps the only time that a Captain had ended up with the steering wheel of the ship that had torpedoed him.

HMS *Kelly* refused to sink and was towed for ninety-two hours back to the Tyne. On arrival, she was virtually beneath the waves, but one year later she was back on patrol off the island of Crete in the Mediterranean. On 23rd May 1941, after *Kelly* had just won a skirmish with German high-level bombers, Mountbatten saw on the horizon an approaching squadron of enemy fighter planes. They attacked his ship, coming down at an angle of about 80 degrees, almost vertically. *Kelly* was hit whilst at full throttle, doing about thirty-five knots.

The control systems were destroyed and with the ship heeling heavily over to port, he gave the order: *Abandon Ship!* Having waited to ensure that, as Captain, he was last to leave his ship, Mountbatten found himself in the water alongside his

Navigating Officer. "Swim like hell, Pilot, get clear!" he is reported to have said. Just at that moment a crew member, stoker Second Petty Officer Garner, swam into view. Seeing his Captain and Navigating Officer struggling in the water, he is said to have commented: "Funny how the scum always comes to the top on these occasions!" Mountbatten loved telling that story. Whether true or not, he enjoyed its naval humour and ignored any perceived offence.

HMS Kelly's heroes were immortalised in the film *In Which We Serve. Kelly's* name was never used in the film. The setting was Dunkerque where *Kelly* never sailed, but the story was unmistakable and the star, Noel Coward, wore Mountbatten's cap throughout.

Mountbatten became a Vice-Admiral at the age of forty-one — two years younger than Nelson had been when he was promoted. He served on the Chiefs of Staff Committee alongside Naval Officers from a totally different generation. Despite this, he had a lot in common with Prime Minister Winston Churchill. Their wartime thinking was aligned and Mountbatten accompanied Churchill at the famous Allied Forces conferences at Casablanca and Quebec.

It was at the Quebec conference in August 1943 that Churchill appointed Mountbatten to be the Supreme Allied Commander Southeast Asia. Leaving those planning D-Day, he returned to India where, twenty years earlier, he had fallen in love with both that continent and Edwina.

After two more years of bitter fighting, Japan surrendered on 15th August 1945, and on that day Mountbatten broadcast to the soldiers, sailors and airmen of his so-called 'Forgotten Army'. His words were these: "You have fought a great campaign under hardships and difficulties that have probably never been equalled. You have beaten on the ground, in the air and on the sea a most stubborn enemy. A fanatical enemy from whose vocabulary the word surrender is officially deleted and is replaced by the word suicide. Yet, never once have you faltered or failed, never once has your courage or your dash been dimmed. The long list of VCs and other decorations for gallantry indicate the spirit that has animated all ranks and the ascendancy over the enemy that your bravery won for you."

Some of those who listened to that broadcast would hear him speak each year at the annual Burma Star Reunions, held at the Royal Albert Hall in London. According to him, to have fought in Burma made you something very special.

Following the surrender of the Japanese forces, Mountbatten was tasked with engineering a peaceful solution to the problems that were simmering in the Indian sub-continent. This is when his career as a statesman came to the fore. During World War II, he had fought for the freedom of one fifth of the world's humanity; now he had to intervene between those who were fighting for their right to rule themselves. It was a daunting prospect. Hindus, Muslims, Buddhists, Sikhs and Christians all had very different ideas of what 'Independence' meant and how it should be obtained.

The Muslims wanted their own new, independent, country to be called Pakistan. Thousands were killed or injured in riots, and against this background of unrest, Mountbatten decided to move ahead fast. He brokered an agreement to partition British

India into two independent Dominions: India and Pakistan. The Dominion of Pakistan spans what has become the Islamic Republic of Pakistan and the People's Republic of Bangladesh.

Mountbatten served as last Viceroy of India from February to August 1947, and then as the first Governor General of the new India from August 1947 to June 1948.

While the main political conflict had been resolved, at least temporarily, the partition displaced between 10 and 20 million people along religious lines, creating refugee crises in the newly constituted Dominions. More than half a million were killed in religious riots as non-Muslims (Hindus and Sikhs mostly) migrated from Pakistan to India, across the newly created borders. Chaos ensued as religious refugees criss-crossed between Pakistan and India. Lady Edwina Mountbatten worked tirelessly, flying from camp to camp, often working ankle-deep in mud as she tried to soothe thousands dying of cholera. She and Mountbatten worked closely with Mahatma Gandhi to defuse the crisis, notwithstanding Gandhi's opposition to Mountbatten's partition plans.

Mountbatten, whose uncle, Emperor Nicholas II of Russia and his family, had been executed thirty years earlier, was profoundly affected by Gandhi's assassination in January 1948. Following this tragic event, which helped reduce the tension between the leaders of India and Pakistan, Mountbatten returned to Britain to a mixture of adulation and criticism. Churchill thought that he had pushed everything through too hastily.

Back in the UK, the former Vice Admiral returned to the Royal Navy in the less exalted rank of Rear Admiral. He would soon step up the ladder of promotion again, becoming in turn Vice Admiral, Fourth Sea Lord, NATO Commander in Chief in the Mediterranean and then, like his father, First Sea Lord.

In 1959, Mountbatten became Chief of the Defence Staff, but that appointment was over-shadowed by the sudden death of Edwina. the following year while she was on a tour of the Far East on behalf of the Save the Children Fund. This was a cause that became increasingly important to him in the years that followed. He once made this dramatically clear at a humanitarian awards ceremony when he said that he preferred personally not to disguise the poor and needy by using the term *under-privileged*. "This euphemism may ease our conscience", he said, but in his opinion it distorted the truth.

Mountbatten didn't personally think it a privilege to have enough to eat or clothes to wear. He once said: "It is not a *privilege* for children to have medical help when they were sick. It is not a *privilege* for children to have enough education to enable them to earn their living when they had grown up. It is a basic human right, and children who are denied this are not *under-privileged*, they are damned well poor and needy, and we should face up to it."

As a widower, Mountbatten sought refuge in hard work and was persuaded to remain in the Navy well past his normal retirement age. He eventually retired in 1965 as an Admiral of the Fleet. Invested with the Order of Merit, he found time to record details of his colourful career in a TV series *The Life and*

Times of Lord Mountbatten. This resulted in lots of fan mail from those who had served with him through the years.

One of the programmes in the series entailed a visit to Malta, where much of his time in the Royal Navy had been spent. Whilst there, he was asked to take part in a promotional interview for Maltese television. He agreed. The interviewer said: "Lord Mountbatten, I understand that the series of programmes being made is to be called *The Life and Times of Lord Mountbatten.*" He asked if this was so. On being assured by Lord Louis that it was, the interviewer said: "Would you mind telling me what part you are playing in this?"

Mountbatten was appointed Life Colonel Commandant of the Royal Marines in February 1965. Together with Prince Philip, Captain General of the Royal Marines, he worked tirelessly for the next four decades to enhance the reputation of Royal Marines worldwide.

Mountbatten received awards and decorations from many countries throughout the world. He was made a Freeman of the town that was to be his home for many years, Romsey, as well as a Freeman of the cities of London and Portsmouth. It was during the installation at Portsmouth that his sense of humour took over. He reminisced about his early days in the city as a young sailor, and recalled a ceremony that he had attended, when Prince Philip had been made an Honorary Fellow of the Royal College of Surgeons of Edinburgh. In this hallowed atmosphere, the President solemnly announced: "Your Royal Highness, we are deeply honoured that you have graciously deigned to accept honorary membership of the Royal College of Surgeons of Edinburgh. We, the College, wish to present you with a souvenir and I ask Your Royal Highness to accept this ancient *Bleeding Bull.*" Whereupon, Prince Philip stood up and is reputed to have replied: "All I can say is that it is bloody kind of you!"

Lord Mountbatten's view was that so long as it remained an island at the centre of a Commonwealth, Britain must retain a navy. It was the spirit of the Royal Navy in the old days that had made this country great, and he often said that if he were to have his time all over again, and they would have him, he would go straight back into the Royal Navy. It was therefore greatly significant when, following his assassination, it was decreed that he should be given a State Funeral, with a guncarriage carrying his coffin pulled by sailors of the Royal Navy.

Mountbatten's funeral

Arrangements for Lord Mountbatten's funeral were carefully planned during his lifetime, and he certainly had some input into his own. He was not to know, however, that his life would end in 1979 when he and several members of his family, enjoying their annual August holiday in the Republic of Ireland, would be assassinated by the Provisional IRA while sailing from the harbour at Mullaghmore in their 29-foot fishing boat *Shadow V,* lifting the lobster pots that had been set the previous day.

Those on the boat were Mountbatten, his eldest daughter Patricia, Lady Brabourne, her husband Lord Brabourne, their twin sons Nicholas and Timothy Knatchbull, Lord Brabourne's mother Doreen, Dowager Lady Brabourne, and

Paul Maxwell, a young crew member from Enniskillen in County Fermanagh.

Mountbatten was killed instantly, together with his grandson Nicholas Knatchbull and crew member Paul Maxwell. Doreen Knatchbull died of her wounds the following day.

As Director of Music to the Flag Officer Naval Home Command in Portsmouth, it became my duty to arrange for a large Royal Marines Band, comprising 119 musicians, to march with the funeral cortege from St. James' Palace through the silent crowds to Westminster Abbey. In accordance with Mountbatten's wishes, the band's formation, with twenty-three side drummers and three bass drummers, was to be seven across and seventeen deep. The drums of all these percussionists were draped with black silk, in accordance with Service regulations. Likewise, the Drum Major's staff and gold-braided sash were similarly covered.

Rehearsals with the sailors, one hundred to pull the guncarriage and another hundred behind to steady its progress, took place at Eastney Barracks in Southsea. It was fortuitous that at Eastney, there was an archway of almost identical size to the one leading from London's Horse Guards Parade to Whitehall. Practice at negotiating this narrow point whilst towing a three-and-a-half ton guncarriage was vital. A full rehearsal of the procession, but with bass drum beating only, took place in London in the early hours of one morning a few days before the actual ceremony. The timings had earlier been determined by the London Garrison Sergeant Major, who presumably had measured the route by walking it with his pace-stick.

The State Funeral of Lord Mountbatten on 5th September 1979

On the day of the rehearsal, however, we reached the Abbey some seven minutes later than the Garrison Sergeant Major had scheduled. There was much consternation as I insisted that there must be an adjustment on *the day*. A State Funeral is possibly the only time where a procession's rate of progress along its route is determined by the weighty guncarriage carrying the coffin. The Sergeant Major had overlooked the fact that a hundred sailors pulling a heavy guncarriage, and having to negotiate bends and narrow arches, were never going to march with a regular thirty-inch pace. The timings were altered and the guncarriage reached the door of Westminster Abbey on the day of the funeral just as the Abbey's clock struck the appointed hour.

British ceremonial is the envy of the world and much of its success is based upon timing. I didn't want to be remembered as the person responsible for getting it wrong on this most significant occasion. I schooled myself into knowing exactly what it felt like to march at a funeral pace that is between the normal slow and quick-march tempos. In the procession, I marched in a position to the left-hand side and slightly behind the Drum Major at the front of the band, where I could be seen at all times by the master bass drummer. He was instructed to beat his drum as my feet touched the ground, and this he did throughout. Nowadays, of course, he could carry a hand-held electronic metronome for accuracy, but I was working in less innovative times. It was quite an experience, for ceremonies such as this occur very rarely.

Some weeks after Lord Mountbatten's funeral his family held a wedding ceremony in Romsey Abbey, wherein he is interred to the right front of the nave. I was privileged to conduct a

Royal Marines fanfare team inside the Abbey on that wedding day. A survivor of the bombing at Mullaghmore, Mountbatten's daughter Patricia, Lady Brabourne, attended the wedding lying on a litter. Her shattered figure was shrouded from head to slippered feet in Irish green satin. It was a demonstration of British phlegm that I have never seen bettered. Years later, when I was in her company socially, I was able to tell her how significant I thought her gesture had been on that day. She was pleased I had noticed. I cannot have been the only person to be impressed by her resolve that her family should not be beaten. That indomitable courage was, and remains, a Mountbatten trait.

GOLD ON BLUE

CHAPTER 11

THE ROYAL HONEYMOON CRUISE – THEN A SURPRISE
1981

'Her Majesty's Yacht Britannia'
Depicted in needlepoint by Miss Valerie England of Southsea

It is likely that Royal Yachts had been used on previous occasions by royal honeymooners, so it was not surprising that arrangements were put in hand for *Britannia's* use when Prince Charles married Diana, Princess of Wales in July 1981. The couple joined *Britannia* at Gibraltar, a few days after their wedding at St. Paul's Cathedral and after spending some time at Lord Mountbatten's home at Romsey.

After the honeymooners had embarked, we sailed into the Mediterranean with many small craft chasing after us. Planned stops along the North African coast were a well-kept secret. On shore, a well-briefed member of Royal Staff kept in touch with *Britannia's* progress and advised where best it may be for the royal couple to make use of uninhabited beach areas.

On one of these brief stops, the Officers of *Britannia* arranged for an evening beach barbeque to which the royal couple were invited. Several of us went ashore early and erected a large tent, put up fairy-lights and prepared the small area of beach. Martin Orbidans, the pianist with my band, then joined us ashore with an accordion and song-sheets. Everything was in hand by the time the Royal Yacht's *jolly-boat* appeared, carrying the honeymoon couple. The barbeque was sizzling and the lights were twinkling in the background.

A royal detective had accompanied the couple from *Britannia* and was first out of the boat, followed quickly by the Prince and Princess. The two men immediately ran for the sea, leaving Princess Diana on the beach, where she quickly became involved with the preparation of the food. She was intrigued to see that we had brought with us a large thermos flask containing borsch soup that we knew she particularly liked. She held up she the cups while I poured. The evening that ensued was totally relaxed for us all and remains a joyous memory.

Amazingly, the press was kept at bay throughout the honeymoon and the precise whereabouts of the royal yacht went undetected. A meandering itinerary took us through the Greek Islands before reaching the head of the Suez Canal, where Egypt's President Sadat and his wife joined the Prince and Princess on board *Britannia* for dinner.

The next morning, our planned transit of the canal began at about 6am. Passage through the Suez Canal is taken in convoy so on this day, *Britannia* headed an early morning line of ships heading south. Soon there was consternation on the bridge when it was noticed that a small Egyptian bumboat was sailing up the canal from the opposite direction. As it reached us, it was seen to be loaded down to the waterline with mangoes. The Suez Canal pilot on board *Britannia* soon ascertained that these were intended for the Royal Yacht and were a gift to the Royal couple from President Sadat.

No vessel was ever allowed close to the pristine paintwork of Britannia's side, but on this occasion dispensation had to be given and the Royal Yachtsmen quickly produced fenders to limit possible damage. I had forgotten all about this story until reminded of it by Princess Diana a year or so later when she was Guest of Honour at one of my Royal Albert Hall concerts. In conversation with her during the interval in the Royal Retiring Room, I asked her what, if any, were her special memories of her time in *Britannia* following her marriage to the Prince of Wales. She recalled how, during the dinner party on board for President Sadat, he had asked her if there was anything she didn't have that she perhaps may like. She apparently mentioned that she liked mangoes, so as soon as President Sadat left the Royal Yacht, he arranged for this shipment to be delivered to her.

Princess Diana almost whispered the story to me because she was a little embarrassed to think that she had received such special treatment. She laughed hugely when I explained that a whole boatload had arrived, and that as they were so ripe, all but those that she had found on her breakfast table had been distributed around *Britannia*. Everyone had mangoes that day!

Dining in their shared cabin each evening hardly required the attendance of an orchestra, so I suggested to Prince Charles that instead we provide a trio of musicians who would play to give a relaxed ambience to these evenings. The trio consisted of piano, bass and drums. It was led by Musician Martin Orbidans (he of the accordion on the beach) whose remarkable talent and ability to play music of all types was exquisite. It was salon music that could have graced the finest hotel and made for the most relaxing end to each day.

Up on the Royal Deck, a small portable pool had been placed for the convenience of the royal couple if they felt like a splash at any time. There was some doubt as to whether they used it, for it was not in general view. It was decided that we could probably find out by a simple jape. A visit to the galley produced a small bag of carrots that were then each shaped into goldfish, before matchstick heads were poked in for eyes. Someone crept up onto the Royal Deck late one evening and emptied the bag into the pool. Over the next twenty-four hours we heard absolutely nothing from the Royal Apartments, so I think we can assume that the pool was surplus to requirements for our royal honeymooners!

Princess Diana on board Britannia, 1981

A couple of years after this had happened, Princess Diana was again Guest of Honour at a Royal Marines Massed Band

Concert at the Royal Albert Hall in London. Directors of Music of each band conducted during the concert, and I had to wait backstage until it was my turn to conduct and to draw the concert to a close with an extended finale. Each conductor was in turn introduced to the audience by the BBC's Susannah Symons, who also gave details of the works they were to conduct. Susannah and I were waiting together for my turn to go on stage, when she began to ask me all sorts of light-hearted questions about my career, and in particular any interesting things that may have happened while I had been on board *Britannia* during the Royal Honeymoon trip. In an unguarded moment, I told her the story of the carrots in the honeymoon pool. She laughed and I thought no more about it. Imagine, then, my embarrassment as she went forward to make my introduction and, directly addressing the Princess of Wales in the royal box, relating at length the story I had just told her!

After transiting the Suez Canal, we headed for the port of Hurghada on the shore of the Red Sea, where the royal couple were to disembark at the end of that stage of their honeymoon. The evening before our arrival, the Royal Yachtsmen gave one of their delightful impromptu concert parties on the fo'cstle. It was great fun and inevitably had many references to the honeymoon and *Britannia's* part in it. The royal couple enjoyed themselves immensely and the Yachtsmen knew that their contribution to the honeymoon had been huge.

The following morning, a Saturday, *Britannia* berthed alongside in Hurghada to allow the Prince and Princess of Wales to disembark, together with their small retinue of no more than five Staff. They went straight to the local airport and took off for Aberdeen in Scotland where the honeymoon was to be continued at Balmoral. *Britannia* was to remain in port for a couple of days before continuing south for the long voyage to Australia, where Her Majesty the Queen would join by air for a Commonwealth Heads of Government Conference.

A big disappointment for the crew of *Britannia* was that while alongside in Hurghada, the local telephone network was out of action, so making telephone calls home was almost impossible. On Monday morning, just two days after the concert party given on board Britannia, a British tabloid newspaper published full details with pictures of it. Fingers were pointed at Royal Yachtsmen for having been in contact with the press in UK from Hurghada, and it became very uncomfortable for us all on board *Britannia*. However, given the reality of the disrupted telephone lines, it was quickly realised that the culprit was most unlikely to have been a Royal Yachtsman, particularly as they all knew that their careers would have been jeopardised by such stupidity.

The person who had been in contact with the press just *had* to be one of the five members of the Royal Staff who, having witnessed the concert party and accompanied the royal couple to Balmoral, would have been able to pass on the information. Sure enough, after an enquiry it eventually transpired that one of the Staff had a relative who worked for the newspaper in question and that he had passed on the information. Whether he was retained in Royal Service or not I have no idea, but he certainly didn't foresee the significance of Hurghada's defunct local telephone network. He thought he was safe and that any blame must surely bypass him. Not so!

When not embarked in *Britannia,* the Royal Yacht musicians were part of the Eastney-based Royal Marines Band fulfilling their duties in support of the Royal Navy and Royal Marines. I was particularly keen on demonstrating the orchestral prowess of Royal Marines musicians, for this is often not appreciated by members of the public, who generally only attend military band concerts. Eastney Barracks had a superb church within its boundary wall, and using this as a venue, I arranged a series of public orchestral concerts. They were very well supported, and I found that funds were being generated that could be put to good charitable use. Thanks to the audience's generosity, we were able to sponsor several guide-dogs for the blind and a complete set of sports-wheelchairs for disabled athletes living in Portsmouth.

Gradually, Eastney Barracks came into prominence as a place where Royal Marines musicians could be seen and heard. Naval and Royal Marines Officers from nearby establishments were invited to entertain their guests to supper in the Officer's Mess before each concert. The old barracks began to spring to life again after many years of seeing everything gradually run down for want of money or enthusiasm. The days of it being a hub of Service activity had long gone when I arrived there, and it was a joy for me to be able to begin some form of renaissance.

It also gave the musicians an opportunity to play classical music that would not normally fall into the general daily repertoire. Some were featured as soloists on the concert platform, other musicians premiered works they had composed that would otherwise never have seen the light of day.

A surprise

Returning from Australia in the Royal Yacht after the Royal honeymoon cruise and the Commonwealth Heads of Government Conference in 1981, I was informed that one of my colleagues, Captain Peter Heming, was to be interviewed by the Admiral on *Britannia's* arrival in the UK to confirm his suitability to be my relief. Having only a couple of years left to serve until I reached pensionable age, I expected that once my relief had taken over my duties at Portsmouth, I would be absorbed within the Corps to serve out those years.

I knew that unless the incumbent Principal Director of Music Royal Marines, Lt. Colonel Jim Mason, was given an extension of service, then he would shortly retire. Traditionally, promotions to senior positions for officers are published at least six months in advance. Although I was aware that there was a possibility that I might be a contender for any Principal Director vacancy, my name was not on an awaited promotions list when it was signalled from London during *Britannia's* voyage back from Australia. To me, this meant that an extension of service must have been arranged for the incumbent PDM. I sensed that having served for four years as Bandmaster in the 1960s and latterly four as Director of Music, this was to be my last trip in the Royal Yacht, and I prepared myself to welcome my successor on board.

Entering Portsmouth harbour in *Britannia* for this last time was highly emotional, for I was faced with the end of my musical career in the Corps that had begun in 1949. From just nine miles up the road at Fareham, my mother and father had come with my wife Margaret to see the Royal Yacht arrive, and they were waiting on the jetty where we were to berth.

Part of me died as the main engines of *Britannia* were stilled and we waited for the gangways to be placed against the Royal Yacht's side. Sadness was quickly forgotten, however, in the excitement of reunion with family and friends over drinks in the Wardroom. After about half an hour, I was called by a steward, who told me that I was to report to the Admiral's Secretary in his cabin. I apologised to my family for having to leave them for a moment and went to where I had been bidden.

Om my arrival, I was given an opened letter that had just been delivered by courier from the Department of the Commandant General Royal Marines in London. I was told to read it. With the Admiral's Secretary looking on I scanned its contents, but the words began to swim in front of my eyes. It appeared to say that I had been selected to be the next Principal Director of Music and that I was to be promoted immediately to Major Royal Marines. I was also to be given a lengthy sabbatical before being elevated to the acting rank of Lieutenant Colonel six months hence.

As PDM, I would have overall responsibility for eleven Royal Marines bands with a compliment of some 500 musicians spread around major Royal Navy ports, Royal Marines barracks, and some buglers still serving on ships.

Totally stunned, for this had come right out of the blue, I was told that the Admiral was now waiting in his day-cabin to congratulate me, and I was taken to see him to receive his best wishes and congratulations. In total shock, I then made my way back down to the Wardroom, where I found the composure to relate my experience to my family. The news quickly flashed around and within no time at all the wardroom stewards ensured that champagne was splashing into everyone's glass.

I was so pleased that my nearest and dearest were there to share in my emotional roller-coaster. It really was strange that meaningful things always seemed to happen for me at odd times. My initial promotion to Lieutenant had been on Christmas Day 1968. I had been told of my instant promotion to Captain on April Fool's Day 1976 and now, without previous indication and against all usual administrative procedures, I had been given the unprecedented news of my accelerated promotion and the job of leading the Royal Marines Band Service.

GOLD ON BLUE

CHAPTER 12

SABBATICAL AND RETURN TO DEAL
1981 - 1985

Former Principal Director of Music Lt Colonel Sir Vivian Dunn, who was knighted following his retirement from the Corps in 1968, was involved with arranging a sabbatical for me before I took up my new appointment as Principal Director of Music. He invited me to his home at Hayward's Heath, where several ideas were suggested for my further musical education in the forthcoming months.

It was agreed that during the spring and summer of 1982 I should have regular tutorials with Malcolm MacDonald, a Royal Academy of Music Professor, at his home at Harrow-on-the-Hill. The curriculum would include Harmony, Counterpoint, Orchestration, Musical History, Arranging and the Technique of Conducting. The latter led to an invitation for me to appear as a guest conductor with a well-known London orchestra.

I was also provided with a season ticket to enable me to attend each of the 57 BBC Promenade Concerts that had been programmed for that year. This was more than I could reasonably manage - actually it was impossible for me to spend so much time in London attending every concert.

There was a lot going on in my life at this time that more urgently needed my attention. In April 1982 the Falklands War had broken out and I was acutely conscious that whilst I was out of uniform, standing 'on the sidelines,' bands of the Royal Marines were in the South Atlantic, on board the *SS Uganda* and the P&O ship *Canberra*. At the age of 47 I felt that my place was to be involved with them in some way, rather than honing my musical skills.

I also suspected that what I was learning would probably be surplus to any requirement for my new role, as it was likely that I had already achieved the standard considered necessary, otherwise I would not have been appointed. I was uncomfortable during the months of my sabbatical, for it was the first time in my lengthy career that I was marking time without a real hands-on job.

I greatly valued Malcolm MacDonald's tutorials. We became friends and, in the years to come, I was able to include one of his musical compositions at a Royal Marines Massed Band concert at the Royal Albert Hall in London. He was thrilled to have the opportunity to be present in a tiered box seat and to be acknowledged by the capacity audience.

When the victorious fleet returned to the UK at the end of the Falklands War in July 1982, I at last had a small opportunity for involvement and I grasped it with both hands. The wife and family of Trevor Attwood, Bandmaster in SS *Uganda*, had no transport to get them to Southampton for the arrival home of the ship. It gave me the greatest pleasure to drive to Deal from where I was living in Hampshire and to deliver Trevor's family to the dockside. This one useful duty slightly assuaged my guilt at being *out of the firing line* during those difficult months when I wanted to be useful with colleagues and friends but couldn't be. Eventually, Trevor Attwood went on to become my personal secretary. His loyalty, ability and generosity of spirit became the mainstay of my tenure as Principal Director of Music. My gratitude to him is boundless.

Towards the beginning of summer of 1982, before I was due to take up my new position at Deal, I was unexpectedly called for an interview with the Commandant General Royal Marines, Lt General Sir Stuart Pringle Bt., in London. He advised me that changes to the initial succession plan had been made and that my new duties would be those of Principal Director of Music only, whereas my predecessor, Jim Mason, had also been appointed Commandant of the RM School of Music.

This news was in many ways a big disappointment, and to make things worse, David Watson, the Royal Marines Officer who was now to be Commandant had initially been gazetted as one of my team, reporting to me. Immediately prior to his appointment, he had been on the Staff of NATO and based in Naples. I had previously met him during a Royal Yacht deployment when he came on board *Britannia*. He would now move into the Commandant's residence, Zeebrugge House, that would have been for my use, and he would also have use of the staff car and driver.

It wasn't until I had talked matters over with an experienced friend that I realised I was probably very lucky to have just one role - a musical job to which I was suited and for which I had been fully trained. Someone else would be responsible for military matters and the logistics of feeding and administering a complex training facility. When I was informed, in London, of the changes, I was concerned that it was because the Commandant General considered that I was ill-equipped for the dual role. This didn't boost my confidence, as it happened at a time when I was emotionally torn by not being alongside my colleagues in the South Atlantic.

Investiture ceremonies at Buckingham Palace

On 11th June 1982 I was able to tell my friends and family that my name was on the Queen's Birthday Honours list which had been announced that day. I was made a Member of the Royal Victorian Order, which recognises personal service to the Sovereign. It was the Queen's way of marking my term as her Director of Music on board *Britannia*. Margaret and my daughters would accompany me to Buckingham Palace where I would in due course receive my honour. I had known of the impending announcement for a couple of weeks but had been sworn to secrecy.

Those receiving their honours were required to attend the Palace at 10.30am for an 11.00am start. David Watson loaned me his staff car and, as the driver neared the venue, we joined a long queue of taxis along the Mall that were also waiting to disembark their passengers inside the palace courtyard. Once inside, those to be honoured were invited into an ante room, while their guests were ushered to their seats in the State

Ballroom. In the ante room, we were corralled into groups, according to the honour we were to receive, and then invited to form a queue in alphabetical order. We were then briefed on what would happen next.

In a line, we were to leave the ante room and be escorted behind where our guests were seating in the State Ballroom to a door at the other side of the ballroom, which took us down a long side corridor to another door that allowed access to the front of the ballroom. At that door, a retired senior officer in full dress uniform pinned a hook to our chest and explained that, on his signal, we were each to take ten paces forward, turn to the left and take another four steps forward. This would put us in front of the Queen. Women would curtsey while men would offer the Royal Salute, or the *Royal Nod* as we called it in *Britannia*. A *Royal Nod* involved standing to attention and placing one's chin on one's tie knot for two seconds.

As the senior officer signalled for me to take my ten steps forward, I heard an equerry quietly tell the Queen who the next recipient was and that he had been *Britannia's* Director of Music. Appropriately briefed, we exchanged a few words as she placed my medal on the hook. The Queen then held out her hand to shake mine, and with a distinct push indicated that my time was up. I took four paces back, made my *Royal Nod* once more, turned to the right and walked to another side door. Here, another retired senior in full dress uniform removed my medal and pin, put the medal in a box and presented it to me, and explained that I could now join the audience to witness others obtaining their awards.

Once everyone had been invested, the audience rose as the Queen silently left the Ballroom, I found Margaret and the girls and we all went outside into the Palace courtyard to have our photographs taken. We were then driven in the staff car to the Royal Free Hospital's student nurses' home in Hampstead where we all, including the staff car's driver, crammed into my eldest daughter's room to celebrate my investiture with a mug of tea and a slice of cake. After that, we were driven back to Deal.

This procedure was repeated in 1988 as my name was published on that year's New Year Honours List. This time, I was to be made an Officer of the British Empire, which recognises prominent national or regional achievements. On this occasion, Margaret, my daughters and my son accompanied me to Buckingham Palace. The only difference to the routine I've described above was that rather than celebrating afterwards at the student nurses' home in Hampstead with tea and cake, we all enjoyed a delicious lunch at *The Ritz*!

Deal

I arrived in Deal to take over my appointment as Principal Director of Music in November 1982. A Naval officer occupying No. 1 Royal Buildings, now designated to be my residence, was only too pleased to move his young family the short distance into a house in nearby Infirmary Barracks to make room for us. Two reasons became quickly obvious. One was the fact that he knew from personal experience that No.1 Royal Buildings presented huge problems for anyone living in it, and the other was that he was able to receive financial assistance to relocate.

This imposing property, arranged over four floors and a basement below, was designed by Naval Architect and Surveyor Edward Holl in 1813 during the Napoleonic Wars to accommodate the Senior Physician of the new Naval Hospital – the building which would eventually become the School of Music. However, living there became an ongoing nightmare for me and my family.

Originally, the house was heated by a system that served the entire Barracks complex in Deal – where warm water had been pumped to the residence free of charge. Now, the three-inch diameter pipes that ran throughout the house would contain water that was heated by an industrial sized gas boiler in the basement, and I was expected to meet the heating costs. My gas bills were huge, yet the water was never hot enough for the upper rooms of the house to feel warm.

For our first three weeks in No. 1 Royal Buildings, no hot water was available in the property at all because the new boiler in the basement was still being installed. To take a bath, we had to go out of our front door and walk through a communal garden to one of the entrances of the adjacent Commandant's house. The Commandant had kindly allowed us to use one of his bathrooms in our hours (that turned into weeks) of need. Suitably dressing-gowned, and in full view of the passing public, we would make as dignified a journey as was possible in the circumstances.

The heating bills quickly became a serious problem, so I made representations to the Headquarters of the Royal Marines explaining that it simply wasn't fair to expect me to pay such a significant proportion of my salary to live in that residence. I didn't have a private income to supplement my Service pay, but I did have a family to support. My points were accepted and some financial assistance was provided, but the residence remained cold and miserably uncomfortable. It was the time of a defence spending moratorium. The décor could best be described as (very) shabby chic. Although the heavy curtains in the dining room, which we used to entertain official visitors to the Barracks, were shredded in places, the Admiralty could not afford to replace them.

What had been anticipated as a most exciting period to crown a long career was quickly turning out to be a desperate disappointment.

I intended to use my new position to promote the School of Music and invited local dignitaries to attend regular fortnightly orchestral concerts within the barracks, as Vivian Dunn had when he had been in Deal. Margaret and I invited up to eighteen people on each occasion. They came for drinks and supper at our house before going to the concert hall, and afterwards we entertained them to drinks in the Officers' Mess. This arrangement had its difficulties, however, for with no staff available to assist us, Margaret and I would provide the drinks, cook and then serve the food to the guests ourselves.

Once the meal was over, we needed to get our guests to the concert hall in good time for me to greet the audience and make announcements from the concert stage before the music began. Later, after conducting a substantial part of the second half of the concert and attending to the guests in the Officers' Mess for an hour or so, Margaret and I would make our way back to the house, where we would round off the evening by tackling the washing up. We did all this because we wanted to provide a standard of hospitality that mirrored the unique nature of the Royal Marines School of Music in the town of Deal.

Lt. Colonel Hoskins, 1982

Some of our guests expected more hospitality than others, and many worthies of the town who often featured on the guest list were under the impression that anything that was done for them was being paid for by the taxpayer. They felt that their position in the local community had earned them the right to be invited to each concert, and they took every advantage offered. It was difficult, and in a couple of cases impossible, to get our guests to appreciate that this hospitality was not met by any Service expense account, but that I was personally paying for everything.

We continued to entertain in this manner until changes in the running of the Officers' Mess made it possible for that venue to be used rather than our house for the pre-concert activities. Gradually, the hospitality for the concert evenings began and ended in the Mess, and this greatly relieved pressure on Margaret and me. We were almost back to the situation we had enjoyed during my tenure at Eastney Barracks. Fortnightly orchestral concerts at Deal once again became more than just vehicles for the training of embryo Bandmasters. They reclaimed a role as the hub of happy social occasions for the many local supporters of the Royal Marines School of Music, with both Sergeants' and Officers' Messes fully involved.

The exam invigilators

Having arrived in Deal, I knew that one of my first important duties would be to oversee the annual Bandmaster's examination. Students would have spent the previous twelve months in the Theory Rooms in the company of the Professor of Theory and his assistant, a serving Bandmaster with considerable experience as a teacher. Having been Director of

Music Training some years before, I knew that the annual examination papers, always set and marked by the Royal Academy of Music, would have been forwarded to the School of Music and locked in a safe within the Commandant's office to await the examination day. To ensure fairness, the Royal Academy required packets containing the examination papers to be unsealed in the examination room immediately before the examination commenced. Just prior to that day I went to see the Commandant for him to confirm that the examination papers were in his possession.

The officer acting as the Commandant at that time was a Captain Royal Marines with an acting rank of Major who, for this duty, was wearing the insignia of a Lieutenant Colonel! He had no knowledge of any examination papers and there were none in his safe. I saw I huge problem looming, for specially prepared sets of examination papers from a professional body such as the Royal Academy of Music are not easily replaced. I spoke to the Chief Instructor Bandmaster to ascertain whether papers had been requested from the Academy. I needed to know this before contacting the RAM in London to notify them that the papers had not arrived.

He told me that they had in fact reached the School some days before and that they had been sent across to his Theory Room, where the students were studying. I was concerned that this compromised the in-built security of the Commandant's safe, but was relieved that I had been able to locate these important documents. I ordered the Bandmaster to bring them immediately to my office. When he arrived, he looked extremely flustered and uncomfortable, and on taking a large brown envelope from him, I knew why. The package had been opened and re-sealed.

The papers had been in the Theory Room for some days and although the Bandmaster said they had merely been opened to check the contents, I could not be sure that the examination for that year had not been compromised. I reserved judgement and sent for the current Director of Music Training, whose responsibility it was to secure the examination papers. He explained that he had spent almost all of his time with the junior musicians under training at the School and had left the administration of the Bandmaster's Course to the Theory Room staff. He had not even checked whether the papers had been requested from the Royal Academy, let alone whether they had arrived.

My immediate reaction was to contact the Royal Academy to request a new set of examination papers. Not surprisingly, a new set could not be made available in time and in any event I then realised that no money would be made available to pay for any new papers. We were, at that time, in the middle of a defence spending moratorium where even pencils for junior students were being halved in order that they went round to all! The theoretical examination for Bandmaster had to go ahead with the students using the only set of papers we possessed, and so it did.

The Chief Instructor Bandmaster was relieved of his duties and moved elsewhere, whilst the Director of Music Training was left in no uncertain mind as to what I thought of his failure to oversee the vital task of invigilating all aspects of such an important examination. It was a dismal start to my role as

Principal Director of Music, and further up-hill struggles were in the offing.

The Music Professors

Since Vivian Dunn introduced the concept of employing civilian music tutors in the 1950s, they have been a constant asset. Originally they were contracted on an hourly basis and received no pay for leave periods when students were elsewhere. As competent instrumentalists, they were recruited from professional orchestras, etc., usually at a time in their careers when constant travel to and from engagements was becoming tedious. The idea of taking a teaching job on the coast of Kent, where student numbers were guaranteed, must have been an attractive proposition. The initial draw back was, however, poor financial remuneration.

Eventually, changes were made to recruitment policy and music tutors, by now colloquially known as *Professors*, became civil servants with proper status, pay and conditions that raised their standing considerably. The change meant, however, that recruitment was no longer a matter of locally replacing one-for-one as required. Civil service rules required professional vacancies to be advertised nationally and proper selection procedures gone through before a replacement Professor could be employed.

A Professor of clarinet left unexpectedly, and I was informed that it would take some time for the recruitment procedure to take effect. I was told that a temporary replacement could be brought in for this interim period, and fortunately a former Band Officer, Lieutenant Tom Merrett, newly retired from the

Band Service and now a local peripatetic teacher of clarinet, was happy to step into the breach. This was a satisfactory arrangement and the situation pertained for some months. Inevitably, however, civil service rules had to be observed, so eventually the vacancy was advertised nationally.

Tom Merrett was advised to apply for continuation in his position and he did so but, at the eventual interview, he was not chosen from the short-listed candidates. Instead, a man who had been principal clarinet player of Manchester's Halle Orchestra was selected. The Board that made the decision consisted of a Board Chairman, who was a high-ranking civil servant from London, me as Director of Music Training and another Royal Marines Band officer.

It was my unenviable task at the end of the day to inform Tom Merrett that he had not been successful. It was an unwelcome slap in the face for him and he was not a happy man. For me, it was a reminder of the fact that decisions by Selection Boards must be determined on the day, when the candidates are interviewed one after another. The best candidate is usually well ahead in everybody's judgement. Such was the case in this instance.

A Selection Board made a similar decision some years later when a replacement as Professor of String Bass was required. Among the shortlisted candidates was a Scottish lady. The Chairman quickly ascertained that she was pregnant (which is not a relevant issue today) and that her main interest in the job was that she wanted to get as far away as possible from her estranged husband in Scotland - and Deal qualified admirably.

One of the candidates that day arrived at the barracks with his Double Bass poking through the top of a small French car. When bidden, he appeared before the Selection Board and was asked to temporarily place his String Bass on the floor while he sat in front of us to answer the various questions we had compiled. He was very flustered throughout and seemed very ill-at-ease. Answering questions was definitely not his forte! Eventually, and before the time when we were going to invite him to do so, he pointed to his instrument lying on the floor and asked: "Do you mind if I play that thing!" He then perched on a bass player's tall stool, cuddled his instrument to his body and, now comfortably at home, freely answered any and all questions that followed.

To the Board, this man was only at ease and confident when coupled with his String Bass. His selection looked like a foregone conclusion from that moment on, and it was with great joy that when invited to demonstrate his technique on his instrument, we found that he really was a talented and highly accomplished professional musician. Ron Peters went on to become a most respected Professor at the School of Music where his teaching skills and musical prowess produced remarkable student results over many years.

On manoeuvres

One of the most senior Royal Marines officers I engaged with during my time in Deal was Julian Thompson, now a renowned military historian. As a Brigadier, he had led 3 Commando Brigade in the 1982 Falkland Islands Campaign. He was subsequently promoted to Major General and given command of all Royal Marines Training. This duty brought him to Deal on several occasions, where he showed great interest in the activities of the Royal Marines School of Music. I walked around with him during one of his periodic inspections of the facility, going from classroom to classroom, witnessing the young players of the varied instruments as they struggled with their scales and arpeggios.

Eventually, we got as far as the boatyard just inside the barrack wall, where a line of sailing dinghies greeted his eyes. They were looking 'well used' and forlorn all except for one. This was a ten-foot-long white Mirror Dinghy. It was mine, and I had spent most of my summer leave period that year painting and varnishing it. I was very proud of my boat as it stood out pristinely in the line, but the General had no idea that I owned it. He went inside the boatshed where there was a man mending a large hole in the bottom of a boat, like mine, that was upside down on a pair of trestles. "What sort of boat is that?" said the General. "A Mirror Dinghy" was the reply. "Oh!" said the General: "They are alright until you are about fourteen, but after that anyone in one looks like a gorilla in a hat-box!" After he had gone, I painted my cap size, *6 & 7/8,* on the front of my boat - and that was its name from that day onward.

About every ten years an exercise is held to test the country's readiness for a possible war scenario. All reserve forces as well as UK-based units are tested in realistic conditions. The bands of the Royal Marines all have secondary military roles and spend time each year training for them. In my time, each band had a designated geographical area to which they would be sent in the event of a threat to national security.

On one of the occasions when the country's readiness was being tested, it was decided that I should accompany General Julian Thompson as he toured the country visiting all Royal Marines personnel deployed. I was to be with him for his visits to installations in Wales and Scotland, where my bands were placed. My orders were to report to the Royal Marines Commando Establishment at Bickleigh in Devon. This I did and was then told that the General would arrive by helicopter at 9am the following morning. Dressed in unfamiliar camouflaged combat kit and carrying my overnight things in a small canvas grip, I waited for the helicopter to land on the parade ground.

The General smiled a welcome and told me to get aboard and secure myself in a seat behind the pilot, whom I noted was a Royal Marines Sergeant. The aircraft, a Lynx, then took off heading for a secret destination on the north coast of Wales where the first of my bands was deployed. I was impressed by the helicopter's array of instruments both for flight and warfare, which were spread out before the pilot and his navigator who was sitting alongside. I was then slightly less impressed as we seemed to need to follow the A38 road to Exeter, before turning left looking for Wales! The flight was very smooth and untroubled. We reached our destination and spent some hours on the ground with the musicians as they fulfilled their war roles with determination and considerable panache. Once again it was demonstrated that when members of the Band Service are given essential non-musical tasks, they will intelligently apply their skills and carry them out.

After a most interesting period at this location we reboarded our helicopter and took off to travel north. Our eventual destination was in Scotland, and arrangements had been made for an overnight stop en-route. Deep in some distant countryside, we landed in a remote field alongside a small road, whereupon the General, his Staff Officer and I hopped out. We headed towards the gate of the field where, to my great surprise, the General's staff car and driver were waiting to transport us to a delightful country inn nearby, where we just happened to be booked in for the night. At dinner that evening before a roaring log-fire, my thoughts were for the men on the top of that mountain in Wales acting out their war role in the damp mists of that location.

The next day, the Admiral Commander in Chief joined us and boarded the helicopter in place of the Staff Officer. We then set off along the coastline towards Scotland. Unfortunately, the weather deteriorated badly and north of Prestwick the helicopter became totally fogbound. We were cocooned in 'cotton-wool' and flying blind by instruments only. There was imminent danger ahead, for we had to negotiate narrow passes in a mountainous area. We came to the end of a valley where the pilot knew he would have to climb to a higher altitude.

Being in the general area of Prestwick airport, where fixed wing aircraft were taking off and landing, our pilot sought clearance from ground control to fly at a higher altitude. He was told that with further deterioration in weather likely, he should turn back and land his helicopter at Prestwick. He was given the appropriate heading to follow and was talked through the air for about half an hour with no visual contact with the ground at all. Eventually he was advised to reduce altitude and, when he did so, we found ourselves right above the apron of the airport terminal building. Brilliant!

With weather abated, we eventually took off again and flew to a Royal Naval facility north of Glasgow, where 45 Commando was guarding a nuclear submarine base. Here again, we saw intense professionalism as the marines went about their tasks. The General and I were taken to a jetty at the head of Loch Long, where two small inflatable rigid-raider craft were waiting. The General leapt into the first and immediately took over the controls. He told me to travel in the second boat, which was to follow him. A Royal Marines Corporal stood at the central control position and once I was on board he insisted that I take over from him. He started the engine, thrust the gear lever right forward and we were away at high speed in the wake of the General.

It was enormous fun but, as we headed out into the loch, increasing mist and drizzle turned my spectacle lenses into grey discs, through which I could see virtually nothing beyond the area just in front of the bow. I realised that all I needed to do was follow the wake produced by the now-unseen boat ahead of us to safely arrive at the agreed destination a mile or so down the length of the Loch. I thought that if the General was prepared to go fast in these conditions, then I must at least attempt to emulate him. I held rigidly to any alterations to his course that his wake showed. Suddenly, the General's wake began to veer all over the place so, thinking that he must have been avoiding some driftwood or something equally dangerous, I did the same. At speed, we bounded around like a mad thing.

Later, I asked what the General had been so anxious to avoid halfway down the Loch. He replied that he had not been trying to avoid anything, but the boat had run low on fuel and he had to change the supply tanks whilst under way. This switching manoeuvre, whilst quickly achieved, had caused the boat to suddenly slew about. I had motored through this patch of water at speed while attempting to hold to the course he had taken. Greater experience might have made me less adventurous, but I was following my leader like never before!

The next phase of the trip entailed being transported up into the Scottish glens by Chinook helicopter. These huge machines fly at an angle with the front higher than the back. Some minutes into the flight, the pilot hovered over some rough ground that, from where I sat, seemed well covered with Scottish heather. The order was given for the General's party to disembark, so together with a couple of other officers, I jumped out of the doorway only to disappear up to my chest in thick, wet and prickly scrub. The Chinook flew off and I was left to pretend that I had done all of this before and was perfectly at home in such conditions. Struggling to find a way through the boggy terrain, and never even having fired a rifle before, I had never ever felt more inadequate or out of place.

The Edinburgh Military Tattoo and the Mountbatten Festivals of Music

The Band of the Royal Marines School of Music was not only a vehicle upon which to train Bandmasters and Directors of Music. It was also required to maintain an engagement diary for performances at venues throughout the country. Band engagements fell into four categories of precedence. *Category I* engagements were for royal occasions involving major ceremonial events and this category also covered normal barrack duties. *Category II* engagements covered performances where Ships or Establishments didn't have a band of their own to call upon. *Category III* engagements were those where Service charities would be the beneficiaries, while *Category IV* engagements were those involving non-military organisations, where fees and other charges were levied.

The band from Deal was often required to take the lead at significant events in support of the Royal Navy and the Royal Marines. In the first year of my appointment as PDM, I found myself the organising Director of Music for the 1982 Edinburgh Military Tattoo. The event was produced by Lt. Colonel Leslie Dow, whom I had known from my days as Director of the Flag Officer Scotland and Northern Ireland Band. He allowed me full rein and my musical ideas were quickly incorporated into his plans for the year. I enjoyed it all immensely. There were no rolling oranges or frothy trails on the esplanade that year, so I must have done something right!

The tradition of giving an annual concert by the Massed Bands of the Royal Marines at London's Royal Albert Hall started in 1973. Established during the tenure of Lt. Colonel Paul Neville as a publicity vehicle for the Royal Navy and Royal Marines, the annual concert's main beneficiary was initially the Malcolm Sargent Cancer Fund for Children. Sir Malcolm Sargent, a renowned British conductor, had been in his lifetime the Honorary Advisor in Music to the Corps of Royal Marines. In 1980, after the assassination of Lord Mountbatten of Burma, the event became known as the *Mountbatten Festival of Music* with a broad range of Service charities sharing the profits with the Sir Malcom Sargent Cancer Fund for Children, and began to be held on two consecutive nights.

In such a vast venue with seating for over five thousand spectators, it was possible to combine at least three large Royal Marines Bands on stage for a really impressive performance. This also enabled the individual Directors of Music of each band to share conducting duties.

Rehearsals were held at Deal, with the nominated bands arriving there on the Sunday prior to the concert. Rehearsals began on Monday morning and had to be completed by Tuesday lunchtime. Tuesday afternoon was taken up with administrative matters and the packing, etc., of all instruments and equipment ready for a move to London on Wednesday morning. A full rehearsal at the Royal Albert Hall would be held on the Wednesday afternoon, followed by the first public performance on Wednesday evening. For an event of this magnitude one would imagine that it would be proceeded by a longer rehearsal period, but each year we had to make do with just two days!

Several eminent BBC presenters were used over the years, including well-known personalities such as Richard Baker, Angela Rippon, Susannah Simons, Desmond Carrington and Kate Adie.

I was initially very impressed to find that copies of the souvenir programme of the concert that would be presented to those occupying the Royal Box each year were bound in tooled and gold-embossed leather covers. This arrangement suddenly ceased without explanation. I later learned that the person responsible for producing them was spending time at Her Majesty's Pleasure because he had also been making covers for fake passports!

Well before the concert, I would propose a programme of music that had interest and balance. Within it, there would be items selected because of historic or other significance for that year. I was then required to forward my programme suggestions to the office of the Commandant General in London, together with a tape recording of each piece. This was for assessment to be made (possibly by people with no musical or performing experience) about the suitability of the music I had chosen.

This event was one where the Corps invited those with influence, both politically and personally, to witness the best in military musical performance. It was an annual opportunity to showcase the musical expertise of Royal Marines musicians and to programme some innovative and adventurous music. I did not always have an entirely free hand and was sometimes a little economical with the truth when asked what my plans were! I never told lies, but I might sometimes have omitted certain details. This approach enabled me to get away with things that, had they been previously known about, would almost certainly have been vetoed by an over-sensitive Staff Officer with an eye to possible adverse publicity.

For the 1984 concert, I arranged for a compilation of music from the 1940s to be featured. It was the year of the 40th anniversary of D-Day, and tunes from the war period were appropriate. One of the bands on stage was from Plymouth, and I knew that one of its musicians was a very convincing 'Al Jolson.' The Commandant General happily accepted *Music from the 40s,* but he probably wouldn't have done so if he had known that the compilation was to end with a fully blacked-up 'Al

Jolson' coming to the apron of the stage to sing *Mammie!* to his mum, who was to be sitting in the second row of the stalls!

Although each week the BBC was then happily screening *The Black and White Minstrel Show,* political correctness was beginning to make its mark. There was absolutely no problem on the day regarding this item until the soloist, still blacked-up and with white-painted lips, left the Royal Albert Hall at the end of the concert to hail a taxi for his mum. Not such a good idea!

Another detail that I kept quiet about until it happened was when a spectacular arrangement of music from the London Stage entitled *The Magic of Andrew Lloyd Webber* was being played at the 1988 concerts. As the volume of music reduced to barely a whisper at the ending of *Cats,* and the hall was in almost total darkness, the figure of The Auctioneer, a character from *The Phantom of the Opera,* appeared at the top of the steps to the side of the auditorium.

Under a spotlight, he was in evening dress with top hat and Malacca cane. He appeared in white gloves and a black cape with scarlet lining thrown back over his shoulders. The cape had, unbeknownst to the audience, previously been the property of Sir Vivian Dunn, and it was now mine. "Lot six six six – What am I bid? ... A chandelier in pieces," he announced, as he descended the steps with a spotlight leading him onto the stage. The words were from the prologue of *The Phantom of the Opera.* He continued his short monologue before sweeping off-stage as the massed bands and Royal Albert Hall organ crashed out the huge descending chords of this exciting music. For the audience, it was an unexpected surprise and one of the highlights of the night. The man who had played this mesmerising (and unrehearsed) part so well in that vast arena was Bill Howie, the Regimental Sergeant Major from Deal.

How could I top that? I conducted the finale, Zehler's *Viscount Nelson*, which led into Albert Elms' *The Battle of Trafalgar*, with narration by BBC presenter Richard Baker. The climax, complete with pyrotechnics, was hailed by the *Blue Band*, the journal of the Royal Marines Band Service, as one of the most spectacular moments yet seen at any Royal Marines concert. Watch it on YouTube!

The Corps of Drummers and Buglers always came into its own during these concerts. It was their opportunity to shine like no others could; their stick-drill and ceremonial bearing has become the yardstick by which others throughout the world are judged. Great effort goes into making their routines both spectacular and slick. Today, they are in every way as professional as their musician colleagues and, as masters of their craft, deserve the high accolades they now regularly receive. Their technique, as demonstrated in David Cole's superb arrangement of *Riverdance,* performed at the Mountbatten Festival of Music concerts in 2009, was a revelation to all who witnessed it. The drummers managed to incorporate the original sound of Irish tambours with scintillating cross rhythms that have yet to be bettered by percussionists from the other Services.

During my six-and-a-half-year tenure as Principal Director of Music, I was able to increase the profile of the concert and thanks to public demand, by 1988 they were held on three consecutive days, broadcast by the BBC and recorded on LP and VHS video format for commercial sale.

Every year, EMI would produce a vinyl LP of the concert for the Royal Marines Association. I would visit the famous Abbey Road studios on the Monday immediately following the concert week, when the whole day would be spent analysing the tape recording of the show to determine what material could be included or would have to be omitted from the record.

Time was the operative factor, for in those days an LP could only play about twenty-five minutes of material on each side of the vinyl record. Somehow, a two-hour live concert of music had to be reduced to fit the available space, yet still be marketed as "Recorded 'live' at the Royal Albert Hall". It was not easy to achieve this. The original live recordings were made using EMI's 15 inches a second, reel-to-reel tape recorder, a machine which was state of the art for its time, as digital technologies were not yet in common use. Unwanted material was gradually deleted from the master tape by a sound engineer who as needed, expertly cut out sections of the tape with a razor blade.

Our sound engineer at EMI, Stuart Eltham, was also known to be *The Beatles'* producer George Martin's favourite engineer. Stuart was wonderfully talented and after a whole day of editing bits of tape, the finished product would be taken to the disc's master-cutter. He was the lynchpin at Abbey Road, for it was he and he alone who produced the metal master-discs from which all LPs would be made. His expertise concerning the technical side of record production was second to none, and he was one of the main reasons why the Abbey Road Studios had such a great reputation. If he was good enough for *The Beatles*, he was good enough for the Royal Marines!

Over the course of my career I was invited to record with my various bands, through EMI and other studios, some 23 LPs and compact discs. These recordings are listed in *Appendix II* and include a double album of Sousa marches, the original sheet music for which I was able to obtain from the US Marine Corps *President's Own* Band in Washington. This unique compilation of forty-three marches using the original scores, won critical acclaim. A leading international music magazine carried the following review:

This collection of marches is music that will stir the soul of any military man, veteran, or lover of the finest in marching band music. It is like a good book, at first reading it gets to you and you become a part of it as it becomes a part of you. On further readings you discover avenues untouched on the first reading. Likewise, on further playing of this recording you discover that the excellence of the band exceeds even that which you thought you heard before. The sounds of every instrument are identified as the work of artists, masters of their art coupled with the spirit of fighting men, the kind that have sacrificed for freedom through the ages. In pride and admiration these men are part of their music, bugle-clear trumpets, thunder-shaking trombones, baritone and bass sounds that literally shake your frame apart.

You can hear plainly the heart and soul of John Philip Sousa, who mastered his trade as a US Marine Bandmaster from 1880-1892, in music that has meaning in every bar, painted in master strokes to yield a sound picture relating to the title of each march. No military man will listen to such music without recalling in brilliant detail the events he experienced while serving his country. Underneath the entire performance is unmistakable leadership and direction that gives life, spirit and colour to the entire collection.

Twenty years after their initial release, a double CD of the original LP recordings became available for world-wide distribution under the EMI Classics label: *Gemini – The EMI Treasures.*

Horse Guards Parade and London Duties

For many years the three Services have been able to present outdoor musical ceremonies on Horse Guards Parade in London. This has allowed for greater use of the tiered seating erected for the annual Trooping of the Colour ceremony, which would have taken place the previous week. While the seating is still in position the Royal Navy, Royal Air Force and Army annually take it in turn to perform. When it is the Royal Navy's year, the Massed Bands of the Royal Marines carry out a *Beat Retreat* ceremony that often coincided with the actual birthday of Prince Philip, who had been appointed Captain General of the Royal Marines in June 1953. I was fortunate to be able to organise this ceremony on two occasions, in June 1985 and in June 1988.

Prince Philip always attended and took the salute from a central dais, near the archway leading onto Whitehall. Members of the Royal Family would watch from windows of the rooms above. The Queen and Prince Philip were usually driven the short distance from Buckingham Palace to Horse Guards Parade in a car for the *Beat Retreat* ceremony but in June 1988, to celebrate the 35th anniversary of Prince Philip's appointment as

Captain General, they chose to travel in an open carriage procession. On this special occasion, seven Royal Marines bands were on parade.

The large Corps of Drummers and Buglers is always given a central position for the *Beat Retreat* ceremony and for this occasion, inspired by the tune that 1984 Winter Olympic Ice-Skating Champions Jane Torvill and Christopher Dean had adopted, I also used the music of Ravel's *Bolero* to accompany the drummers' intricate display. In slow time, they marched out to the far reaches of the parade before returning to turn individually into position facing the front for their final *tour de force*. As the last chord in the music was reached, the last drummers slotted into place and the whole team was stretched across the width of the parade ground. All were at exactly the right distance from those alongside, although there had been no marks on the ground to guide each drummer into position. In triumph, the music of the bands and ceremonial drill movements of the drummers ended with a crashing chord at exactly the right moment.

It was a moment to savour, much like another occasion that occurred in 1986 during a Tri-Service early evening ceremony at the Royal Naval College in Greenwich. The Queen was taking the salute from the tiered steps between the chapel and the painted hall, while I conducted the musicians from a dais on the grassed area immediately in front of her. My band completed the marching and counter-marching part of the ceremony, halted and ceased playing in front of me. In the silence of that summer evening, as I raised my arms to begin the finale, I saw approaching from dead ahead the RAF's Red Arrows aerobatic team. I didn't even know that they were involved in the event, so it was more than a surprise to me when they appeared.

Flying low at high speed and trailing coloured smoke, they roared straight through my up-stretched arms, over the head of the Queen, to disappear into the distance. Thinking that the timing could not have been bettered, although in truth it was entirely coincidental and certainly nothing to do with me, I felt like turning round to the Queen and saying: "How about that, then?" Instead, in the silence, I used my baton to indicate the first beat of *The Day Thou Gavest, Lord, Is Ended*. This gentle hymn seemed singularly appropriate as a prelude to the traditional bugle-call of *Sunset* that followed. As one of many events held to commemorate the 40th anniversary of the ending of the Second World War this one was, for me, particularly memorable.

Over the years, it has been rare for Services other than the Army to carry out what are known collectively as *London Duties*. These largely ceremonial duties centre upon guarding Buckingham Palace, St. James's Palace and Windsor Castle. Mounting daily guard at these places has become part of the British 'scene' and attracts many thousands of foreign visitors each year. For various reasons, including the ever-increasing deployment of the British Army throughout the world, these duties are now shared with other Services personnel.

During my tenure, it was the turn of the Royal Marines and 42 Commando from Plymouth to carry out these duties. Together with the band of the Royal Marines School of Music, 42 Commando personnel paraded each day at Wellington Barracks, before marching across to the forecourt of

Buckingham Palace for the traditional *Guard Mounting* Ceremony. Having placed sentries there, the band would march down the Mall, turning left at Clarence House and proceeding to St. James's Palace to place sentries there as well. Meanwhile, an equivalent ceremony was taking place at Windsor Castle, where the Royal Marines Band of the Commander in Chief Fleet provided musical support.

Sir Robert's device

From time to time, a member of the Royal Family would contact me to ask if some of my musicians might perform at an event they were associated with, or to ask me to pass on their thanks to those that had performed, or to raise another matter. On one such occasion, I was unable to accommodate Prince Edward, who had hoped that my band could be with him in Dover when he made an official visit to the town.

Prince Philip once informed me that Sir Robert Mackworth-Young, a senior member of the Royal Staff at Windsor, had developed a piece of equipment that he wanted to donate to the Royal Marines. I met Sir Robert at his home in the grounds of Windsor Castle and learned that he had been involved with the development of radar during the Second World War and that he had continued his interest in electronic devices.

He showed me his latest invention, contained in a beautifully polished wooden box with inlaid brass handle and lock. The box carried an inscribed silver plate explaining that this device had been donated by Prince Philip to the Royal Marines School of Music. It was an electronic aid for musicians when tuning up before a concert!

Sir Robert's device could be calibrated to the frequency of any musical note. When a nearby instrument sounded that note, a dial would register if the note played was flat or sharp, and if so to what degree. It seemed a very useful item, and I accepted it with thanks.

On returning to Deal, I took the presentation box and contents to the Musical Instrument Store, where I hoped that it could be tested as to its usefulness. I went into some detail with the Officer in charge, particularly regarding what these tuning devices would cost when they became more widely available. When I mentioned the figure, the Officer smiled slightly before going to a cupboard and retrieving several electronic instruments. "These little things," he said, "are easily carried in a pocket, are manufactured by Casio and cost a fraction of the price you are suggesting for Sir Robert's device. They do the same thing as his, and we already have lots of them readily available."

Although I didn't know it at the time, electronic tuning devices had been around for many years. A former Royal Yacht musician later told me that, while serving on *Britannia* during the Queen's State Visit to Sweden in 1956, it had coincided with the visit of the BBC Symphony Orchestra to Stockholm and *Britannia's* band was invited to attend one of the orchestra's rehearsals and meet to its conductor, Sir Malcolm Sargent. After the band had been introduced, Sir Malcolm stepped onto the podium and pushed a hidden button which produced a loud concert *A*, to which his musicians tuned!

I didn't fancy another trip to Windsor for a potentially difficult discussion with Sir Robert, so I quietly arranged for his device, with its silver inscribed box, to be immediately displayed in the Band Section of the Royal Marines Corps Museum at Eastney Barracks.

Ewan Sale and Lympstone's new statue

The Commandant I first worked with as Principal Director of Music was David Watson. On his retirement from the Corps, he was succeeded at Deal by Ewan Sale, an officer of distinction who had also come to serve out his final years in the Corps. Having previously been a British Defence Attaché in Sri Lanka, Ewan's gentle, sensitive and thoroughly professional nature was ideal for one whose main task now was to represent the Royal Marines School of Music at the highest levels. This he did with grace and aplomb.

During the summer of 1986 a new bronze statue was commissioned for the Commando Training Centre at Lympstone in Devon to replace the existing figure of two bent arms with clenched fists - which had had few admirers and allegedly had always been mocked rather than appreciated. An appeal was sent to all Commando Units and to the Royal Marines School of Music at Deal requesting donations towards the newly commissioned work. It was a request that was not generally as well supported as perhaps the Corps had hoped for, as I was later told that one particular Commando Unit had donated an extremely modest sum. Ewan Sale and I were not to know this as we raised over £10,000 from the proceeds of special concerts and personal donations.

Most people remain blissfully unaware that the bronze statue of a Commando in full combat kit now erected outside the

Administration Block at Lympstone in Devon was largely paid for by the musicians, buglers, instructors and ancillary staff of the Royal Marines School of Music in Deal!

Commemorating lost comrades

A set of silver drums commemorates the 143 Royal Marines Bandsmen who lost their lives during the First World War. Their names are inscribed around the outside of the bass drum. The drums were paid for by voluntary subscriptions from all ranks of the Royal Naval School of Music and were dedicated at Eastney Barracks on 5th March 1921. They are now displayed in the Royal Marines Corps Museum.

On 1st June 1948 a set of 14 silver fanfare trumpets with banners was dedicated at Burford in Oxfordshire as the Royal Naval School of Music's memorial to those lost in World War II. From then on, an annual reunion of Band Service personnel was held on that date at the Royal Marines School of Music in Deal.

On 1st June each year wherever I was serving I made a point of holding a five-minute ceremony at midday, during which I reminded my musicians of the huge wartime losses sustained by their forebears. A fanfare was then sounded before the men were dismissed.

At Deal, I helped plan the reunion weekends and would conduct the full Royal Marines School of Music orchestra at the Memorial Service in the Barracks church. I incorporated the whole of the Saint-Saens *Organ Symphony* in one of these services, conducting the first half before it began, and the second half as an extended outgoing voluntary, during which I featured the 14 memorial silver trumpets. Normally, these trumpets were only used each year to sound the 1948 memorial fanfare *To Comrades Sleeping*, composed by Leon Young, who had been a *Hostilities Only* wartime Royal Naval School of Music musician.

Leon Young was an accomplished composer and arranger who in 1960, worked with composer Lionel Bart, noting down the melody lines for *Oliver* as Lionel sang them to him, because Lionel could neither read nor write music. The experience caused him to decline the offer to make the orchestral arrangements as well. Leon was also closely associated with the clarinettist Acker Bilk. Their hit single *Stranger on the Shore,* the tune that I, as Mr Utter Bilge, had so often lovingly played whilst Bandmaster onboard the Royal Yacht, remained in the charts for 58 consecutive weeks following its release in November 1961.

When Leon's fanfare was originally written, it was decreed that only Senior Non-Commissioned Officers of the Band Service should play the memorial silver trumpets and that whilst doing so, their caps and not their white ceremonial helmets should be worn. In time, the original trumpets became quite fragile and were passed to the Corps Museum to be displayed along with the 1914-1918 memorial silver drums. Later, each Royal Marines band was issued with their own modern set of fanfare trumpets and it was decided that it was no longer necessary to adhere to the outdated dress code. It was now possible for members of Royal Marines fanfare teams to wear ceremonial uniform and white helmets when sounding the trumpets.

Influenced by the many churches up and down the land that had managed to obtain decorative kneelers for their pews, Margaret and I launched a project to provide a set for the Royal Marines School of Music church of St. Michael & All Angels as personal memorials to lost comrades. Advertising in the *Blue Band* magazine, distributed throughout the world to former members of the Band Service, the idea bore fruit. In due course, well over a hundred individual kneelers were made and either sent or brought to Deal. My own mother made and presented ten.

The diversity of design shown throughout the range is remarkable. The only stipulation we gave concerned their size, because we wanted the set to have some uniformity. They became a colourful and welcome addition to the ambience of the church. When the School of Music was relocated to Portsmouth in the 1996 the kneelers were presented to St. Ann's Church in the Royal Naval Dockyard at Portsmouth, where their intricacy, individuality and colour is much admired and will remain a lasting tribute to the fallen.

Supporting the sea cadets

Having been a sea cadet myself as a youngster, I maintained an ongoing interest in the way the Sea Cadet Corps was run. Whilst Director of Music at Portsmouth, I had taken my band to Lincoln each year to give a public concert on behalf of that city's cadets. Always superbly organised by the unit's Commanding Officer, Lt. Commander Larry Pogson RNR, they would be attended by the Lord Mayor and other civic dignitaries. When I became Principal Director of Music, I was invited to become the President of the Lincoln Sea Cadet Corps - a position I proudly held for many years.

This link concentrated my mind as to how I could help the local Deal Royal Marine Cadets. The unit was well run by former Royal Marines who were able to maintain high standards of turnout and discipline. Like so many organisations what they needed most was cash! Over several years, Margaret and I made, designed and marketed Christmas cards with all proceeds going to the cadets. It was a task that kept us both very busy throughout several festive seasons.

Lt. Colonel Hoskins presenting a ceremonial sword to a Sea Cadet, 1990

The Milton Glee Club

The Milton Glee Club, a Portsmouth Choral Society, was for many years a part of my life as I first became involved with it in 1965 after my appointment as Bandmaster of the Royal Marines Band at Eastney Barracks. On many occasions throughout my career I appeared on concert platforms with the Glee Club, initially as an orchestral player and subsequently as the conductor. In 1982, the Club presented me with an engraved crystal bowl to mark my elevation to the role of Principal Director of Music Royal Marines. I became President of the Society in place of Lt. Colonel Paul Neville in 1984 and held that position until 2006, when I passed the Presidency to Lt. Colonel Chris Davis on his appointment as Principal Director of Music Royal Marines. Nearly sixty years of unbroken liaison between the Club and the Royal Marines was thus maintained. Being no longer President, I became a Patron and continued my personal involvement with the Club for a further decade.

Kingsdown

One day in 1985 Lt. Colonel David Storrie came to see me in my office to ask if I knew of anyone from my band who might rent his cottage in Kingsdown for a year or so. He was about to take up an appointment as a British Military Attaché in Barbados and the time for his departure to the West Indies was fast approaching. I was unable to find anyone and discussed his problem with Margaret later that day. We were still having considerable difficulties with our residence in the barracks, although I had never considered not *living over the shop*, so to speak. Margaret was, however, so unhappy in the circumstances we found ourselves that she had even applied for a job as Superintendent of a nearby British Legion housing complex, which carried with it a flat on site that we could use.

Later, clutching the letter informing her that she had not been successful, Margaret drove to nearby Kingsdown, where she intended to take a walk along the beach to reassess her options. There, she met Linda, David Storrie's wife, who was very distressed as, in only four days, she and her husband were to fly off to Barbados and they still had no one to rent the cottage in which they would be leaving a teenage son who was about to take his final school examinations. Margaret intimated that she and I would rent their cottage if they would like us to do so! Her offer was accepted, and we duly moved out of No. 1 Royal Buildings in the barracks to a new home at Kingsdown. My duties as Principal Director of Music were not compromised by my changed circumstances and, for many reasons, life became much better for us both.

GOLD ON BLUE

CHAPTER 13

THE TOUR OF NORTH AMERICA
1985

I had always wanted to take my band to tour North America, so in 1983 I approached the London agent of the American concert promoters Columbia Artists Festivals to ascertain whether they would be prepared to underwrite such a tour. After two years of negotiations, an agreement was reached for a tour to proceed.

Columbia Artists explained that if a tour was to go ahead, they would like my band to be combined with pipes and drums from a Scottish regiment, who were known to always be a big draw. Their stated preference was the Black Watch, who were exceptionally popular in America. Enquiries with Army authorities revealed that the Black Watch were not going to be available for the period specified, but that the Argyll & Sutherland Highlanders could be. This was an ideal solution as far as I was concerned, for the Royal Marines and the Argyll's have a strong historic link from a time when they served together during World War II.

As plans became firmer and the Army realised that the tour would go ahead, they wanted to send one of their Colonels to be in charge. I knew this would be problematic as, in my experience, when on tour boredom quickly sets in for those with little to do. Travelling many miles by road each day is not fun and I knew that if a senior officer came, he would have very little to do except occupy a seat on a coach. Our touring party only required one non-musical role, and for that I had nominated Captain Nigel Scott, Adjutant of the Argyll's. He was to be responsible for looking after the VIPs that would attend each show. Tall, slim and dressed in his kilted Argyll & Sutherland Highlander ceremonial uniform, he was ideal for such a task.

My views eventually prevailed, and it was accepted that I would be the overall Commander for the tour that would last for thirteen weeks. In this period we would travel 16000 miles, have only four clear days, and perform in 74 cities across the USA and Canada. We travelled around America in a roughly clockwise direction, eventually arriving back where we had started from. The schedule included performances in the states of New York, Pennsylvania, Ohio, Kentucky, Virginia, Georgia, Florida, Texas, New Mexico, Arizona, California, Oregon, Washington, Idaho, Colorado, Nebraska, Illinois, Michigan, Maine, Massachusetts and New Jersey.

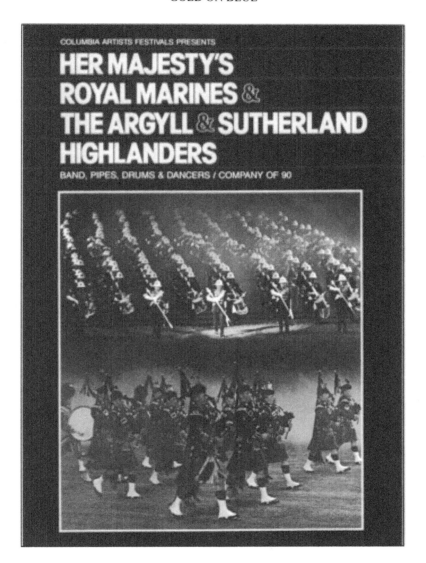

Publicity leaflet for the tour of North America and Canada, 1985

There were 86 people in the touring company. We travelled aboard two Greyhound touring coaches while an eighteen-wheeler pantechnicon carried our equipment. Columbia also provided us with drivers, a tour manager, an announcer and a stage manager. Each touring coach consumed one gallon of fuel every five miles. A full tank held 270 gallons, but the drivers still had to gauge progress carefully and take advantage of all the available fuelling points. Overall, this was a highly successful venture that grossed over $1,090,000 - a huge sum for its time.

Throughout the tour, the Royal Marines travelled in the first coach whilst the second accommodated the Argyll & Sutherland Highlanders and those Marines who needed to smoke. Most days I was struck by the continuing excellent behaviour of those in my coach. It seemed always quiet and peaceful and without the laughter and verbal obscenity often found among travelling Service personnel. There was a thoroughly professional attitude of commitment and acceptance that *what will be, will be,* for it was appreciated that every effort had been made to ensure our days ran smoothly and with minimum fuss.

Before leaving the UK, my band members were each provided with a new pair of grey shoes, three pale blue shirts, two pairs of grey trousers, a maroon blazer with gold wire RMSM badge on the pocket, a tie, travelling bag and suitcase. Our standard of dress ensured that we were treated with respect wherever we went. On our initial arrival in New York, we were greeted as if we were returning Olympic athletes!

It soon became clear that the wearing of clothing made only from man-made materials was perhaps not such a good idea when one is required spend long hours sitting on nylon covered coach seats. We all became intimately aware of the build-up of static electricity. Having been quizzed by the Lady Mayoress in one city regarding any difficulties the tour party was encountering, I explained our predicament. The following morning, she arrived at our hotel and presented me with 86 cans of anti-static aerosol spray, one for each member of the touring company! My problem then was explaining to the men how she could possibly have known what problems we were experiencing within our underwear!

The musical programme had been devised to show all aspects of playing ability with the accent always on entertainment. The Royal Marines and Argyll bands played individually and in combination, with pipers, drummers and dancers being used to great effect. Musical styles for all tastes were included and the presentation was arranged so that it could fit and be performed at any venue, from a theatre stage to an ice rink. The amount of travel between venues meant that very little rehearsal time in each city was available, yet each performance had to be exciting and polished. We were, after all, flying our country's flag throughout North America and Canada.

My assistant Director of Music for the tour was David Cole who later in his career would become Director of Music on board the Royal Yacht *Britannia* until it was decommissioned in December 1997. Following his eventual retirement from the Royal Marines Band Service, he has been the British Legion's much respected Director of Music, arranging the music for the spectacular Festivals of Remembrance at the Royal Albert Hall each November. For me, his musical arranging skills were invaluable and brought an exciting and unique sparkle to our shows. From arrangements of Andrew Lloyd Webber's music to inventive fanfares and themes from the silver screen, he did much to ensure our success wherever we performed.

Initial rehearsals for the show were carried out at Deal, where the final dress rehearsal performance was given in front of the people of the town, who came in large numbers to see it. Prior to crossing the Atlantic, my band and I performed in that year's Royal Tournament at Earls Court in London. This provided an opportunity for photographs to be taken for the tour's souvenir programme. As well as using the arena at Earls Court with dry-ice effects and vividly coloured lighting, we went before dawn to be photographed as a ceremonial band in the Mall, processing through Admiralty Arch. Personnel from both bands also posed for photographs at Greenwich Royal Naval College.

The souvenir programme was a sell-out item throughout the tour. EMI produced an LP of music from the show and the sale of these, together with the obligatory T-shirts and other memorabilia, added considerably to the tour's net profit.

To keep customs problems to a minimum, British Airways sent cargo containers to us at Deal so that, with a Customs Officer available to bond items as they were sealed, we could load everything directly at our band room. The next time we saw our instruments and equipment, they were on the floor of 20,000-seater Madison Square Garden arena in New York City. Once everything had been checked there, it was reloaded into the pantechnicon.

Army administration was not at its best prior to our leaving the UK, so by the time we left for America, not all the Argyll team had obtained the necessary visas to work in the USA. We had begun our tour light-handed but within a week, two more pipers with the correct documentation had joined us.

Our New York dress rehearsal took place on the flight deck of the *USS Intrepid* aircraft carrier. Co-incidentally, it was berthed at Pier 90, where *HMS Sheffield* had berthed in 1953 and from which I, as a member of its band, had enjoyed my first 'run-ashore' on that vast continent. For this rehearsal, we were joined by a small US Marine Corps Colour Guard team, such as would be present at most of the venues across America. They added greatly to each performance and made the *Colours* and *Sunset ceremonies* visually authentic for our audiences.

The accommodation provided for us throughout the thirteen weeks was generally of a high standard, but occasionally we were in areas where even the best hotel was a bit dodgy. In New York, where we were booked into the same hotel that many airline staff used, the raw side of America was quite noticeable.

With the dress rehearsal completed and local radio and TV stations informed of our itinerary, it was time to begin the tour. Bandmaster Trevor Attwood, together with Corporal Donald Campbell a piper from the Argyll's, would travel ten days ahead of the touring company, confirming the arrangements at each city and venue and making sure that we were expected. On our eventual arrival at each hotel, bedroom keys were in envelopes with our names on the front, any mail that had arrived was ready for distribution and any other messages were passed on.

Trevor Attwood and the piper kept the public aware of our approach by appearing in ceremonial uniform for TV interviews and school visits, whetting appetites for the colour and pageantry of what was to follow. They travelled alone, in a hire car, driving the whole 16000-mile route themselves. We did not see them from the moment they left Deal until we arrived three months later in New York City for our final shows.

In light of the vast distances we were to travel, I intended that each member of the tour party should have as much freedom outside of their performance times as possible and that petty regulations should be kept to a minimum. I made just one stipulation: Anyone late for anything, for any reason, was to be fined $1 per minute! Captain Scott of the Argyll's was seventeen minutes late on the very first morning. He was seen to pay up before he took his place, somewhat sheepishly, in the second coach.

Every two weeks, the tour manager went to a bank in the city we happened to be in and drew cash that was then paid to the individual performers. The agreed fortnightly payment that they received throughout the tour was $270 for officers, $226 for Senior NCO's and $188 for others. The performers didn't immediately receive all the money that was due to them because I was determined that at the end of the tour, everyone would receive the balance of their fee so that they had some money available to spend on presents for their families in the UK, should they wish to do so. There was therefore no need for anyone to save while travelling across the USA, they were free to spend such money as was in their pockets.

Each performance began with the reception of an invited VIP, who was greeted with an appropriate fanfare and musical salute before taking his seat. We had with us a specially constructed cabinet containing bottles of alcoholic drinks and glasses so that Captain Scott could offer appropriate refreshment in the VIP box during the show's intervals. Throughout the tour, however, all anyone seemed to want was Coca-Cola from the nearest vending machine, for which they happily proffered their own coins. We returned home with probably the most well-travelled unopened bottles of sherry, etc., since the voyages of Captain Cook!

From Colonial days, the Pipes and Drums of Scottish Regiments have been very popular in North America. Several times in the Deep South, among those queuing for tickets we saw people wearing outrageous combinations of kilts and sporrans. One chap appeared with a Scottish Dirk inside his right stocking and a fork down the left! Few had much idea of what truly constituted Highland Dress. Many seemed to have made theirs up as they went along. For a laugh, and to prove a point, one of the Argyll pipers, who was splendidly costumed in his authentic highland dress, stood in the foyer of the theatre prior to a show with his sporran slung crosswise over his shoulder with the hairy bit prominent against his chest. Within minutes, several of the arriving audience had theirs similarly positioned!

I was keen to ensure historical accuracy in our performances and to demonstrate the link between the Royal Marines and the Royal Navy. With this in mind, members of my fanfare team dressed in authentic sailor's rig from the days of sail and, at an appropriate time in the show, danced a hornpipe to a selection of British sea shanties. It was an appealing part of the entertainment, for they appeared in white cotton trousers, blue and white striped *Breton* shirts, neckerchiefs and round straw hats like those worn by British seafarers in the days of sail. We had obtained the hats from a UK fairground but had replaced their *Kiss Me Quick* hatbands with authentic *HMS Victory* cap tallies.

Whilst at Anaheim, near Los Angeles, the team visited Disneyland for a morning's fun. They appeared in the show arena that afternoon for their hornpipe dance wearing eye-patches, hooks on their arms and one or two even had stuffed parrots on their shoulders. These had been bought from a Disneyland shop, and their appearance added greatly to the show. After all, we were in America to entertain.

To ensure across-the-board entertainment for all age groups, band music, piping, sword dancing, and spectacular drumming routines as well as the hornpipe dancing were featured in the show. The ever-popular *Post Horn Galop* was an essential item and was performed, sometimes twice a day, by the same two soloists throughout the whole three months of the tour. They played together and developed remarkable personal techniques involving copycat phrases, in which they in turn attempted to out-do each other. One, Band Colour Sergeant Jon Yates, had the exceptional ability to keep a note sustained for very long periods without appearing to take a breath. It is a technique known as circular breathing, where muscles of the face are used to keep a mouthful of air passing into the instrument, whilst at the same time breathing in through the nose to keep the lungs inflated. It was very clever stuff and it left the audiences baffled!

Musically, the show was very diverse. The combined bands rendition of *Scotland the Brave* had the audiences stamping with delight. Band Colour Sergeant John Pring's playing of his electric violin, specially made for the show, was memorable. His performance of music from Andrew Lloyd Webber's *Song & Dance* whilst accompanied by the band was riveting.

Capitalising on our ability to use colour and movement, David Cole had made an arrangement of the music from the film *Chariots of Fire* that incorporated the Argyll & Sutherland Highlanders Pipes and Drums. It was made even more memorable on one evening when the UK and South African Olympic athlete and barefoot runner Zola Budd attended the show. Our arrangement of that film score must have brought her many memories of an illustrious sporting career. Unfortunately, we could not make any public reference to her attendance because of her nationality and possible trouble over the still simmering apartheid situation. Nelson Mandela would remain in prison in South Africa for another four years or so.

Many amongst our audiences were of an age that meant they had seen wartime combat. We were also aware that ex-patriots from the UK would make every effort to see the show as it went around America. They made their presence felt as soon as the songs of Vera Lynn began. *Land of Hope & Glory* was wildly applauded and gave us an indication of whereabouts the *ex-pats* contingent was seated.

Because of the constant interest in our tour shown by the United States Marine Corps and their provision of Colour Guard teams at each of the performances we gave in America, we always included *The US Marine Corps Hymn* within our programme. We also inserted local tunes known to be appropriate for the area we were in. The playing of *Dixie* in the Southern American states, for example, always brought about cheers and the vigorous waving of Confederate flags.

The tour begins

We received a standing ovation from a large audience at our first performance, which took place in an Ice Stadium at Hanover in New Hampshire. Moving on to Worcester, Massachusetts we unexpectedly found ourselves in the path of Hurricane *Gloria,* so the performance was cancelled. Returning to New York, prior to our appearance at the Nassau Veterans' Coliseum in Uniondale, we realised that we could not expect a warm welcome at every venue. We performed on a boarded ice-rink whilst outside, a full-scale IRA demonstration against us had been organised. It was contained by the police but worrying, nevertheless. We still managed to entertain 33,000 people over two performances in that city.

Inclement weather the following day forced the event organisers to move our show from the planned outdoor venue in Elkins, West Virginia, into a large gymnasium at the local university. Thousands of people turned up and we were late starting because of the numbers vying for seats. However, all who needed to got in eventually and they all enjoyed a spectacular show.

Our next performance, in Charleston, South Carolina was given on the large stage of an indoor theatre. This was the first such venue, though there were to be others, and we found that we were able to condense the show within the confined space and still carry out movements as planned. Later performances in theatres would see the pipers entering the auditorium through the audience from the back of the stalls to gain access to the stage.

The next day's journey took us to Knoxville, Tennessee where we were accommodated in a superb Hyatt Regency hotel with a huge open plan interior lobby and glass astro-lifts streaking between floors. No greater contrast could be imagined than this with our performance venue: the nearby car parking area of the 1982 World's Fair.

The salute for the show at the Arthur Ashe Centre in Richmond, Virginia was taken by a triple amputee US Marine Corps Vietnam veteran Lewis Burwell Puller Jr. His late father, United States Marine Corps Lieutenant General Lewis "Chesty" Puller, was the most decorated US Marine in American history, having served with distinction in both World War II and the Korean War.

No less than five US Marine Corps Generals attended the next show in Wilmington, Virginia together with over a thousand *rapid-reaction-force* US Marines. The senior General gave an impromptu speech honouring *The British* at the end of a memorable evening.

We had an audience of 12,000 in Raleigh, North Carolina and because we knew we were far enough south for the audience to appreciate it, we ended the show with *Dixie*. It brought rapturous applause. Hundreds of balloons were released, and I found a young boy close by me in the audience to help conduct *Auld Lang Syne* during the finale of the show.

Travelling south

Colonel Tom Seccombe, former Commanding Officer of 41 Commando Royal Marines, and his wife Jacqui, on holiday from UK attended the show in Atlanta, Georgia. They were welcome visitors, and I spent an enjoyable time in their company before they moved on to Florida for the next stage of their holiday.

As we travelled further south, I noticed that the cities were becoming bigger and more sprawling. Taking any exercise by walking around in any spare moment was difficult because there were so few sidewalk pavements, and the road intersections were so busy. We tried to arrive at the show venues as early as possible so that there was time for impromptu games of softball, etc., to take place in the arena. One musician had brought his weightlifting gear from the UK. We all thought he was mad at first, but later acknowledged that it was a good idea to bring the equipment after all – so long as he did all the necessary humping of the weights in and out of the side locker of the coach.

When we reached Jacksonville, Florida the Scottish dancers decided to give the first few rows of the audience more than they bargained for. At the front of the elevated stage, they performed a particularly vigorous sword dance. There was more hooting from the audience than from the dancers, for it may have been that it wasn't only their knees that were seen to be bobbing up and down. I guess the age-old question of what is worn under a kilt was well and truly answered that day.

Our contract with Columbia Artists allowed for dry-cleaning of our uniforms on three occasions during the tour, and the first of these was arranged for our stop in Fort Lauderdale. The dry cleaning was a disaster, as uniforms were returned with all sorts of damage to them. Hooks were ripped out, buttons were lost, and in my case, the silver globe of a collar badge was missing. An investigation by our embarrassed tour manager unearthed a catalogue of errors. Clearly, the wrong firm had been given the work and it had not expected to clean so many uniforms. The wrong vehicles had been sent to the hotel to collect everything, and dirty litter bins had been used to transport our soiled uniforms to another hotel to be cleaned.

Fortunately, I had a spare uniform with me, so I was not overly inconvenienced by the damage to my tunic, but I realised that we could not risk this sort of thing happening again. This was the only time during the tour that our uniforms were sent to be cleaned.

As the tour progressed, the audience in the front seats might well have been able to smell the musicians as well as hear them. The ceremonial uniforms were close-fitting and of winter weight. We perspired freely every day under the arena lighting and our clothing became unavoidably stained and smelly. After each performance, our uniforms would be packed away and were often still damp when they were required at the next venue. Florida in late September was hot, and we would continue to experience this heat for some weeks as we crossed

America to the West Coast before our itinerary took us northwards, where the weather became cooler and where we would eventually be glad of the warmth that our heavy uniforms gave.

Throughout the trip tour merchandise was sold in the shape of LP recordings of the show, T-shirts and souvenir programmes. Responsibility for these sales fell on the civilian members of the Columbia Artists team, and in particular the driver of the lead coach. He earned a decent commission for selling the merchandise and had fitted a lockable safe under the floor of the coach to keep the proceeds as they mounted up. Several of the performers, dressed in their uniforms and awaiting the start of each show, were only too glad to assist in selling the concession items in the foyers of venues in which we appeared. This was much appreciated and resulted in the Columbia Artists team arranging a hotel poolside party for them

Our venue in Clearwater, Florida was a small theatre, and when we arrived I had to hastily reorganise the show to enable it to fit. Our venue, in Pensacola, Florida - the Saenger Theatre - was also rather small. The entertainer Bing Crosby fell from its stage into the pit just before he died, and there is much speculation that this sad event contributed to his demise.

According to a newspaper report of the show in Pensacola, *Bagpipes are heathen instruments* and I, as the Tour Director, was quoted as having said so! I may have thought it, but not out loud, surely. I also learned that day that one of the Argyll pipers has lost hearing on the left side of his head. In the circumstances I suppose that this could be considered fortunate!

We were aware that a tour of this magnitude, often involving travel through areas far from towns or cities, meant that we would be wise to take some health precautions. Before we left the UK, one of my Band Sergeants volunteered for a course of instruction in advanced first aid and basic patient care, so that at least we had someone who could help if anyone became ill. He was called upon many times to assist with minor medical problems and was able to obtain professional help from military clinics whenever there was one in our vicinity.

His first patient was a piper who had contracted a mild venereal disease. Fortunately, we were close to a US Navy clinic that treated him immediately, so we were still able to get on the road again by 8am the following morning.

Travelling through Texas, one soldier started to complain of haemorrhoidal discomfort after all the coach travel but was advised that what he really needed was just a couple of bulldog clips!

I saw some large strangely shaped objects for sale in the foyer of the *Holiday Inn* at Tucumcari, the next stop on the tour. They turned out to be the scrotums of slaughtered bulls that had been cured and were being sold as indoor plant pots for people who didn't mind answering questions from visitors as to what they really were. I didn't bring any home!

Still in New Mexico, Albuquerque's *Regent Hotel* was very swish indeed. I was not at all surprised to learn that it was owned by the same hotel group that managed London's *Dorchester Hotel* and I appreciated, not for the first time, that throughout this tour the performers had been given the best possible accommodation. We had played in some small towns where there had been no good hotels, and we had to make do with whatever was available. Happily, these hotels were in the minority, and the *Regent's* experience put into perspective how generally fortunate we were.

Nearly halfway through the tour, we were booked into a Holiday Inn in El Paso, Texas and some brave souls went off to buy trinkets and Mexican hats at a nearby market before our performance in the Civic Centre Theatre. Inside the hotel, the Royal Marines Buglers' efforts to celebrate the 321st birthday of the Corps in style came to fruition with the presentation of a cake by the local Community Concert's Association.

The West Coast

In California, we stayed for five nights at a *Ramada Inn* near Disneyland while performing at arenas within a reasonable distance of the hotel. The venues included San Diego, Los Angeles and Pasadena, so there was still more than enough travel involved. At Pasadena, I was introduced to two elderly American sisters who proudly told me that two of their ancestors had been prominent musicians in UK Service bands. One had been in the Grenadier Guards and had risen through the ranks to become Director of Music of the Regimental Band. His son, thanks in part to a letter of recommendation from Sir Arthur Sullivan, was appointed Bandmaster of the Portsmouth Division Royal Marines Light Infantry Band in 1884 and remained in that post for 33 years.

I was given the latter's name as Major George Miller and was told that I couldn't possibly know of him. Actually, I did, and

I took John Trendell's excellent book *A Life on the Ocean Wave – The Royal Marines Band Story* from my suitcase to show an article on the man, with his photograph in full dress uniform as Director of Music of the old Royal Yacht *Victoria & Albert*. The sisters were thrilled and we struck up a lasting friendship. On my return to UK after the tour, I arranged for the sisters to bring memorabilia of both their forebears to England to be donated to their respective Regimental museums, where they were gratefully accepted for display.

I was delighted to learn that just two of the shows we had given in the vicinity of Disneyland and Hollywood had grossed the equivalent in US dollars of £92,000. The tour's financial news wasn't always good news, though. In San Francisco, our coach driver placed $15,000 from the sale of tour merchandise in a leather bag which he took to a restaurant, where it was stolen. The theft was reported to the local police and an investigation was carried out, but there was no conclusive result. This was $15,000 the performers would have ultimately shared with Columbia Artists, and it had gone. We were all devastated. The money should never have been in the custody of our already overworked coach driver.

Our performance venues over the next few days were at the Coliseum, in Oakland, and the University of California in the city of Davis. I managed to briefly take in some of the sights. In San Francisco, after dinner at Fisherman's Wharf with representatives of Columbia Artists who had flown from New York to see how we were fairing *on the road,* I was taken across the Golden Gate Bridge. Sadly, the experience was spoiled by a thick sea fog that regularly obscures even the uprights of the bridge. Below and in the distance, I could just make out the shape of Alcatraz Island with its infamous prison and realised that it must have been a shocking place in which to face a life sentence. I was also taken for the obligatory car ride up and down the steep roads in San Francisco's city centre. They really are as Hollywood films have portrayed them over the years, the streetcars still noisily jerk their way along with clanging bells to advertise their approach.

After a successful show at the Portland Coliseum in Oregon and a good night's sleep, we left early from our hotel to travel to Canada, to board a large ferry that would take us across to Victoria in British Columbia. The plan was that after the lengthy crossing we would book into our hotel and go immediately to the city's Victoria Arena for an evening performance.

We reached the Port Angeles terminal in time to have coffee before boarding the ferry and crossing the Strait of Juan de Fuca. Whilst we stretched our legs, the tour manager and our drivers went about the business of dealing with the Customs and Immigration officials. We were back on the coaches and waiting to proceed when two US Marshalls stepped into our lead coach and began to question our driver, who seemed unable to fully satisfy them and he became very flustered. They did no more than ask him to turn off the engine of the coach and to accompany them to their car. It later transpired that, amongst other things, they had not accepted his paperwork regarding the sums of money and tour merchandise he had said he was responsible for and that were on the coach. Without further warning, he was arrested and taken away.

We were in a coach with no driver, in an international ferry terminal lane, with vehicles behind waiting for us to move so that they could follow us onto the ship, and we had a deadline for a performance within hours in Victoria, a Canadian city still many sea and land miles away. It was not a pleasant position to be in.

At this point the Drum Major of the Argylls explained to the tour manager and I that, as he held a current UK PSV licence, he would drive the coach onto the ferry, which he did, thereby freeing up the traffic behind us. All we then had to do was await what we expected to be the speedy return of our driver from police custody. Unfortunately, when the time came for the ferry to sail, it did so with him still locked up ashore!

During the lengthy crossing, I tried to find out what had happened to our driver and what offence, if any, he was to be charged with. Without him, the touring schedule was going to be totally compromised. At sea and heading for Canada, I received a message explaining that the driver had been released from custody in the US and that he would join us in Canada as and when he could. Given the time-constrained circumstances, it was necessary for a light aircraft to be chartered to fly him from the USA to where we now were.

Berthing at Vancouver Island, the Argyll Drum Major drove us off the ferry to a point where we could await the arrival of the proper coach driver. Everything was fine until we got off of the ship, whereupon our relatively inexperienced driver carried out a manoeuvre in the confined space which caused the rear of the coach to collide with a pillar holding up the roof of the Arrivals Hall. It was decided that he had better turn the engine off and retire to his passenger seat. The look on our real driver's face when he eventually reached us and saw the scars on his coach had to be seen to be believed.

We now had to convince the Canadian authorities that we were who we said we were, and that there was no contraband hidden in the eighteen-wheeler pantechnicon. Time was ticking away; the start time of the evening's performance was fast approaching and we really could not afford further delay. Getting a piper to play loudly outside of the coach while waiting for the immigration check certainly helped to speed things up! We made it to the venue and the audience remained in blissful ignorance of what had transpired during our journey. The show must go on!

At the hotel in Vancouver, I learned that Her Majesty's Consul has been trying to reach me for advice regarding protocol for *salute taking* at the start of a performance we were to give in Seattle in the next few days. I was then informed that, together with David Cole and Captain Nigel Scott, I had been invited to dine immediately after the show with a party of Canadian officers and the Lieutenant Governor at the city Armoury. The invitation must have been made weeks before, but this was the first we knew of it. However, we went along, only to be horrified to discover that the venue was an Officers' Mess and that everyone else was in Mess Dress uniform whilst we were wearing our tour rig of blazer and flannels!

Our hotel in Walla-Walla in Washington State was the nicely appointed *Whitman Motor Inn*. In this small town our performance was given in the gymnasium of the local high school. A good dinner afterwards in the high school was arranged for the performers whilst officers are taken to the home of the Dean of the Faculty, where eighteen guests had assembled for a delightful supper party. During the evening I learned that the Dean planned to be in London in February of the following year, when I would be presenting a Massed Royal Marines Band concert at the Royal Albert Hall. He was delighted to accept my invitation that he and his wife should join me there as my guests.

The long journey east

Arriving in Boise, Idaho, we were promised a mail-drop, so were all very hopeful. Mail deliveries to us had been one of the poorer aspects of the organisation associated with this tour. Columbia Artists Festivals HQ in New York knew where we would be on any given day but mail for us, delivered to them in New York, was not given any priority. Mail *was* awaiting us when we reached our hotel but, it was weeks old. Many of us tried to telephone home but the call quality on the telephone lines was very poor and the attempts were largely fruitless. Our show that evening was given in the gymnasium of Boise State University for which event the wooden basketball flooring had been carefully overlaid! We had a small but very responsive audience on that occasion. I woke early next morning and made a further attempt to telephone home. This time I was successful and felt much more relaxed as I boarded the coach for a 375-mile journey that day to the city of Ogden in Utah.

On our arrival in Ogden we were very comfortably accommodated in the local *Hilton Hotel*. We gave our performance in a fully carpeted circular arena with *Bishop purple* seating all around. The City Mayor even appeared in a purple suit!

Our matinee performance in the Denver Coliseum clashed with a major football game that took place in the city. The football had an audience of 75,000. We didn't! I later learned that the tour organisers had even given away free tickets to increase the numbers attending. In America, one cannot be seen to be unsuccessful. Immediately the show finished we were taken 75 miles to Colorado Springs to give an evening performance on a theatre stage in the Pikes Peak Centre. Here, we were delighted to meet the eminent Australian horn player, Barry Tuckwell. He was also on tour for Columbia Artists but was travelling in the opposite direction to us.

Arriving in Iowa, I had a deputation from the Argyll & Sutherland Highlanders who asked when they were to be paid their *Local Overseas Allowance*. Not having studied Service rules governing such activities, they thought they were entitled, when away from the UK, to get the same sort of extra payments as soldiers serving their country in theatres of war. It took them some time to accept that their case was different and, as they were being paid for their services by Columbia Artists, as well as getting their normal salary, they could hardly expect the British Government to spread even more largesse. I also explained that the contract with Columbia Artists allowed the UK Government to take a considerable percentage of the income we were generating in America, and that this was a key reason we had been allowed to undertake the tour. When that had sunk in, I reminded them that on their return to the UK, they would need to declare for taxation purposes all that they had been paid, from whatever source, over the duration of the tour.

The Argyll's mood soon improved though, as on completion of our performance at Iowa State University, a reception was arranged by the local St. Andrews & Caledonian Societies. Tickets for drinks were distributed among the men and because we have not had much access to beer or spirits over recent weeks, I foresaw the event deteriorating as the evening progressed. I left at a reasonable time but was woken in my hotel at about 3am by a family of raucous Scots attempting to find their room. One of the Argyll pipers had relatives nearby and they had come, with friends, to the St. Andrews party. They had not arranged accommodation, so all headed for the Corporal's room and were still playing bagpipes there at 8.30am. Even with all this racket, seven other pipers were absent when the muster took place by the coaches at 9am. They each paid the usual fine before being allowed to board.

In my hotel room at Champaign, Illinois, I found a bottle of bourbon awaiting my arrival and learned that was it the gift of the parents-in-law of one of my musicians. They managed to catch a performance of the show whilst on holiday here. I was able to meet them and to pass something appropriate to them in gratitude for their thoughtful gesture.

During the interval of our next performance, I was visited in my dressing room by a huge policeman wearing a brown Stetson hat and with his body festooned in lethal hardware. I feared the worst, but quickly learned that in fact he was here with his family because he had won a local radio competition for which the prize, unknown to me, was this visit and the chance to speak with me and obtain my autograph. I did what I could to make him feel special. He didn't let on to me, but he may have been collecting the booby prize!

Another instant and unannounced reception was laid on for us after the Champaign Arena show. The party, attended by the great and the good of the city, was the nicest so far. I spent much of the time with a US Air force General, his wife and his Director of Music. We were given a set of USAF Band recordings that David Cole was able to distribute among my band members. Dizzie Gillespie performed as a guest artist on one of the discs, so I ensured that my Principal Trumpet player was given that one.

We had a large and very appreciative audience for our performance in the Rosemont Arena, Chicago: perhaps the most buoyant since the *Dixie* days in the Deep South. I was delighted, because the Guest of Honour was the British Consul General and it was obvious that he greatly enjoyed the show. I hoped he may include his appreciation in despatches sent back to London and this may persuade the authorities to allow similar tours to go ahead in future years.

Next morning I was up early and together with David Cole went for breakfast in a nearby café. It was David's 37th birthday, so we had a second cup of coffee to celebrate! Back at the hotel our departure was delayed. Two Senior Non-Commissioned Officers were absent and found to be still asleep in their shared room. They arrived dishevelled and harassed. The mandatory fines were awarded and they boarded the coach, to be greeted by a certain amount of slow hand-clapping. The senior of the two waved a pair of gold earrings taken from, or given by, a lady with whom he had spent most of the night. His compatriot, who normally shared the room, was late having made himself scarce during the action and he had consequently overslept once he had been able to get to his bed!

Our hotel in Detroit was the *Ponchartrain*, a very good one but, unfortunately for us, was undergoing major refurbishment. A bottle of white wine in an ice bucket had been placed in my room, courtesy of the management, which David Cole and I drank to celebrate his birthday. He was also presented with an iced chocolate cake in the arena that day during his part of the show. We had another IRA demonstration, but it didn't cause us real problems and was easily contained outside the building by the police.

The last stage performances of the tour took place at the Potter Centre in Jackson, Michigan. The theatre was excellent, but the people running the venue were unbelievably pompous. I was invited to the *President's Room* for a plastic beaker of neat whisky and met the President of the Jackson Community College, who was also trying to establish a cultural tour business. He hoped that the Royal Marines School of Music in Deal would be included on the list of possible places for his groups to visit. Nothing transpired from this.

Our next show was at the Richmond Coliseum in Ohio, another large and modern facility. Afterwards, I received another unscheduled call to dine, this time with the British Consul from Cleveland. The venue for the meal was the restaurant attached to the arena, so my acceptance caused me no difficulty. It was nice to relax and enjoy stimulating conversation before returning to my hotel for the night.

The performance in Port Huron, Ohio, was given in a very shabby ice-hockey stadium where the audience was disappointingly small, responding to our efforts with only muted enthusiasm. While it was always nice to have a supportive audience, I could never assume that the same show would be warmly received everywhere.

Ottowa and beyond

The next stage of our journey took us back to the Canadian border, where the immigration and customs officers were yet again very thorough before allowing us to proceed to Kitchener in Canada. Everyone had to leave their coach and queue in alphabetical order to have their passports checked. The driver of the eighteen-wheeler pantechnicon again had enormous problems explaining that it would be thoroughly impractical to unload for verification all the instruments, uniforms and band equipment that was contained in his vehicle. Eventually, after a certain amount of persuasion from the tour director, we were allowed to proceed.

At the Kitchener Memorial Auditorium Ice Rink we were greeted by an audience that made up in enthusiasm for its lack in numbers. Afterwards, we were treated to a very nice reception that was attended by the Mayor of the City, who presented plaques to both Royal Marine and Argyll contingents.

Next, it was on to Ottawa, where we were accommodated in the *Lord Elgin Hotel,* surely one of the world's finest hotels and certainly on a par with the best in London. Here we were treated as very welcome guests. It was for just the one night, but it was long enough for us to enjoy something quite out of the ordinary. Not only did the *Lord Elgin* have the most comfortable bed I had slept in on the tour, it was also the one I was able to lie in for the shortest time – just five and a half hours. Mr Sod has a law about such things, I believe.

This being the performance to which members of the British High Commission were invited, I was delighted when Major Ian Healy Royal Marines, an old friend and Military Attaché to the British High Commission, came to my dressing room to discuss protocol. The performance went well, with many autograph hunters besieging the performers at the end. So many, in fact, that our departure from the venue was considerably delayed. We then moved on to the Headquarters of the Governor General's Foot Guards, where Royal Marines personnel were entertained by the army band and the Argyll's by the Pipers of the Canadian Cameroons. This was an enjoyable though hurried occasion and one in which many friendships were renewed, for we had all been together two years before at the Edinburgh Castle Military Tattoo.

We continued to Lake Placid, New York State, in time for an afternoon's performance at the Olympic Centre. Lake Placid promised to be a winter wonderland, with snow scenes and mountainous terrain; it did not disappoint. We would then have a free evening before next day crossing back into Canada, heading for a venue in Montreal.

The delay at the border this time was because the Canadian immigration officials were concerned that we were British Servicemen performing for a civilian company. The officials asked for documentation that we simply didn't possess, and once again it was the pantechnicon driver who took the brunt of their concern because his vehicle contained such a vast amount of our kit and equipment. Eventually we were allowed through, but my chief concern was that we would have it all to face again the next day when we crossed back into North America - and that involved a different crossing point!

By the time we returned to New York State, members of the company had a number of health problems that affected the show. One of the hornpipe dancers had developed a very painful ankle and could not manage the 'hornpipe' dancing. Luckily, we had a substitute dancer. Another musician had developed an abscess under a tooth. A bugler had a painful inner ear, while Band Sergeant John Pring, our solo violinist, had slipped on the ice at the Lake Placid Olympic Centre and had cracked a couple of ribs! Musician Steve Kent stood-in for John Pring, performing the violin solo part of Andrew Lloyd-Webber's *Song & Dance* admirably. An amplified violin can sound remarkably effective with wind band accompaniment rather than an orchestra. So much depended on the excellence of David Cole's arrangement, of course, but the item was consistently popular with our audiences.

Normally, the soloist stood in full view in the arena and played a violin that had been fitted with a radio-mike. This is how Steve Kent began, but sadly he had to alter his playing position after his first performance because he dropped a packing case on his foot whilst loading the pantechnicon after that show and

326

couldn't get his shoe back on! Until the swelling on his foot subsided, he had to perform his solo from the side of the arena – in the case of ice rinks from the 'sin-bin'! This allowed the audience to see a musician under the spotlight smartly dressed in Royal Marines ceremonial tunic, etc. but they couldn't see that, actually, he was playing in his slippers!

After the show in Lake Placid, I was confronted by an American Army reservist officer who went to great trouble to tell me that our choice of music during the show had been far from satisfactory! He only enjoyed marches, and anything else was quite unacceptable. I was reminded of the words of Albert Einstein who is reported to have said: *"He who enjoys only the sound of martial music was given his great mind by mistake. His spinal column would have been amply sufficient!"* I think I further angered my antagonist by mistaking his wife for his mother-in-law! Oh dear!

A good deal of musical composition went on during the trip. David Cole was deep in the production of an arrangement of the music from *Cagney & Lacey* that would be performed by the massed Royal Marines Bands at the Royal Albert Hall the following year, while the members of the fanfare team composed individual fanfares that they rehearsed in the arenas before the public was admitted each day. They were learning from experience how difficult the writing of music can be and learnt quickly from their initial mistakes in harmony and structure. All credit to them, however, for attempting what they otherwise might never have done.

Trouble in Troy

Driving into the town of Troy in New York State brought a moment of humour. Before reaching the *Holiday Inn* where we were to stay, we passed through the main street. A large sign said we were in *Troy Town*. As if by design, a red open-topped escape ladder turntable fire appliance was parked in the sun outside the fire-station. It only needed Noddy in the front seat to complete the scene!

After booking into our hotel rooms we were off to the arena at the Rensselear Polytechnic ice stadium. We weren't made to feel very welcome and were advised that only half of the arena would be made available to us, with the other half curtained off. Then, we had to wait for an age before the ice was covered with wooden sheets to allow us to carry out a quick rehearsal. Finally, just before the commencement of the show and with the audience already in their seats, we were told that twenty-five IRA protesters who had been waving placards outside the main entrance had suddenly dispersed. At about the same time, a telephone call was received notifying the management that a bomb had been placed in the venue. The message was: *Eleven sticks of dynamite have been set and timed to explode at 9pm!*

No pre-searching of the arena had been carried out and, with hundreds of people, including many children, sitting awaiting the start of the performance, there was no alternative to an immediate cancellation. The police advised us that even if the show were to be postponed to allow for a thorough search, the venue would have to be cleared for at least an hour and a half. I then realised that the main stage doors at the rear opened directly onto the street and that there had been a delivery that day of a large consignment of brochures, T-shirts, long-playing records and tapes from the headquarters of Columbia Artists Festivals in New York. Could a device have been planted within this consignment?

The police arrived in droves and took over my dressing room as their headquarters. After a good search, the building was cleared. Quickly and efficiently, the performers had changed back into civilian clothes, dismantled the show and were in their coaches ready to leave the arena some twenty minutes before the bomber's deadline - which eventually proved to be a hoax.

From then on, I insisted that all future venues were properly searched and secured before we arrived to give our performances. I was concerned that the security situation was likely to deteriorate in this part of America as the tour ground towards the final part of this continent-wide extravaganza.

Subsequent discussions in the coach amongst the tour management team concerned whether we were too hasty in deciding to cancel that show. No bomb had been found after all, and Columbia had lost a guaranteed $10,000 plus a percentage of profits. The reality of the situation was, of course, that there was no option but to cancel. Such is the business of responsibility! The newspapers carried reports of that evening's IRA activity, and we were pleased to note that the report of the bomb scare was both accurate and unbiased. But what could we do? Everyone understood that they just had to grit their teeth and get through the last twelve days of this tour as best they could.

As if this wasn't bad news enough, the large consignment of tour merchandise that had been delivered that day had been badly damaged, both in transit and as it was being searched by the police. The boxes had been broken open and their contents, containing the tour's souvenir records, tapes, t-shirts etc., scattered in the backstage area of the auditorium. I saw no way of obtaining any compensation for the damage, but strangely, I appeared to be the only member of the management team who was upset at this.

Fortunately we had no security problems at our next venue in New Haven for support for the IRA thereabouts was silent and unseen. Police, with dogs, carried out searches of the venue to allow our performance to proceed. I did receive some good news - David Cole had completed his draft score of *Cagney & Lacey* music and had managed to get the individual parts transcribed. This allowed a partial run-through of the music to take place in the arena we were booked to play that day before the public was admitted. We now knew that the arrangement, once honed, would be immensely successful when featured on the stage of the Royal Albert Hall.

There really was no way of stopping David's tremendously effective expertise flowing endlessly onto the score paper that he managed to balance on his knees in the cramped conditions of his coach seat. No sooner had he finished *Cagney & Lacey*, he turned his hand to his next project – re-arranging his *Rocky* score, a version of which would be performed at the Mountbatten Festival of Music concerts at the Royal Albert Hall in 1999!

Health problems continued as the tour entered its final phase. The tour manager had a very bad cold that was developing into some form of laryngitis. Our coach driver was sneezing constantly, so obviously he had the bug as well. I kept my fingers crossed as I enjoyed a newly found general fitness that came with my loss of weight. We still had to hide Steve Kent, our stand-in solo violinist, away at the side of the arena for each performance as his blackened toe still prevented him from wearing a shoe on his damaged foot. John Pring, our principal solo violinist, was now able to cough, which to me was good news as it meant that his ribs must be healing satisfactorily.

Kit and equipment were also beginning to show wear and tear. The plastic covers of some of the side drum shells had cracked badly through the icy conditions of transit in the unheated interior of the pantechnicon and would need to be replaced once we reached the UK. Fortunately, this was not generally noticeable.

In Boston, we encountered Irish-American protesters buying lots of tickets from the box office at full price, only to burn them outside the theatre in support of their IRA principles. What sort of reception could we expect from now on? Thankfully, this was an isolated incident, and I was delighted that at the next show, at the Cumberland Community Civic Centre in Portland, Maine, we received a standing ovation at its end.

Returning to Boston, another expected IRA demonstration failed to materialize into anything more than a few banner-waving protestors grouped around the main entrance to the venue. Inside, an audience of over six and a half thousand was rewarded with a super show at which the British Consul and his wife were guests of honour. After the performance they hosted a small party at their home for a selection of invited personalities from the tour party. During the evening I was introduced to an American Air Force General and his wife. Although medically unfit, he had been retained with the US Air Force because it was considered not appropriate for him to be discharged in the normal course. He had spent five years in captivity during the Vietnam War and these mental scars would remain with him for the rest of his life.

At our next venue, the Civic Centre in Providence, Rhode Island, local newspapers carried reports that IRA sympathisers again intended to disrupt our show, but everything went ahead unhindered. The ever-present threat of the tour being spoiled by such people wasn't easy to dismiss, however.

The performance in Landover, Maryland, was memorable as it was attended by many British Embassy staff, including Lt. Colonel Andrew Whitehead of the Royal Marines. The salute was taken by a senior USMC General who was Deputy Commandant to General Paul Kelly, Commandant of the US Marine Corps. After the show, Colonel Eugene Allan from *Pershing's Own* US Army Band, together with representatives of *The President's Own* US Marine Corps Band, met me in my dressing room, where I was able to discuss my plans to record the lexicon of Sousa marches for EMI. They were interested in this project and offered to help by providing my band with Sousa's original scores from their music library.

Before leaving Maryland, we were advised that many complimentary letters regarding our extensive tour had been received by the British Ambassador in Washington and that each letter had received a personal reply.

Whilst in Washington the performers received their final pay packet. This included the money that had been held back since the tour began as savings. The extra $220 each meant that everyone had money to spend on presents, etc., as they enjoyed a free day – only the fourth in the three months we had been travelling. Most people were able to save considerably from their weekly allowance anyway so were very happy to have this extra cash in hand. Mine went towards the purchase of a smart Pulsar dress watch that I had bought earlier in Ottawa.

Our next performance venue was at an ice stadium in the city of Hershey, Pennsylvania, for some years the largest unsupported structure in the world. I was surprised and delighted to find old friends waiting outside my dressing room that evening; Lt. Colonel John Rhine of the US Marine Corps and his wife Betty had travelled from their home to see the show. I last saw them in Scotland in 1970 when John was attached to RAF Edzell and I was directing the Flag Officer Scotland & Northern Ireland Band. It was a joyous reunion, made more significant by also meeting up with an American GI from World War II with whom Margaret and I had lunch in Dover in 1984. That lunch had followed a ceremony when a plaque to the memory of American military casualties was unveiled in Dover Town Hall. As a surviving veteran, this man had travelled all the way to Dover to be present at the ceremony and I had not thought to ever see him again after that day.

Advance news of the success of the show's format meant that we were increasingly being asked to incorporate local uniformed ensembles into our performances. It was difficult to do this without reducing the impact of our own show, which become slicker by the day throughout the tour. In Baltimore, we were asked to include forty local 'Bennie' Band members in our performance. I took one look at them in their colourful 'garb' and refused outright. But by way of a compromise, I agreed that they could parade in the arena before our performance began. By the time we started, the audience was in hysterics, and they found the contrast between the rank amateur and truly professional most revealing. We rose to the occasion with panache and delivered an excellent show that drew an enthusiastic response from the paying customers.

The enthusiastic response from the citizens of Baltimore might have been influenced by the unusual amount of civic pageantry that had greeted our arrival in the city earlier that day. The City Mayor had even proclaimed the date as *Her Majesty's Royal Marines and the Argyll and Sutherland Highlanders Day*! His solemn proclamation read:

Whereas, *the great military tradition of the United Kingdom has been unsurpassed throughout history and that tradition will be brought to our City this evening by Her Majesty's Royal Marines and the Argyll and Sutherland Highlanders; and*

Whereas, *the citizens of Baltimore will be treated to precision and pageantry, traditional Highland dances, the stirring skirl of the pipes, as the Band of Her Majesty's Royal Marines and Argyll and Sutherland Highlanders perform at Baltimore's Civic Centre; and*

Whereas, our nations share a special friendship and heritage, one which has enabled our nations to grow and prosper through the years and we are honoured and proud to welcome these distinguished members of Her Majesty's forces as they bring their extraordinary talent and great tradition to our city; and

Now, therefore, I, William Donald Shaefer, Mayor of the City of Baltimore, *do hereby proclaim December 13 1985 as **Her Majesty's Royal Marines and the Argyll and Sutherland Highlanders Day in Baltimore** and do urge all citizens to welcome these special ambassadors of good will.*

What else could happen on such an eventful tour? Or on a Friday 13th? Spookily, we were all awoken at 3am the following morning by the clamour of fire-bells ringing throughout our hotel. Joined by at least a hundred other people, we assembled in the lobby to await instructions, but no-one from the hotel's management team was on duty!

Fireman and police were quickly on the scene. They moved around with dedication but, seemingly, no co-ordinated purpose. No words of advice or explanation were offered to us as we stood forlornly draped in our blankets. Apart from the incessant fire-bells, there was no other indication that somewhere a fire may be raging.

We put our military training into effect and carried out a head count of tour personnel to ensure that we were all accounted for. Suddenly there was an enormous crash outside the main entrance. A man on the 11th floor had woken in panic to find he could not open his bedroom door. He had not noticed that the door still had the chain across it. In despair and to draw attention to his plight, he had thrown an armchair out of his window, leaving much glass and debris right outside the main entrance to the hotel.

Eventually, the fire-bell stopped ringing and an officer from the fire department thanked us all for our patience and told us that we could return to our rooms. It was a nasty experience, and I was glad that it was over without the loss of anything other than sleep.

After a lie in and an early lunch, we made our way to that afternoon's venue, the Spectrum Arena in Philadelphia, where we gave another performance that drew much support from a large and committed audience. It was a show that gave audiences a taste of the very best and the very worst types of military music. On our arrival, I was told that a large contingent of uniformed *Territorial* personnel had assembled with the intention of integrating themselves into our performance. I forbade them to appear in the arena with us but had no way of stopping them *strutting their stuff* before our advertised show was to officially start. They entered as a band dressed in some form of historic garb *playing* - I have used the term loosely - fifes and drums, etc. They were of almost unbearable ineptitude and, to make matters worse, they appeared alongside a local US Army Band.

The noise was just so awful that when the Royal Marines Fanfare Trumpeters announced the opening of the real show, it was like the first day of spring. Wild applause rather than bluebells followed, but the magnificent colour and spectacle nevertheless opened everyone's hearts to us. They probably didn't have a clue as to how far we had travelled to be with them, or how tired we surely must have been after so many weeks on the road. They was just delighted to see spirit and enthusiasm still uppermost in each performer.

Arriving back in New York, we went directly to Madison Square Garden where we had a show scheduled for 1.30pm. This was the penultimate show of the tour, and I had been eagerly awaiting the opportunity to perform to a capacity audience in that venue ever since we had unloaded our kit from the British Airways cargo crates on the Garden's arena floor, before the tour had begun.

However, I had an unwelcome surprise. I learned that no less than seven Colour Guard teams and marching troops from army regiments had assembled, all expecting to be included in our performance! To my great annoyance, their involvement had been agreed by Columbia Artists' management team. I foresaw major difficulties in altering the regular format of our show to accommodate them all, especially at this very late stage of the tour and, as I wrestled with this problem, I heard unusually brash music coming from the arena into which the public were already being admitted.

What was happening now? We had been *invaded* by militia men dressed in American Civil War uniforms fronted by another of the *Fife and Drum* outfits! They too had been given permission by Columbia Artists to enact a historical pageant, with lots of marching about and drill movements with old-fashioned rifles. To compound my frustration, I learned that the Army Brigadier who was to take the salute that day had asked for twelve free tickets for his entourage before he was prepared to do so!

Wherever we performed throughout North America, US Marine Colour Guard teams had supported us during the opening sequence of the show. After some tense discussions, I agreed with the Brigadier that his Army Colour Guard team could become part of the show's finale on this one occasion, and that this part of the performance would be dedicated to the victims and families of a recent US Army air-crash in Canada.

More intra-service politicking was to follow. It had also been proposed that personnel from the US Navy and New York's Merchant Marine Academy should have some ceremonial input at the Madison Square Garden performance, but common sense prevailed, and they eventually decided against the idea. It was, for me, a very difficult afternoon.

Appearing in Madison Square Garden should have been one of the highlights of the tour for all the performers, but in this magnificent arena the show was an anti-climax – which was caused by local interference, arrogance, amateur attitudes to soldiering, lack of concern for professional standards and a thirst for personal glory. Appearing in Madison Square Garden provided an opportunity for publicity that these American soldiers did not normally get. But, grafting themselves onto our show, and with such little notice, lowered the professional standards our audiences deserved - and it was very poor practice. However, Columbia Artists, for reasons of their own, had been prepared to go along with it all.

What else could go amiss that day? In those times, organised labour was a force to be reckoned with at Madison Square

Garden, and we encountered another unexpected problem as we attempted to break down the show after our performance.

Men of the Teamsters union had moved all our equipment boxes down to street level before we had a chance to pack them, and then demanded an extra payment to take them back to the Arena floor, which was a good number of floors above street level. Stalemate ensued until our intrepid tour manager, had a brainwave. He insisted that all our Service equipment was really the property of Her Majesty the Queen and therefore could only be handled by her uniformed service personnel. No additional payments to the Teamsters were made, but the performers did have to hump all the empty equipment boxes back up to the Arena floor themselves.

Emboldened with the success of this negotiating wheeze, the tour manager went even further with his new-found logic and later would tell anyone who would listen that any gaps in marching band formations (when men were unavoidably sick or merely absent) was deliberate and was the continuation of a British tradition of honouring the Regimental dead!

Our final performance was given the following day at the Meadowlands Arena in East Rutherford, New Jersey. To my delight, it was perhaps the best we had done. Total commitment from every performer gave an extra sparkle to what had always been a colourful and exciting show, and our standing ovation at the end was just what they deserved. Before that show commenced, I addressed everyone and explained how pleased Columbia Artists was at the unrivalled success of the tour and at the overall amount grossed. It was a remarkable achievement, for which much credit must be attributed to our advance team of Bandmaster Trevor Attwood and Corporal Donald Campbell, whose publicity campaign had been conducted in the best *Barnum and Bailey* tradition. They were waiting for us on our return to New York and looked surprisingly chipper after their self-drive 16,000-mile journey through North America and Canada.

After this final performance we spent two hours packing and labelling crates before loading them onto the pantechnicon for the last time and sending it off to JFK Airport.

My closing meeting with Columbia Artist's management team was held the following day to discuss what, if any, lessons could be learned from our experience. A key concern was that of delayed mail, for urgent items from UK and postmarked on receipt in New York had then taken a further three weeks to reach us. In those days, none of us had email accounts, we were totally dependent on letters and post cards from our loved ones to maintain our morale. A jacket, tailored in the UK especially for the tour was never forwarded to us on tour, despite it having arrived in Columbia's New York office. Somehow, however, all mail from that office that was addressed to Columbia's staff who were touring with us was always delivered to the recipient within twenty-four hours, no matter where we were on tour.

I also raised the matter of the stolen $15,000 – a proportion of which should have been shared with the performers - and was told that the tour's insurance policy did not cover such claims, so it would just be written off as an unfortunate experience. In my view, this was totally unacceptable - but there was nothing I could do about it.

We said our final farewells and I made my way to the airport for an overnight flight to Heathrow. What an experience! In thirteen weeks, the touring party had entertained many thousands of people and had given performances in seventy-four cities in North America and Canada. We had been threatened by some IRA sympathisers but, except for one cancelled performance, they had not managed to interfere with our touring schedule. 58 Royal Marines and 27 Argyll & Sutherland Highlanders had lived and worked together without a single punishable offence being recorded. The response to our reception in America was so positive that when we returned to UK, arrangements were quickly made for the Pipes and Drums of the Argyll & Sutherland Highlanders to join again with their Royal Marines musician colleagues at the Mountbatten Festival of Music concerts at the Royal Albert Hall in February 1986.

Tours like this leave so many wonderful memories. *Of such stuff, dreams are made on.* I'll continue to enjoy many of these dreams in what I hope will remain a long and peaceful retirement.

GOLD ON BLUE

CHAPTER 14

THE LAST LAP
1985-1989

In many ways, it was refreshing to return to my desk and deal with the running of a complex School of Music, rather than being constantly on the road, giving daily performances in different venues on the American continent each day. Although I had only been away for thirteen weeks, it did seem that an amazing amount of administrative detail had passed me by, with changes both inside and outside the barrack walls.

At home, Margaret had been advised by the owner that his own coastguard cottage, two along from the cottage we were renting from David Storrie during his absence in Barbados, was for sale. He had not yet advertised its availability but without hesitation Margaret asked if we could have the first refusal. Having experienced the peaceful tranquillity of Kingsdown, I was soon persuaded of the merit of staying there permanently now that an opportunity had presented itself. We were able to move into our new home with a minimum of delay to allow Donald Berryman, from whom we bought it, to move to Dover. Donald had been a Solicitor throughout his working life and was a partner in a firm based at Blackheath in London. He was totally steeped in the past and had hardly altered his cottage in all the years he had lived in it. Now, he needed a home that better suited his ailing health and had spotted an ideal property just a few miles away.

The cottage in Kingsdown had originally been built in the 1850s as part of a row of terraced cottages for the use of Royal Naval personnel who then formed the Coastguard. Donald had bought his cottage in the 1920s as a country retreat when the coastguard station closed and the buildings became surplus to Admiralty requirements. He had used it as a weekend pad to relieve the stress and strain of working in London. His only concession to modernity was to convert a downstairs room into a fully stocked private bar with oak panelling, bar stools and a foot-rail around the bar. His boast was that he could provide any drink asked for and brought friends from London at weekends to enjoy the ambience of this unique place.

The row of cottages was closed to residents during World War II because of its position adjacent to the beach and immediately opposite the coast of France. Our cottage, however, was used intermittently by Vice Admiral Sir Bertram Ramsay when he needed to take a short break from his war duties. As Commander in Chief, Dover, he was responsible for Operation Dynamo, the evacuation of the Allied soldiers at Dunkirk in late May and early June 1940 and Operation Neptune, planning and commanding the naval forces in the invasion of France in 1944. Ramsay maintained an ongoing wartime friendship with Donald Berryman.

A Tri-Service School of Music?

Back in my office, I learned of a proposal for a Tri-Service School of Music to be set up somewhere in the country where the three Services could centralise all musical instruction. Meetings at Kneller Hall in London came thick and fast as much opposition to the idea, particularly from those who would be directly affected, surfaced. Convinced that it would save money, the Government was keen to move ahead with an amalgamation of the existing Service music schools - but the more the idea was investigated, the more obvious it became that many hurdles would prove to be insurmountable.

The key problem was that the Army, Royal Air Force and Royal Marines had entirely different training templates that had evolved over the years to suit their individual Service requirements. If these individual requirements could not be consolidated into a single requirement, the prospects of realising any financial savings in terms of training costs would be non-existent.

The Army recruited soldiers who would be taught by their Regimental Bandmaster to play wind-band instruments. In time, some of the better players would be seconded to the Royal Military School of Music at Kneller Hall for extra tuition, and here they would become members of the Kneller Hall Band that was the vehicle on which Student Army Bandmasters and foreign and Commonwealth personnel were trained. In terms of training requirements for Bandmasters, as Army Bandmasters trained band instrumentalists within their regiments, they needed a three-year course of instruction at

Kneller Hall to ensure they were sufficiently competent teachers of all band instruments.

The Royal Marines recruited young musicians who would play in both band and orchestra, so each recruit was taught combinations of instruments that allowed for this. They were taught by civilian music tutors (*Professors*) at the Royal Marines School of Music. In terms of training requirements for Bandmasters, the course for Bandmaster in the Royal Marines lasted only one year and focused on enhancing their conducting, composition and orchestration skills.

The Royal Air Force recruited mainly adult musicians who had already graduated from civilian music colleges. Advanced musical tuition for their future Bandmasters and Directors of Music was carried out at RAF Uxbridge.

A further complication was deciding where, if there was to be one, a combined facility should be sited. The Army were totally against leaving Kneller Hall, with its proximity to London and all that the city offered, but that site was not large enough for a combined school. The Royal Air Force had no interest in moving from Uxbridge and could not see benefit to them of any meaningful association with the two other Services anyway. The idea of having a combined school at Deal, where there would have been ample space for any expansion needed, was an anathema to both the Army and the RAF. The Royal Marines, however, were quite happy to stay on the Kent coast for, with little outside the barrack walls to distract young trainee musicians, Deal was an ideal, but expensive, place for diligent instrumental study.

Was it possible to find a format that would suit all in any combined school that would result in financial savings for the Ministry of Defence?

A study group was set up to scrutinise and publish a comprehensive report on the proposal. It was led by Captain Jim Rider, a Royal Marines Director of Music who had valuable IT skills and an analytical brain. Jim was supplied with forward projections concerning the likely number of annual recruits that each of the Services needed and what particular instruments they would be required to play. He went at his task with great enthusiasm and commenced work on a curriculum where students attended instrumental classrooms that were delineated in a tabletop model of the school.

In his tabletop model, each recruit was represented by a coloured disc: red for the Army, blue for the RAF and green for the Royal Marines. Each training period in a day could be represented with the coloured discs placed within each of the classrooms that were set out in the tabletop model. This method enabled the study group to show where each student would be for each training period of the educational term.

I met the study group to see how things were progressing and was shown the representation of the first period of week one of the proposed new school's curriculum. I registered some surprise that only Army and RAF coloured discs were in the classrooms and there was no sign of the green of any Royal Marines. My attention was then drawn to an area to the side of the tabletop where all the green discs were lined up in three files. "That is Deal beach," I was told. "The Royal Marines students are carrying out a basic fitness run during this period!"

I was then shown the module for the Bandmasters' Course and found that only the Royal Marines and RAF students were present in the musical theory classroom. "Where are the Army students?" I asked. "They are elsewhere learning to play fanfare trumpets" was the reply. This was a necessary requirement for the Army trainee Bandmasters, as they would eventually have to teach these instruments to their regimental colleagues. What this really meant was that the training staff wouldn't be able to teach their class as a whole during this period because a third of the students would be missing.

These were just a couple of the programming difficulties that the study group highlighted if the three Services were to try to train together. The group's final report concluded that any change to current practice would ruin what for each Service was being done very successfully. As there would remain a divergence of students' ages, abilities and training requirements, it was easier to run separate Schools of Music.

Accordingly, the proposal to combine musical tuition at one venue for the three Services was shelved. I was left with no doubt, however, that the subject would return in the years to come.

This training stalemate didn't mean that the future of the Royal Marines School of Music in Deal was secure. Far from it.

Leaving Deal?

When I had marched into East Barracks as a Boy Musician I joined some 3,000 servicemen that were based in Deal, but the Royal Marines presence in the town began to wind down in the late 1970s and early 1980s. First, the Royal Marines Commandos moved their training operations to a bespoke training establishment in Lympstone, Devon in September 1977. Then, with the disbandment of 41 Commando Royal Marines in May 1981, just 300 Royal Marines Band Service personnel were left as the sole occupants of the entire Barracks complex.

By 1988 the Band Service requirement was to train between 55 and 90 Royal Marines musicians at the School of Music each year, but it was costing over £11.2 million a year to keep the Barracks complex open do this. Something needed to be done, at a time of huge pressure on public finances, to reduce the training costs. Accordingly, Lieutenant John Perkins was posted to Deal in the role of Supply Officer Music. Amongst his tasks was that of acting as the project officer to move the musicians under training from Deal to a new home in Portsmouth.

The decision that the School of Music would leave Deal was finally taken and an official announcement was planned for the autumn of 1989. It was a decision I had reluctantly supported as the broad economic case for leaving the town was overwhelming, even though the social impact of the loss to the townsfolk of Deal, and its impact on the local economy, had not been sympathetically considered. All the groundwork had been done. Everything was in place. Plans had been made for a new concert hall and a new swimming pool to be built on Whale Island in Portsmouth. That announcement, however, was derailed following a tragic event that occurred shortly after my retirement.

Westminster Abbey, 23 July 1986

In 1953 as a young musician I had marched in a Royal Marines band in the procession as the Queen was conveyed from Buckingham Palace to Westminster Abbey for her coronation. On a sunny day 33 years later, I was inside Westminster Abbey on another Royal occasion. It was the marriage of Prince Andrew and Sarah Ferguson, who would become Duchess of York during the ceremony. The event didn't pass without incident.

I was sitting in my office with David Cole two days before the wedding of Prince Andrew and Sara Ferguson when I received a telephone call from London. It was Prince Andrew who, knowing that my fourteen-piece fanfare team was going to be there, said that he wanted a bright new fanfare to greet his wife-to-be just as she arrived at the door of Westminster Abbey. Learning of this request David, my loyal assistant, put pen to score paper and composed one while I drank my coffee!

The next day at the rehearsal in London, my fanfare team was positioned above the Nave, facing the tomb of the Unknown Warrior and the open Abbey door. From a central position, in the only space available, I conducted the fanfare at the appropriate time. All went well. Next day, when we arrived at the Abbey for the actual wedding, I found that overnight a huge flower arrangement had been installed where I was to stand to conduct that completely blocked my view of the Abbey door. With the Abbey filling with guests, the flowers couldn't be moved. So, how was I to know when the bride was at the Abbey door?. With typical panache my principal trumpet player, Colour Sergeant Jon Yates, came to my rescue. He explained that with seven trumpet players inclining inwards on either side of the flower arrangement he, as one of them and nearest the centre, with an unimpeded view of the door, could indicate the start of the fanfare with the bell of his trumpet! And, having started the fanfare team, he would ensure that they all ended together.

His initiative solved the problem and the eventual performance was exemplary. The resulting BBC LP recording of the wedding ably demonstrates this fact. The person who wrote the sleeve notes explained that the fanfare had been conducted by Lt. Colonel Graham Hoskins. But it wasn't - I was in the crypt with my fingers crossed, watching the event on TV.

Late for a Sandringham date

Just about the most embarrassing thing that could have happened to me in my long career occurred at the end of the following week, when my band and I were to perform for Her Majesty the Queen Mother at the Sandringham Flower Show on 30th July 1986.

We left Deal at 4.30am that day, travelling by coach to Sandringham in north Norfolk, some 175 miles away. Driven, as always, by the owner of the coach firm, Bob Bailey, it should have been an early but otherwise normal day for us all. Without the benefit of Satnav, which was not widely used in coaches at that time, Bob relied on his instincts to drive to Norfolk. I dozed off en-route, knowing that there was nothing for me to do until we had arrived at Sandringham. A few hours later, I was woken by an animated conversation between Bob Bailey and one of the bandsmen, who had realised that Bob had taken a wrong turning at some point past Newmarket and was now miles off course and driving in the wrong direction, approaching the outskirts of Ipswich.

It was vital that we reached Sandringham by 10am in time to play the National Anthem to greet the Queen Mother when she first appeared at the show. With this in mind, it was decided that Bob should not try to retrace his steps, but rather to take a more cross-country route, thereby cutting out a lot of miles. Unfortunately, we came across many slow-moving farm vehicles that delayed our progress along increasingly narrow roads and it became obvious that we were going to be late arriving at Sandringham.

From at a BT telephone box in a small village in Suffolk, the Drum Major explained our predicament to the Royal staff at Sandringham. He was told that our arrival there in a big yellow coach, probably just as the Queen Mother was making her own entrance onto the grass, would be singularly inappropriate. Instead, we were to wait outside the gates of the Estate until she had entered the first pavilion to judge the exhibits.

This is what we did, and once it was possible to do so we drove inside the Estate, changed into our uniforms and carried out our pre-arranged entertaining programme of music. It was the first time in over a century that the playing of the National Anthem had not greeted a Royal visitor to this event, and the next day's national newspapers were not slow in saying so. The Daily Mail reported the incident with the eye-catching headline: *Sound of silence as band gets in a jam.*

Immediately on my return to Deal, and with humble duty, I sent a letter of abject apology to the Queen Mother. Her response was that she was sorry we had had such an early start to our day and that our journey to Sandringham had been so frustrating! To my great surprise, there was no hint of censure either then or later.

Australia & old comrades

In 1988, the Band of the Royal Marines School of Music performed at the Royal Easter Show at Sydney, Australia. This six-week long agricultural show was the largest in the southern hemisphere and was held each year at a venue adjacent to Sydney's Cricket Ground. David Cole, and I were invited by the show organisers to take our wives with us, which we did.

Sadly, the weather was abysmal throughout our time in Sydney and with performances every day at the showground, we had little time to see much other than the immediate confines of the city of Sydney. Even so, Margaret and I managed to visit Darling Harbour, and drove once to Bondi beach, which we were only able to view through the arcs of the windscreen wipers as we sat in our car avoiding the torrential rain.

I did manage one trip north of Sydney to visit an old Royal Naval School of Music colleague. Tom Shacklady had served in World War II before leaving the Band Service to become the Bandmaster of the Royal Papua New Guinea Constabulary Band from 1964 to 1980 with the rank of Superintendent. He is the composer of Papua New Guinea's national anthem, first heard when the country gained its independence from

Australia in September 1975. Towards the end of his time in New Guinea, he won a National Lottery prize which enabled him to move to Australia to live out his retirement in some comfort north of Sydney. He made David Cole and I, and our wives, very welcome when we went to visit him.

Another Band Service personality, familiar to many at the time, also lived in Sydney, although I saw little of him during my visit. Captain Tom Lambert had retired early from the Band Service to work in Australia. His initial plan was to take up a musical position with the Australian Navy, but instead he became an officer within the Australian Naval Careers Service. Maintaining his considerable ability as a cellist, he later became a much-travelled music teacher in Australia before being appointed Director of Music of the Police Band in Sydney. This was the position he held while we were at the Royal Easter Show, although it was ages before I realised that he was nearby. Amazingly, he and his band were also giving regular performances at the showground. I had been his Bandmaster at Eastney Barracks and on-board *Britannia* in the late 1960s, so it gave me great pleasure to invite Tom and his wife Margery to dine with Margaret and me in the showground restaurant before we left Australia to return to the UK.

Blue Sky Country

In 1988, during his year in office as Master of the Worshipful Company of Musicians, former Principal Director of Music Royal Marines Sir Vivian Dunn arranged for a competition to be held with a £1000 prize for the winner. Participants were required to write an original work in several movements for concert wind band. A similar competition had been held with considerable success in the early part of the 20th century. Entries were whittled down to five by a panel from the Worshipful Company, and these scores were then sent to me at Deal. Sir Vivian arrived a couple of days later to oversee my rehearsal of these works because he had arranged for me to take the Royal Marines School of Music Band to London to perform them at the final adjudication ceremony, at which the overall winner would be selected.

Sir Vivian, when in the Corps, had a reputation as an authoritarian, and he had not changed his ways in his retirement. There were difficult moments, both for me and for the musicians, as he behaved as he always had, and demanded rather than asked for things to go as he wished. Eventually, we went to London for the adjudication ceremony. The winner was Bram Wiggins whose composition, *Big Sky Country*, is evocative and stimulating. I was later able to give the work its UK premier at a Mountbatten Festival Concert in the Royal Albert Hall and for the composer to be present. Sadly, I have not seen the work programmed nor heard it played in its entirety since, but Bram did develop an international reputation as an author of instrument tuition books and as a composer of music for both brass and wind bands.

Final Mountbatten Festival Concerts

For my sixth and final series of Mountbatten Festival Concerts at the Royal Albert Hall, in 1989 I invited the Royal Netherlands Marine Band, De marinerskapel ser Koninklijke marine, to take part and we heard their superb arrangement of symphonic dances from *West Side Story*. The logistics were challenging. Could we arrange for them to have a grand piano on the stage for 26 bars of *West Side Story*? In the fullness of time, this little problem was resolved.   The Netherlands Marine Band much preferred to play alone on stage, although for these concerts they were massed with the Royal Marines. Their individual performances that we included in the programme were exhilarating.

Lt Colonel Hoskins 1989

At the end of the third concert, the compere Richard Baker surprised everyone by announcing that this was my final appearance with the massed bands and inviting me to say a few words to the audience. This was the first time that a Director of Music had been given the opportunity to address the audience in that vast auditorium, for the concerts always featured a professional announcer. I held my composure and found the words to thank everybody for making my career so memorable.

Handing over

Prior to his appointment, I had intimated to John Ware, Director of Music of the Plymouth Band, that he was being considered as the person to replace me. When this had been confirmed, and on his return from a sabbatical, we discussed what the future might hold. Our Service backgrounds had been very similar, so he needed little advice from me.

What a career I had enjoyed! Not bad for someone who had joined the Royal Marines at the age of fourteen and one week, having failed his eleven plus exam and without any academic qualifications to his name. My 6 ½ years as the professional head of the organisation had seen a reduction in the number of bands from eleven to seven. But I helped ensure that the Royal Marines retained large bands (staff bands were 70 strong and the standard bands 40 strong), making it certain that Royal Marines musicians would always produce a powerful sound on parade or as an orchestra. It was also still possible for smaller musical combinations from within bands to meet requests to perform for the Royal Navy at different locations and on different ships in harbour at the same time.

I had performed everywhere, from intimate gatherings of the Royal Family to very large audiences on occasions of national significance. I had directed two massed bands *Beat Retreat* ceremonies on Horse Guards Parade and six Mountbatten Festivals of Music. I had increased the profile of these festival concerts which, thanks to public demand, were now held on three successive days, broadcast by the BBC, with the concerts recorded by EMI for commercial sale.

As a Royal Marines musician, I had travelled widely with my bands: Europe, North America, South America, Asia, Australia, the length and breadth of the UK, and I had sailed the oceans of the world on *HMS Sheffield, HMS Hermes,* the *QE2* and the *Royal Yacht Britannia,* always upkeeping the highest standards and always looking for something new.

I offered John my best wishes as he completed his preparations for this most challenging of roles and assured him that I would not offer any criticism from the side-lines. I intended to maintain a dignified distance from the day-to-day life of the Band Service, once I had left it.

At my final dinner in the Officers' Mess at Deal, which was attended by most of my fellow Directors of Music, as well as a set of golf clubs, I was presented among other things with the clarinet that I had lost in Durnford Street Barracks in Plymouth in the 1950s. On its barrel, it bore the same serial number of the instrument I had been fined for losing. Now, it had miraculously been found and had been restored to a playing condition. I picked it up, joined the small jazz orchestra that had been playing that evening and we performed a few more *Extras* for the assembled diners. What an evening to remember!

Captain Ted Whealing presents a set of golf clubs on behalf of fellow Directors of Music, 1989

I gave my final orchestral concert in St Michael and All Angels Church in Deal on 2nd March 1989. Earlier that afternoon, members of my family, including my mother and two of my sisters and their husbands, had surprised me at my cottage in Kingsdown. Unbeknown to me, Margaret had arranged for them to travel from Hampshire and to be accommodated in the Officers Mess after the concert.

To have my mother present as I conducted for the final time was a very moving experience. She had seen my entire Royal Marines career unfold. She had been present in the Barracks gymnasium in 1952 when I had performed an extract from the Mozart Clarinet Concerto, the item with which I had won the *Cassell Prize* Bronze Medal; she had been present on board the Royal Yacht *Britannia* in 1981 when I had been surprised with the news that I had been selected to be the next Principal

Director of Music; and now, she was present as I conducted my last orchestral concert.

The following morning, it was time for the official handover to my successor and for me to make my final farewell address to the assembled musicians.

At 10.30 am on 3rd March 1989 the last of the *Burford Boys* was escorted out through the same gateway in East Barracks that he had entered as a Boy Musician in 1950, when the School of Music moved from Burford to Deal. The procession was led by the Junior Band of the Royal Marines while I was seated on a decorated handcart that was being towed by some of my musicians. Whoever organised this insisted that I carry a white painted broomstick as a music baton throughout. Disembarking just outside the East Barracks Main Gate, Margaret and I were taken by the Commandant's staff car to our home in nearby Kingsdown.

Then, I began to plan my retirement – something that up to this point I had not given much attention to!

CHAPTER 15

RETIREMENT & THE DEAL BOMBING
1989 -

I should have retired from the Corps in 1985 on attaining the age of fifty but, for reasons known only to those at the Department of the Commandant General who made the decision, I was asked to serve on past that milestone, and I eventually retired from my position as Principal Director of Music Royal Marines four years later. My career in the Band Service had lasted for one week short of forty years.

In Spring 1987, Ministry of Defence officials received intelligence that members of the Provisional IRA were planning an operation that potentially impacted servicemen in East Kent. Deal Barracks was not considered to be a sufficiently high-profile target, so no resources were made available to improve the existing perimeter security controls. Servicemen in units associated with soldiers of the Parachute

Regiment around East Kent were considered for more likely to be terrorist targets. The Commandant relayed the news of this threat to everyone in the establishment, and we then carried on as usual. Military uniforms were a familiar sight in Deal until the late 1970s when, for security reasons, the wearing of civilian clothes when out of barracks became the norm for Service personnel.

Perimeter security around the barrack blocks in Deal was best described as *slight*. Just as I and my fellow *Sheffield Five* conspirators had so easily managed to remove the *ceremonial gong* from its hook at the edge of the main parade at North Barracks, and bury it in the beach in 1955, any Deal-based Royal Marine might find some reason to pop over a barracks wall after lights out. Everyone knew how easy it was to leave the barracks at night, including the then Royal Marines School of Music Commanding Officer, Lt. Colonel Richard Dixon.

However, with persistent rumours of plans to close the Barrack blocks and to move the School of Music to another, as yet unannounced location, there was very little evidence to support the argument that it was necessary to spend public money on better physical security measures.

22ⁿᵈ September 1989

Just four months after I had left the Corps, IRA terrorists planted a 15lb (6.8kg) bomb in North Barracks. It detonated at 8.22am on 22nd September 1989, killing eleven young men with whom I had served. Many more were injured physically and emotionally. The atrocity's impact was felt right across the Corps.

At the time of the blast a group of trainee musicians were practicing their drill movements on an adjacent parade ground, just one hundred yards away. They were first on the scene to help move some of the injured to a safer place before the emergency services arrived. Some of these young men, just sixteen or seventeen years old, had joined the Band Service only a few weeks before and most were profoundly shocked at the carnage they had encountered.

Living by the sea some two miles from the site of the explosion, I had not actually heard it, although I was quickly made aware of it by people who had been nearer at the time. I immediately left to see if I could be of assistance in the barracks, but by the time I reached it, the area had been sealed off. Access to me was denied.

Wanting to be of help, I drove to the local married quarters area to offer any worried wives without transport lifts to the barracks. Being unable to find anyone who needed any help, I drove to the local hospital to see if I could be of assistance there. On arrival, I was shown into a room and spoke to some of the young musicians who had earlier witnessed the horrors of the incident. All were suffering from shock. Other musicians that had arrived at the hospital just wanted a cup of tea and a cigarette. I was eventually able to drive a few of them back to North Barracks.

This mission allowed me to pass through the security cordon around the area and, after ensuring that my passengers were safely back with their friends, I visited the incident room that had been set up in the Sergeants' Mess. There, I found a scene of total anguish. The upper floor had been set aside for the relatives of those known to have died, whilst the lower floor was designated for those who had were still awaiting news of the well-being or otherwise of their loved ones. The Commandant's wife, Tricia Dixon, took it upon herself to coordinate the civilian volunteers who had come to the barracks to offer whatever help they could. For this, she was eventually awarded an MBE.

All information about the event was very sensitively handled by the Royal Marines through a single point of contact. No information about a deceased musician was released until a Band Corporal they had worked with closely had visited the mortuary at Buckland Hospital in Dover to inspect their remains and confirm their identity. Some bodies were too badly injured to recognise. The devastation caused by the bomb meant that it was many hours before all those missing had been accounted for.

North Barracks, 22nd September 1989

The device had been placed in or behind a large settee which was set against the rear wall at the top of a tiered lecture theatre that doubled as a band changing room and refreshment area. It had been set off by a pressure trigger that was hidden under one of the settee's cushions. In the immediate vicinity were members of the Staff Band who were arriving for that day's musical activity. Most of the musicians were in the lowest part of the building, near the lectern. The blast blew out the breeze block walls causing the flat heavily reinforced concrete roof to collapse. There was no escape for those in the upper area. Some of the dead and injured were the other side of the rear wall of the lecture theatre, in an adjacent toilet area and office facility.

The passing hours brought news of further casualties. All were people whom I had known well. I couldn't have been the only person to have cried like a baby as the news sunk in that so many talented and remarkable young people had been murdered that day. Many had joined the Band Service because of a successful interview with me, sessions during which I had given my pledge to their parents that they would have a good life in the Corps and be able to enjoy many happy years of music-making. Now they were dead or grievously injured and I would meet these parents again to convey my condolences at this dreadful time.

A Royal Marines Officer was assigned to each of the grieving families. Although in retirement, I was asked to travel to Yorkshire two days after the bombing to visit the parents of one of those killed. Band Corporal Andy Cleatheroe had been a young handsome lad who excelled in playing violin and saxophone. Engaged to be married, he had featured as a soloist with the Massed Bands of the Royal Marines at the Royal Albert Hall and had occasionally led my orchestra. He was very popular with his colleagues and was known to go out of his way whenever there was to be a concert locally to collect an old lady from her home so that she could attend, after which he would return her home safely.

Another of those killed, Musician Mark Petch, a skilled flautist, lived with his family in the village of Kingsdown near my home. His father, a highly talented artist, later produced the artwork for Christmas cards, etc., raising funds for a planned memorial bandstand once it was up and running. It gave me great pleasure to donate one of his original oil paintings for display in the Royal Marines Association Club at Deal in recognition of the unstinting support of Club members for the memorial that now stands proudly on Walmer Green, opposite the Club.

The others that were killed in the explosion were Musician Michael Ball, Band Corporal Trevor Davis, Musician Richard Fice, Musician Richard Jones, Band Corporal David McMillan, Musician Chris Nolan, Musician Dean Pavey, Musician Tim Reeves and Musician Bob Simmonds.

Although awful, the carnage could have been much worse. Several members of the Staff Band had played as an orchestra at a dinner in the Officers' Mess the previous evening, so all members of the Staff Band had been ordered to report for duty at 9.00am on Friday morning, rather than 8.30am. Many were still making their way to North Barracks when the fatal incident occurred.

Precisely a week after the explosion, the entire complement of the Royal Marines School of Music, led by the Staff Band, marched through the crowded streets of Deal. The barracks tailors had worked hard to repair or replace the musicians' damaged ceremonial uniforms. Spaces were left where the eleven men of the band would normally have marched. The mood of the townsfolk was sombre but defiant. Among the crowd, paying his respects, was Falkland War veteran Simon Weston, the Welsh Guardsman who had suffered terrible burns injuries while serving on the *Sir Galahad* in 1982. His presence was greatly appreciated by all who saw him. The route into town for the band was along Canada Road and when they arrived at the site of the bombing they stopped for a moment and turned to face the rubble prior to paying their respects.

At the dais in front of Deal's historic Time Ball Tower, taking the salute was the Royal Marines Commandant General Sir Martin Garrod. Addressing those on parade, He made his contempt for the atrocity and those responsible for it very clear. Immediately after the incident, Sir Martin had appeared on television in uniform to condemn the perpetrators in an angry speech as: "Thugs, extortionists, torturers, murderers and cowards – the scum of the earth." He declared: "We will emerge stronger and more determined than ever before to end and destroy this foul and dark force of evil." Despite an intensive police investigation, no arrests were made, nor has anyone been convicted for committing this crime.

Each musician was given a funeral with full military honours. Many of the funerals took place at the St Michael and All Angels Church in South Barracks, which Margaret and I attended. Before each service, the bereaved families assembled in the Officers' Mess, where the funeral cortege would leave for the short journey to the Church. The Deal Staff Band would march in front of the cortege and, outside the Church, and form a lane through which the coffin would pass. Inside the church, a full orchestra, under the direction of the Principal Director of Music Lt. Colonel John Ware, would play music that each family had been invited to select. Bob Simmonds was a jazz fanatic, so for his funeral, a musician played a piece in that genre on the grand piano. Andy Cleatheroe's family chose *Adagio of Spartacus and Phrygia*, the theme of the TV series *The Onedin Line*.

After the funeral, most bodies were buried by their families away from Deal. Each funeral service was just as unbearably moving as the last. Only four months before, a capacity audience in that same church had generously applauded my last orchestral concert. Now, the congregation was paying their respects to some of those who had performed that evening.

Another consequence of the IRA bombing was a change to the plan to move the School of Music from Deal to Portsmouth. By 1989, some 300 Royal Marines Band Service personnel were left as the sole occupants of the entire Barracks complex in Deal. A decision to leave the town had been taken, the new Secretary of State for Defence Tom King had been briefed, and an official announcement had been planned for the autumn of 1989.

That announcement was scrapped following a pledge by Prime Minister Margaret Thatcher, after visiting the scene of the blast and the hospitals where those who were injured were being cared for on 26th September, to keep a Royal Marines presence in Deal. She did not want to be seen to be giving in to the IRA. So, Royal Marines musicians under training continued their education in Deal for a further 7 ½ years, when it was then considered politically and financially expedient to move them all to Portsmouth.

The memorial bandstand

Within a day of the bombing, people had started to contact the School of Music to ask how they could donate money to a fund for the victims, and many organisations throughout the country collected money for those who had been bereaved. To care for the families affected by the atrocity, the Royal Marines Benevolent Fund helped establish a special trust fund. The fund was closed after 18 months, having distributed over £1.1 million.

The Deal branch of the Round Table Association collected over £30,000 and wanted to erect a permanent memorial in the town to those killed. A former Army bandsman and local resident Denis Atkinson proposed that a Memorial Bandstand prominently displaying the names of those killed should be built. He also suggested that an ideal site would be the raised grass area on Walmer Green, where it now stands and is seen by all as they enter Deal.

As the then President of the Deal & District Men of Kent & Kentish Men, I became aware of this proposal when the organisation was holding a summer event at Deal Castle the following year. Recognising that Denis needed support to get the project started, I offered to help. With the professional assistance of well-known local solicitor, Jonathan Daniell, I negotiated a fifty-year lease on the Walmer Green site and secured the ongoing support of Dover District Council. With the Round Table Association providing the funding, I was able to oversee the building's construction, it's dedication and registering the Deal Memorial Bandstand Trust as a national charity.

Once completed, the memorial was dedicated on 2nd May 1993 at a special service in the presence of local civic dignitaries, senior representatives of the Round Table Association and the families of many of the bomb victims. The Round Table Association then formally passed responsibility for the building to the Deal Memorial Bandstand Trust. I was the Trust's Chairman for ten years and was able to ensure that, annually, the incoming Town Mayor of Deal became President of the Trust on their accession, thus maintaining the Bandstand's high profile within the local community.

Each Sunday afternoon from early May to the end of September, a civilian band is engaged to play on the bandstand, and each year a Royal Marines Band returns to Deal to give a concert at this memorial venue. This is a very special event and remains a high point in the Royal Marines Band Service and Corps calendar. The 30th anniversary concert, held on 14th July 2019, attended by at least ten thousand people, was especially memorable. Two Royal Marine bands performed to an audience that included local civic dignitaries, the Captain of Deal Castle, Commandant General Royal Marines, and the Lord Warden of the Cinque Ports. The emotional climax of the afternoon came during the second half of the concert. For one of the items, the band was joined onstage by a guest performer – Musician Andrew Gronkowski - a former Royal Marines drummer who had been badly injured by the blast and who had not, until that day, performed in public again.

The weekend bandstand venue for music soon became a meeting place for those who had been previously involved with the Corps, and for those with long-gone family connections. I would often be approached at the Sunday afternoon concerts by visitors to the town who knew a relative or Royal Marines musician who had served at Deal. As the Band Service has always been a close-knit family, I found familiar names being mentioned and was glad to be able to give my recollections of such people with whom I had served.

On one sunny afternoon, I was approached by a lady who was anxious to discuss her father, now deceased. All she knew was that he had been a Senior Non-Commissioned Officer when serving at Deal many years previously. She was immensely proud of him and, having told me his name, was delighted to know that I remembered him. I had recognised the name immediately and had then to tread very carefully indeed, for I realised that she must have been unaware of the circumstances surrounding his 'retirement' in the 1950s. I was talking to the daughter of the Senior NCO whose court-martial, dismissal with ignominy from the Service and subsequent prison sentence I referred to in Chapter 2. She departed that afternoon none the wiser. I had no intention of ruining the happy memories she had retained of her father, who had obviously managed to keep his dark past a secret.

The memorial garden

Backing onto the rear wall of the old Canada Road concert hall, a garden of remembrance has been consecrated at the site of the actual bombing. Little had been done to nurture the site for 17 years and by 2006 it had become something of a local eyesore. After I had generated some unwelcome publicity about its sorry state, the local council, agreed to improve the ambience of the area and provide a dignified and private place for the families to pay their respects to the victims of the tragedy. The memorial garden is surrounded by a wall with decorative wrought-iron gates made by a former member of the Band Service. Thanks to an initiative sponsored by former Bandmaster David Yates, a plaque containing the names of these killed was set in the wall in time for the families of those affected to commemorate the 30th anniversary of the atrocity.

Plaque in the Royal Marines Band Service Memorial Garden, 2019

Since it was consecrated, Margaret would visit the memorial garden each week to ensure it was maintained in good order. Here on September 22nd each year, a memorial service is held at 8am to which bereaved families and civic and Service dignitaries come to continue their vigil. Led for many years by the Reverend Jane Walker, a vicar and sister of one of those killed, Musician Bob Simmonds, the service contains these familiar words:

They shall not grow old as we that are left grow old.
Age shall not weary them, nor the years condemn.
At the going down of the sun, and in the morning,
We will remember them.

The congregation also recite the Royal Marines Band Service prayer, written by the Reverend Lovell Pocock, a former Royal Naval Chaplain and vicar in Deal:

Almighty and Eternal Lord God, in whose sight and love live our memories of many generations of those who have served You in the Band Service of the Royal Marines; we thank You for the rich heritage of music placed in our hands, and for the joy and inspiration which it brings to men; enable us with our whole hearts to serve You, that by Your grace and through our gift of music, we may continue to inspire, help and lead men and women; we ask these things in the name of Jesus Christ our Lord. Amen.

Also on September 22nd, two hundred metres away, floral tributes are placed at dawn above each of the named plaques on eleven sides of the memorial bandstand. The lights are lit, allowing those who pass by to realise that although another year has elapsed, those who died at the hands of terrorists on that dreadful day in 1989 have not been, nor ever will be, forgotten.

Cruse, Fundraising & the U3A

The IRA atrocity and my involvement with the victims' families brought me into contact with Cruse Bereavement

Care, a charity now known as Cruse Bereavement Support. Margaret and I trained as Bereavement Volunteers and, after completing the course, benefited greatly from the experience. By giving talks on various subjects resulting from my Service career, I was also able to raise money for the organisation.

At around the same time I was getting involved with Cruse, I was invited to become a tutor with the University of the Third Age, a UK-wide collection of over one thousand locally-run interest groups that provide opportunities for those no longer in full-time work to come together and learn for fun. As a tutor for Canterbury U3A, I held my weekly sessions at the home of a retired Doctor in that city. My students were all professional people whose interest in music had remained dormant throughout their individual careers, but who now had great joy in carrying it forward.

At around this time, Margaret was deeply affected by the TV coverage given to the desperate plight of children in Romania, news of which followed the revolution that was taking place in that country. The removal and assassination of President Ceausescu and his wife in December 1989 brought with it pictures of conditions in the country's orphanages that were horrifying to Western eyes. Margaret lost no time in deciding that she had to do something to help and became quickly involved with relief work, both locally and nationally. She helped to organise the collection of large amounts of aid and went more than once to Romania with a convoy of vehicles to oversee its dispersal.

I was thus minded to focus on fund raising for Romania. My financial support for Cruse Bereavement Care at Dover was no longer so vital for that organisation, so the proceeds from my burgeoning talks schedule were re-directed. I found that there was a considerable interest in my presentations and was soon being asked to travel much further to deliver them than I initially thought would be the case. Interest continued to build and eventually I had to limit the number of speaking engagements I could accept each year to between eighty and ninety. Recognising very early on that people often preferred to be entertained rather than educated, I prepared a range of topics with this in mind. Eventually, I was able to offer:

A life on the ocean wave
An account of my life in the Royal Marines Band Service.

John Philip Sousa
The story of an American musical legend.

Mountbatten of Burma
The story of a remarkable man of our time.

The Royal Marines School of Music
The story of the unique musical training offered to students joining the Corps.

The heritage of the sea
An account of Britain's proud history as a maritime nation.

Beat Retreat & Tattoo
The story of the two military ceremonies.

Britannia, pride of the ocean
Life on board the Royal Yacht.

Royal Albert Hall concerts
The inside story of the annual Massed Band concerts.

Instruments of the orchestra
Strings, brass, woodwind and percussion instruments are discussed in turn before they are combined for a performance of 'The Magnificent Seven' film score.

Entertaining onboard the *QE2*
The story of the Royal Marines Band as it undertook an eight-day cruise in the Mediterranean.

The diary of a nobody
Memories of a lifetime in the public eye.

Music around the globe
Songs of the sea from the days of sail, when muscle-power and rhythm went hand in hand.

The British are coming!
The story of the 16,000-mile concert tour of North America and Canada.

With money now available to address the situation in Romania, Margaret and I were able to use these funds to help some of those who needed it. Instead of trying to help all - an impossible task - we concentrated on a few young people who Margaret had met when she had visited that country, distributing aid. The help we were able to give enabled these people to get themselves educated. Eventually three were able to attend, and graduate from, the University of Bucharest.

Public speaking, 2004

The Royal Marines leave Deal

With the collapse of plans for a combined School of Music for
the three Services maintaining the large barracks at Deal just
for the musicians of the Royal Marines became ever more
difficult to justify. It had already been decided that the Royal
Marines School of Music should be re-located in Portsmouth
alongside the Headquarters of the Royal Marines Secretariat.
The only question remaining, following the Deal bombing, was
when the decision to drop Prime Minister Margaret Thatcher's
pledge to keep the Royal Marines in Deal would be announced

377

GOLD ON BLUE

and the plans put into effect. Margaret Thatcher ceased to be Prime Minister in November 1990.

When the naval authorities in Portsmouth eventually notified the Commandant of the School of Music, Lt. Colonel Richard Dixon, of the impending announcement, they justified their decision by explaining that they considered the Marines had suffered too much emotionally by remaining in Deal and should be moved on.

In torrential rain, I attended the final beat retreat ceremony in South Barracks on 22 March 1996, given by the massed bands of the Royal Marines School of Music, Royal Marines Portsmouth and Britannia Royal Naval College. To conclude that performance, they marched for the last time out of Jubilee Gate, turning left on the Dover Road and on to East Barracks, the original home of the Royal Marines Band Service.

One week later, the Royal Marines School of Music moved into the old Detention Quarters at the Portsmouth Naval Base. This facility had been extensively refurbished and bore little resemblance to the prison of earlier days. It was ideal for the purpose. This was largely because the thickness of interior walls dividing the many small *practice rooms* gave ideal sound-proofing. One of the major difficulties in designing a new facility for music training is isolating the sounds produced by individual and diverse instrumentalists as they undertake their daily practice. Having a cubicle in which to be isolated was ideal and once *cell doors* had been removed and replaced by double-glazed glass panels there was no feeling of being confined. Light, airy and now fully carpeted, the old Detention Quarters took on a new lease of life.

A further development that coincided with the move from Deal was an association between the RMSM and the music department of Portsmouth University. Arrangements were put in hand for Royal Marines music students studying for a career in the Corps to obtain university degrees.

The move of the School of Music to Portsmouth dealt a considerable cultural blow to Deal. It had been very much an integral part of the town and was the last surviving link with the Royal Navy, whose presence in the area had lasted for almost 325 years. Although no longer as visible as before, retired musicians of the Corps continue to entertain and support the local community. Sergeants' Mess pantomimes, written and produced now by former '*bandy*' Brian Short, are always popular and raise huge sums for local and national charities. His productions included *The Sound of Muesli, Pirates of the Curried Beans, Skinderella, Dad's Barmy, Wonky Willy* and *It is Quite Hot, Mother,* the latter a homage to the very un-PC BBC television programme of the 1980s.

After the School of Music had been relocated in its new home at Portsmouth, I was asked to contact the former Officer's Mess Manager at Deal, who was busy carrying out a final closure routine prior to the whole barracks being offered for sale. My farewell present to members of the Officers' Mess when I retired in 1998 was amongst rubbish set aside for removal to the corporation refuse tip. It was a large, framed navigation chart produced by the Hydrographer for the Navy for the Royal Yacht and used when *Britannia* brought the Queen Mother to Dover for her installation as Lord Warden of the Cinque Ports in 1979. To have just thrown it into a skip at Deal was crass and insensitive and, at the time it was found, for me deeply wounding.

Infirmary Barracks was sold to a developer in 1988. It was demolished and the land used to build a new housing estate. The remaining barracks complex, comprising North, South and East Barracks, was eventually sold to a private developer and also converted into private housing.

Tapestry and the Falklands War commemorative kneelers

My mother had been a skilled seamstress and she must have passed some of her skills on to me. Throughout my Service career I had also been fairly adept with a sewing needle, and thought that in my retirement I now might like to attempt some tapestry-work. I sent off for a kit. Once the first canvas was on the frame and I had pulled a few threads, I was hooked. This first tapestry depicted flowers in a large bouquet.

I had nearly completed it when the IRA bombing incident took place at the nearby School of Music. I added a green hill with eleven red crosses to the canvass and, working the word *SUNSET* below the hill, I knew that this tapestry would become a personal memorial to those young men whom I had known so well and whose lives had been so tragically taken. It was therapeutic for me to work this canvas as the reality and aftermath of the event unfolded. Once the *Sunset* tapestry was finished and framed I looked for other designs to which I could give my attention.

Working in wool, cotton and silk I took my new hobby very seriously. Success as an exhibitor followed and I was awarded many prizes.

I eventually learned that a memorial chapel, dedicated to the those who had died during the Falklands War, was to be built in the grounds of Pangbourne Nautical College in Berkshire and that there was a need for volunteers to make kneelers for this chapel. I contacted the college and offered to help. Did a bereaved Royal Marine's family need someone to make a kneeler commemorating their relative? I received by return of post a kneeler kit from the Royal School of Needlework with an invitation for me to complete it.

Once I had done so, with the deceased Marine's name on the leading edge of the kneeler, I sent it off to Pangbourne to be put with the many others that were being produced by willing hands across the country. The aim was to have a kneeler completed for every Falklands casualty by the time the chapel was to be dedicated and then opened officially by the Queen in March 2000. Some 258 British servicemen were killed during the conflict, and a further 777 British were injured or wounded. Knowing that there may be a problem in fulfilling the requirement, I said that I would happily work on another kneeler. In just over a year, I completed nineteen kneelers!

As a result, I was invited to be present at Pangbourne for a service for the bereaved, at which all the kneelers were to be dedicated by the Bishop of Oxford. I arrived at the chapel quite early to find the kneelers forming a wall just inside the entrance. As each bereaved family arrived, they found the kneeler that carried their family name. I didn't see one person put their kneeler on the floor. Each was cuddled tightly throughout the service. I then realised that this might be the only tangible memento that the families had of their loved ones. More than half the casualties had died at sea, most under enemy attacks which sank five ships and damaged eight more, and their bodies had not been recovered from the depths of the South Atlantic. Others had been deliberately, but respectfully and with full naval honours, buried at sea. I was then truly aware of the significance of the nineteen kneelers I had worked. Among my list of names had been officers and men from both the Royal Navy and the Royal Marines and even a Chinese steward from HMS *Coventry*.

The day of the Dedication was a difficult one, for among the congregation was a very dear colleague of mine, Captain David Hart-Dyke. Although badly burned, David had survived the Argentinian attack that destroyed *HMS Coventry*, of which he was the Captain. I had been on board the Royal Yacht when he was waved ashore following his promotion from Executive Commander of *Britannia*. Speaking with him at the reception following the service, David gently explained to me that the Chinese steward I had commemorated on one of my kneelers was his personal steward in *HMS Coventry*. Little did we know then that the bright smile seen on the day he left *Britannia* would later turn to deep remorse following the tragic loss of his ship and his comrades. The sinking of his ship had been a devastating blow to a man at the peak of an outstanding naval career. Although physically recovered from the burns he suffered, he now lives with dark memories that will possibly never be assuaged.

Old comrades

Two former Band Service characters lived close by in the Kentish villages of Martin and Martin Mill. Bill Greasley was one whom I had known for my entire Service career and had retired to Martin. As a Bandmaster in the early 1950s, he had taken us boys for weekend camping expeditions to Sandwich Bay. He did the cooking, etc, whilst we swam in the sea. We thought his were the best sausages ever! I had attended Bill's farewell party as he left the Corps in the late 1950s to command the Barbados Police band, and it was Bill who had presented me with one of Sir Henry Wood's annotated scores and wooden batons to commemorate my graduation from the Royal Academy of Music in 1962.

Bill and his wife Joy had similar interests to Reg and Dorothy Long who lived in Martin Mill, they often went on caravan holidays together. Reg Long had also started his Service career as a musician in the Royal Naval School of Music. Both had served during World War II when, for days at a time, they had been battened down in the Transmitting Stations of their respective ships.

On his retirement from the Band Service, Reg became a schoolmaster in Thanet and was the regular organist at Ringwould Church. For many years he served as a local councillor and was an active member of various Royal Naval and Royal Marines Associations. He died in 2004 at the age of 90, just two weeks after he had arranged for his old violin and clarinet to be presented to the Thanet school in which he had earlier been a teacher. Among the many mourners at his funeral were three former Principal Directors of Music Royal Marines, one of whom - Paul Neville - gave the eulogy.

For over twenty years following the death of her husband, former Professor of Clarinet Kenneth Mettyear, Phyllis continued to live near Deal pier in a basement apartment at Prince of Wales Terrace. Originally a Royal Marines Bandmaster, Ken had been retained at the School of Music as a Professor of clarinet on his retirement. This was the apartment which, for half a crown a time, large numbers of ambitious Band Service personnel, including me, had visited to hone their aural skills. Every evening in term time a steady stream of students would arrive there in turn and, with Phyllis banished to a back room, Ken would conduct his lessons from the piano in the lounge. Through that baby-grand, and Ken's patience as he illustrated his lessons with it, many students in the 60s, 70s and 80s successfully passed musical examinations that they otherwise almost certainly would not have done.

After Ken died Margaret and I took it upon ourselves to ensure that Phyllis wanted for nothing. She became a dearly loved member of our family and was always included in our activities. She was with us for our Christmas and Easter celebrations, and during the summer she came with us if we went on holiday. We were also able to take her to the places she had known during her earlier years as the wife of a *Bandy*. During a visit to Burford, we visited the house in the High Street that had been her home in the late 1940s when Ken was serving at the nearby Royal Naval School of Music. The current owner invited her inside, where she recognised items of furniture and fittings still there from those early days.

Having her in our lives was a bonus but, at the age of 89, she faded away. As a co-Executor of Phyllis's will, I helped to put her affairs in order. Phyllis only had one relative, a lady on Ken's side of the family who lived in Canada. I sent her Ken's MBE, together with its attendant citation from Buckingham Palace signed by the Queen, his war medals and other memorabilia. Phyllis had not stipulated who should receive the engraved silver cigarette box that had been presented to commemorate her husband's twenty-fifth year as a RMSM clarinet Professor so, at her funeral, I passed it to one of Ken's former pupils, Band Colour Sergeant Andy Cunningham. I am sure that Ken would have approved.

Market Bosworth

In retirement I have found time for my grandchildren and watching their development year on year has been a delightful experience. We have taken them on holidays in this country and abroad. When they were quite young, we restricted our adventures to going on the canals in a narrow boat. One such holiday involved a voyage along the Ashby canal. With no locks to navigate, it was ideal for a boat with small children on board. There was a lot of interest all around but little danger of any sort.

The Ashby canal passes very close to the historic town of Market Bosworth. We were there on a Saturday and noticed that a mooring was available. We steered the boat to the bank and scrambled ashore to explore the area and found that, by chance, we were close to the site of the Battle of Bosworth Field. Here, in August 1485, King Richard III had lost his crown. On several nearby hilltops, colourful banners were flying and there was a heritage centre for visitors close by. It had been our great good fortune to arrive on the very day that a re-enactment of the battle was to take place, and which we were able to witness.

The next morning, I left the canal boat to walk the few steps down a bank into a small, grassed area bordering a stream. This was thought to be the place where King Richard had been killed. On the grass, a memorial cairn of stones had been built and a *white rose of York* bush was in flower beside it. It was just before 8am when a Land Rover arrived, out of which stepped a Ranger tidily dressed in a green uniform. Carrying something colourful rolled up under his arm, he went to a centrally placed white flagpole and, precisely as a far-off church clock struck the hour, he solemnly raised King Richard III's personal standard to the masthead.

King Richard III Flagpole

386

I couldn't believe it! I had spent my life travelling the world and standing to attention at 8am for *Colours* ceremonies as flags were raised and music was played. Now, I was here in the tranquillity of an English field, seemingly miles from anywhere. Today, in silence, a defeated King was still receiving tribute where his life had ended centuries ago.

In that place and at that moment, the woven golden threads of his personal standard fluttered against the blue of an English summer sky. I realised anew how fortunate I have been over the years, living a life that has been truly joyous and rewarding.

By land and sea my travels have provided me with uniquely colourful memories. I am humbled by my good fortune. As Margaret and I celebrate over sixty-five glorious years of happy marriage and watch the sun glinting on the sea a few steps from the front door of our coastguard cottage in Kingsdown, I know that the thread that has linked us together throughout our lives has truly been one of spun gold.

Margaret and Graham Hoskins, 2010

APPENDIX I: VOYAGES ON HMY *BRITANNIA*

AS BANDMASTER

1965 **Federal Republic of Germany**
In May Queen Elizabeth and Prince Philip embarked at Hamburg following a State Visit.
Great Britain
Visited Cardiff, Kirkcudbright and Clydebank in June with the Queen and Prince Philip.

1966 **West Indies**
With the Queen and Prince Philip.
Australia, Fiji & New Zealand
From March to May with the Queen Mother.

1967 **Canada**
With the Queen and Prince Philip attended centennial celebrations and visited Expo 67 in Montreal.

AS DIRECTOR OF MUSIC

1978 **Federal Republic of Germany**
A State Visit by the Queen and Prince Philip in May.
Channel Islands
With the Queen and Prince Philip to Jersey, Guernsey, Alderney and Sark.
Western Islands
After Cowes Week, the Royal Family cruised to the Western Islands and paid an official visit to Orkney.
Mediterranean
NATO exercises during October.

1979   **Eastern Arabia**
With the Queen and Prince Philip.
Denmark
A State Visit in May.
Great Britain
The Queen Mother visited the Clyde in June, and in July she was installed as Lord Warden of the Cinque Ports at Dover.
Scotland
Cowes Week and the Western Islands.

1980   **England**
To the Pool of London for a Thanksgiving Service at St Paul's Cathedral for the Queen Mother's eightieth birthday.
Scotland
The Western Isles cruise included an official visit to Islay.
Italy
State Visits to Italy and the Vatican.
North Africa
State Visits to Tunisia, Algeria and Morocco.

1981   **Norway**
A State Visit calling at Oslo and Stavanger.
Shetland Islands
With Prince Philip and King Olav V of Norway, the Queen sailed to Sullom Voe where she inaugurated an oil terminal.
Mediterranean, Indian Ocean & Australasia
The Prince and Princess of Wales joined Britannia at Gibraltar to spend two weeks of their honeymoon on board. They disembarked at Hurghada, Egypt, and the Royal Yacht continued to Melbourne. From Melbourne with the Queen and Prince Philip to New Zealand.

APPENDIX II: RECORDINGS

1976   *'Heritage of the March' featuring the RMSM Junior Band (American publisher)*

1979   *Double album 'Mountbatten Tribute' (BBC Solent RSS 001)*

1983   *'Mountbatten Festival of Music' (RMA 1005)*

1983   *The Stars and Stripes Forever (EMI DS-38016)*

1983   *Edinburgh Military Tattoo' (Ross Records WGR 058)*

1984   *Royal Tournament' at Earls Court (Polydor POLH9)*

1984   *Old Comrades, New Comrades' (Grasmere GRALP 1)*

1984   *Mountbatten Festival of Music' (RMA 1006)*

1985   *RM's & Argyll & Southerland Highlanders tour of USA & Canada' ESE 109*

1985   *Mountbatten Festival of Music (RMA 1007)*

1986   *Royal Wedding of Prince Andrew & Sara Ferguson' (BBC Records REP 596)*

1986   *Hands Across the Sea' (EMI EL2701521*

1986   *Mountbatten Festival of Music' (RMA 1008)*

1987   *Solid Men to the Front' (EMI EL2705871)*

1987   *Mountbatten Festival of Music' (RMA 1009)*

1988   *Mountbatten Festival of Music' (RMA 1010)*

1988   *Mountbatten Festival of Music' VHS video (Bandleader BNV 1982)*

1988   *'Beat Retreat' on Horse Guard's Parade (RMA 1011)*

1988   *'Beat Retreat' on Horse Guard's Parade VHS video (Bandleader BNV 1984)*

1989   *Mountbatten Festival of Music' (RMA 1012)*

2001   *Edinburgh Military Tattoo '50 glorious years' BBC DD/video DD05346*

2002   *Sousa Marches' Double CD (43 marches) Compilation released by EMI under their 'Gemini EMI Treasures' label (EMI 24358 55352)*

2004   *Splice the Mainbrace' Compilation (Bandboy BB21)*

GOLD ON BLUE

GOLD ON BLUE

INDEX

393